PARADISE LOST?

The Beijer International Institute of Ecological Economics

The Institute was established in 1991 as one of the research institutes of the Royal Swedish Academy of Sciences, to promote interdisciplinary research between ecologists and economists. The objective is to improve understanding of the links between economic and ecological systems, in order to ameliorate the management of these interconnected systems. The Institute brings together leading scholars from economics, ecology and related disciplines in a number of research programmes including one on the *Ecology and Economics of Biodiversity Loss*, the focus of this book.

The Institute works through extensive networks with scientists from all over the world, who are involved in the Institute's research programmes, projects, or teaching and training activities.

Beijer Reprints Series and *Beijer Discussion Paper Series* are produced by the Institute. The Annual Report and a Beijer Institute Newsletter, published twice a year, are available on request.

For more information please contact
The Beijer International Institute of Ecological Economics
Royal Swedish Academy of Sciences
Box 50005
S-104 05 Stockholm
Sweden

PARADISE LOST?

THE ECOLOGICAL ECONOMICS OF BIODIVERSITY

Edward B Barbier, Joanne C Burgess and Carl Folke

BEIJER   Beijer International Institute of Ecological Economics
The Royal Swedish Academy of Sciences

EARTHSCAN
Earthscan Publications Ltd, London

To the next generation:
Gustaf, Lara, Peder and Peter James

First published in 1994 by
Earthscan Publications Limited
120 Pentonville Road, London N1 9JN

A catalogue record for this book is available from the British Library

ISBN: 1 85383 181 6

Typeset by Books Unlimited, Rainworth, Notts, NG21 0JE
Printed and bound by Biddles Ltd, Guildford and Kings Lynn
Cover design by Lucy Jenkins
Cover photo of the mangrove area of Surat Thani, Thailand, by Nils Kautsky, courtesy
of the Beijer Institute

Earthscan Publications Limited is an editorially independent subsidiary of Kogan Page
Limited and publishes in association with the International Institute for Environment and
Development and the World Wide Fund for Nature.

Contents

List of Illustrations

TABLES

FIGURES

BOXES

Acknowledgements

We are grateful to many people for making the following book possible. First we would like to thank Karl-Göran Mäler, director of the Beijer International Institute of Ecological Economics of the Royal Swedish Academy of Sciences, who encouraged both the establishment of the Biodiversity Programme, and the writing and publication of this book, and Charles Perrings, director of the Biodiversity Programme, who was responsible for the high quality of meetings, participants and papers that made the programme a success and this book possible. For better or worse, the two are responsible for persuading the three of us to collaborate in this effort.

We would also like to acknowledge with thanks the intellectual guidance provided by the editorial board of the Biodiversity Programme, who include not only Professors Mäler and Perrings, but also Buzz Holling and Bengt-Owe Jansson. However, any errors in thinking or omissions are our responsibility alone and should not reflect on the editorial board, the Biodiversity Programme and its participants or the Beijer Institute.

On 16 December 1993, the Beijer Institute and the Department of Environmental Economics and Environmental Management (EEEM) of the University of York held a meeting to review the preliminary draft manuscript of this book. We would like to thank John Proops and Ian Spellerberg for reviewing the manuscript and providing detailed comments at that meeting. We would also like to thank the following participants at the meeting for their contributions to the very stimulating discussion and comments: Paul Burrows, Mick Common, Richard Firn, Alistair Fitter, Nick Hanley and David Stern. Three additional external reviewers who could not attend the meeting but also provided us with helpful comments were Ian Swingland, Ian Simmons and Frances Cairncross. Finally, we are grateful to Mick Common and David Stern at EEEM for taking the time to provide their own review and comments of the manuscript, and to Tom Van Rensburg and Joydeep Gupta for helping us prepare and distribute the manuscript for the meeting. We have tried our best to do justice to all these extremely helpful and interesting reviews and comments.

This book could not have been written without the support of the London Environmental Economics Centre (LEEC) of the International Institute for Environment and Development (IIED) for two of us, Ed Barbier and Jo Burgess. In particular, core support for LEEC by the Swedish International Development Authority should be acknowledged for partial funding of Ed and Jo's participation in this endeavour. We are therefore grateful to the executive director of IIED, Richard Sandbrook, and colleagues at LEEC and IIED for encouraging collaboration with the Beijer Institute. We would especially like to thank Jacqueline Saunders of LEEC who assisted in preparation of the preliminary draft of some chapters and liaising with Beijer. Carl Folke's work was partly financed through a grant from the Swedish Council for Forestry and Agricultural Research. For all these contributions, we are extremely grateful.

Preface

The Beijer International Institute of Ecological Economics of the Royal Swedish Academy of Sciences was launched in July 1991 with the specific aim of 'promoting inter-disciplinary research between ecologists and economists in an attempt to improve understanding of the links between economic and ecological systems' (Folke et al 1993).

The first initiative of the Beijer Institute was to establish the Biodiversity Programme, which brought together a group of leading ecologists and economists to address both empirical and policy issues associated with the biodiversity loss caused by direct depletion, the destruction of habitat, and by specialization in agriculture, forestry and fisheries. However, it became clear that progress on these issues would require overcoming critical barriers to communication between the two disciplines: rigidness in thinking and lack of confidence in the other discipline's perspective. Although some ecologists and economists had substantial experience working in an inter-disciplinary setting, others had little or no such experience. In addition, a select number of scholars from other disciplines were also invited to participate.

Nevertheless, all participants in the programme expressed a genuine interest in avoiding the 'dialogue of the deaf' that in the past has often prevented inter-disciplinary progress between ecology and economics. More importantly, there was widespread agreement that the current biodiversity problem was a major issue facing humankind, and substantial advances in both theory and policy analysis would be required to tackle this problem. Needless to say, at the beginning of the programme, a good number of participants were sceptical about whether a common ground could be found between ecology and economics so that these advances could be made collectively. Intellectual curiosity as to whether the other discipline had any new and interesting perspectives on the global biodiversity problem was perhaps the major motivation for participation.

The Biodiversity Programme sought to bridge the gap between the ecologists and economists by holding one conference in September 1991 and a follow-up meeting in July 1992. The purpose of the first conference was to discuss broadly issues of common ground, to develop a research agenda, and to identify paper themes and authors for the second conference. The research agenda was formed around four major themes: the role of biodiversity in keeping ecosystems resilient in the face of external disturbances; the value of biodiversity in generating ecological services; the social and economic forces driving the loss of biodiversity; and the measures required to reduce or even reverse the current rate of biodiversity loss. The papers presented at the second meeting were based on these four themes, and provided a specific focus for discussion on ecological–economic progress towards advances in theory and policy analysis.

Although the programme may not have convinced the sceptics, it did demonstrate that both ecologists and economists have important perspectives to bring to understanding the global biodiversity problem. More importantly, substantial progress appeared to have been made in opening lines of communication between the two disciplines. At the very least, the intellectual curiosity concerning what each discipline's perspective had to offer appeared to be satisfied. The emergence of many points of common ground between ecology and economics on the analysis of biodiversity can be found across the various papers prepared for the programme.

The papers prepared for the Beijer Institute's Biodiversity Programme over 1991–3 are to be published collectively through the programme in relevant academic journals and books. For example, already two special editions of *AMBIO*, the journal of the Royal Swedish Academy of Sciences, have been devoted to papers from the Biodiversity Programme. Special editions of *Environmental and Resource Economics* and *Ecological Economics*, plus two edited volumes for Cambridge University Press and Kluwer Academic Press containing Biodiversity Programme papers, will be appearing in 1994.

Although the results of this work are of importance and general interest to a wider audience, they are not particularly accessible in their current form. The aim of this book is to present in a more accessible style the insights from these papers on the current global concern over biodiversity loss. In addition, the Biodiversity Programme initiated progress towards a more integrated ecological–economic approach to the biodiversity problem. This book will also attempt to discuss and assess the progress in developing such an approach. Thus the focus of the book is very much on both biodiversity loss and ecological–economic approaches to this problem.

Biodiversity loss is considered one of the most serious problems threatening the world today. Increasingly, ecologists and economists have been asked to address this problem. However, it is doubtful whether economics, ecology or any other scientific discipline on its own is capable of grasping the full implications of biodiversity loss for human well-being and the biosphere. A concerted effort by economists and ecologists, and possibly other scientists, will be required to understand these implications and to begin designing solutions to this problem. This is the view taken in this book.

We also believe that the problem of managing biodiversity is fairly straightforward conceptually. Biological diversity – biodiversity for short – is generally used to describe the variability among living organisms and the ecological complexes of which they are a part. Without this variability in the living world, ecological systems and functions would break down, with detrimental consequences for all life including humans. Consequently, as biodiversity is essential to ensuring the basic ecological services and resources necessary to maintain human welfare and even existence, then a minimum level of biodiversity is required to sustain the well-being not only of current but also future generations. This implies that biodiversity conservation does not require complete preservation of all species in the world or an immediate moratorium on all uses of the environment, including habitat conversion. It suggests that we must ensure that current rates of biodiversity loss do not take humankind beyond the minimum threshold level necessary to sustain human welfare and even existence.

However, this is where the practical problems begin.

Although species extinction is the most fundamental and irreversible manifestation of biodiversity loss, the more profound implication is for ecological functioning and resilience – the ability of ecosystems to absorb external stresses and shocks. These latter impacts are generally localized, but in many cases they generate wider national, regional or even global effects. Consequently, the biological resources and ecological 'services' available today may not be so abundant tomorrow.

In short, the world will be experiencing greater *ecological scarcity*. Not only will this manifest itself through a growing 'relative' scarcity of essential environmental assets and ecological services on which human welfare depend, but, at the extreme, will also lead to irrevocable ecological damage and possibly the collapse of ecosystems. Coping with ecological scarcity is not an easy task. Biodiversity loss can be irreversible, its consequences uncertain, and the environmental values that are lost are so difficult to assess and often unknown. This would suggest caution in our current efforts to convert and exploit natural resources – particularly as we do not know the preferences and technology of future generations whose welfare and even existence may be affected by the pace and scale of biodiversity loss today. However, caution in resource use is hardly an attribute of modern society today. Thus management of the current biodiversity crisis will require fundamental changes in our economic, environmental and social relationships. It is how we manage these changes which is one important theme of this book.

We realize that our views on the biodiversity problem will not please either the optimists or the pessimists. The optimists will find our concern over the 'biodiversity crisis' to be overly alarmist. In their opinion, humankind's capacity to improve human and technical skills will be able to overcome the biodiversity problem – which will gradually fade away as did past concerns over 'Malthusian' population constraints in the nineteenth century and 'limits to growth' from resource exhaustion in the early 1970s. On the other hand, the pessimists would maintain that humankind is already on a dangerous path of biological destruction, that we are on the brink of ecological catastrophe or heading towards it inexorably, and that the only solution is drastic curtailment of present economic activities and resource use.

From our standpoint, whichever of these views is correct is not the point. Our main concern, as is that of all of our colleagues in the Biodiversity Programme, is to acknowledge that uncertainty and ignorance about basic economic–environmental interactions are inherent features underlying the biodiversity problem of concern to so many today. As scientists and policy analysts, our task is to improve our understanding of this problem and to provide guidance to policy makers on how to begin devising solutions. Consequently, the first step should be to pool our knowledge and intellectual resources into a combined ecological–economic approach to biodiversity loss. What is required is that ecology, economics and other disciplines begin applying their specialized knowledge and analytical methods collectively to extend beyond the current frontiers of their respective disciplines, so that we can be sure of the appropriate diagnosis and remedy for the global biodiversity problem. The result is what we call ecological economics. However, for us it is not a new discipline as such, but a new category of analysis for approaching problems of economic–environmental interaction where a single-discipline approach will not suffice. The Biodiversity Programme papers and this book, we hope, represent the beginnings of this ecological–economic 'learning curve'.

Finally, we would like to acknowledge that this book may not represent the views of all the participants in the Beijer Biodiversity Programme. A diversity of participants were involved in the programme and there were consequently a diversity of views on the biodiversity loss problem. Although we were impressed by the remarkable consistency of views across the papers, there were obvious differences of opinion among some authors. Our task here is to find the areas of common agreement, to give them shape and coherence as much as possible, and to supplement them with further material and ideas where appropriate. Obviously, the end result reflects the views of the three of us on the consensus opinion and on the ecological economics of biodiversity loss. We therefore let our fellow participants off the hook: we alone take responsibility for the views expressed in this book.

We have organized the book into four parts as follows. Part I provides a brief background to current concerns over biodiversity, a general overview of the implications of biodiversity loss, the major driving forces determining this loss, and the similarities and differences in current economic and ecological perspectives on this problem. Chapter 1 discusses the emergence of biodiversity loss as a major conservation issue and current concerns over this loss. We also contrast the popular view of biodiversity loss with the concerns emphasized by the Beijer Biodiversity Programme and this book. Chapter 2 briefly describes the ecological and economic implications of continual destruction of the world's biodiversity. For example, the ecological implications include the impacts of biodiversity loss on ecosystems, the inability of stressed systems to function optimally and the loss of resilience. The economic implications include the loss of valuable resources and ecological services, the problems posed by uncertainty and ignorance, and the concerns for both intra-generational and inter-generational equity. Chapter 3 provides an overview of how ecological and economic disciplines have traditionally approached the problems posed by biodiversity loss. We also discuss the important issue of whether a single-discipline approach is sufficient to tackle the challenges posed by biodiversity loss or whether a more integrated ecological–economic approach is required. Finally, Chapter 4 is concerned with the fundamental causes of biodiversity loss. We first distinguish the underlying from the proximate causes of biodiversity depletion, choosing to discuss mainly the former. These include the impacts of population expansion and the scale of economic activities; the economic incentives for biodiversity destruction provided by prevailing market and policy failures; the failure to develop appropriate institutional mechanisms to manage biodiversity; and cultural and ethical world views that influence attitudes to biodiversity conservation.

Part II utilizes specific applied economic and ecological research papers written for the Biodiversity Programme in order to provide detailed analysis of biodiversity loss in selected natural systems. These include forests, wetlands, island, coastal and marine systems, and rangelands (Chapters 5-8) Although the biosphere contains other natural systems, we selected these four because they were the focus of many of the papers written for the Biodiversity Programme and therefore could be combined most easily to provide examples of system-level analysis.

In each chapter, the papers will be summarized and discussed with regard to the identification and analysis of the ecosystem, the management and policy implications of the analysis, and the challenges identified by Biodiversity Programme papers for future research. In these chapters, the objective is not to provide a comprehensive ecological and economic analysis of biodiversity loss in each system, but to emphasize the specific contributions of Biodiversity Programme papers to this analysis. Other relevant research will be cited to support the arguments where appropriate; however, the focus of the chapters is on the particular contributions of the Biodiversity Programme papers.

Although each chapter is concerned with a different natural system, we have organized all chapters similarly. We begin with a summary of the problem of biodiversity loss in the relevant natural system as identified by various Biodiversity Programme papers, and the insights on the problem provided by ecological and economic analysis as illustrated by case studies drawn from these papers. Much of the analysis has important management and policy implications for the process of biodiversity loss in each system. We therefore discuss these implications very briefly in each chapter.

Finally, it will be clear from these chapters that we are only beginning to understand more fully the implications of biodiversity loss in the four selected natural systems. For example, our basic knowledge of the ecological role of biodiversity in these systems, and its support for economic activity and human welfare, is generally poor. Most of these case studies cited can only illuminate this role indirectly through analysis and valuation of ecological goods and services provided by the respective natural systems. Similarly, many of the management and policy options that are discussed are concerned with conservation of whole-scale ecosystems and ecological functions, because often we are unable to determine 'how much' biodiversity must be lost before ecological functioning and resilience is impaired. Given our ignorance and scientific uncertainty, in situ conservation of biodiversity to maintain its vital ecological role results, by default, in de facto conservation of key ecosystems, sub-systems and habitats that are biologically diverse. Thus an important, final section in each of the chapters is a brief discussion of the challenges that must be addressed if our ecological–economic analysis of biodiversity loss in each natural system is to be improved.

Part III explores further the main implications for biodiversity management and policy introduced in previous chapters and addressed in specific Biodiversity Programme papers. Chapter 9 discusses the concept of ecological limits to economic activity and the role of markets and regulations when faced with such limits. It raises the issue of whether additional 'threshold' instruments need to be employed to deal with the biodiversity problem. Chapter 10 then considers specific management institutions and policies identified by programme papers at the international, national or regional, and local levels. The need for an integrated approach across all levels is an important issue that should be addressed.

Part IV presents the conclusions of our book in terms of future research and policy challenges. Chapter 11 discusses these challenges on two levels: first, how can we best influence human behaviour given our current economic and ecological understanding of the biodiversity problem; and second, to what extent do we need to change this understanding based on a more integrated ecological–economic approach to the problem?

We hope the end result is a stimulating book that will inspire others to further the ecological–economics 'learning curve' on biodiversity loss. On the available evidence, the world needs this sort of progress urgently.

Ed Barbier, Jo Burgess and Carl Folke
York and Stockholm
16 March 1994

Into a Limbo large and broad, since called the
Paradise of Fools, to few unknown.

Milton, *Paradise Lost*

Part I

IMPLICATIONS, DRIVING FORCES AND PERSPECTIVES

1

Background and Overview

Biological diversity – or biodiversity for short – is simply:

> the wealth of life on earth, the millions of plants, animals and micro–organisms, the genes they contain, and the intricate ecosystems they help build into the living environment. Biological diversity is simply the end result of four billion years of evolution. (WWF 1989)

More fundamentally:

> Although the species is generally considered to be 'the fundamental unit' for scientific analysis of biodiversity, it is important to recognize that biological diversity is about the variety of living organisms *at all levels* – from genetic variants belonging to the same species, through arrays of species, families and genera, and through population, community, habitat and even ecosystem levels. Biological diversity is, therefore, the 'diversity of life' itself. (Wilson 1992)[1]

Concern over the rapid depletion and degradation of the world's biological resources, and the implications of this loss for the global biosphere and human welfare, has been mounting in recent years. As much as 25 per cent of the world's species present in the mid-1980s may be extinct by the year 2015 or soon thereafter (UNEP 1992).[2] Loss and modification of ecosystems and habitats are also occurring at an alarming rate, but are much more difficult to quantify or estimate on a global scale. A major danger is that the continuing loss of our biological wealth will leave us not only with a smaller but also a much less 'varied' stock of global biological resources. Our remaining 'pool' of genetic material will show less variation, there will be less 'species richness' in a given site or habitat, and our ecosystems will become increasingly managed and more uniform. The result could be to put both human livelihoods and the future of the biosphere at risk.

In this book, we put forward the view that, although species extinction is an important manifestation and indicator of biodiversity loss, it is not the crux of the problem. Conservation of biological diversity is of vital importance to humankind because some level of biodiversity is essential to the functioning of ecosystems on which not only human consumption and production but also existence depends. Although we do not equate biodiversity conservation with the complete preservation of all species nor the maintenance of the environmental status quo, we are concerned that current rates of resource exploitation and habitat modification may be leading to excessive biodiversity loss. In order to

---

1 Wilson (1992) defines a species, or what he calls the 'biological-species content', as 'a population whose members are able to interbreed freely under natural conditions.'

2 However, as indicated in Table 1.3 and discussed below, this estimate of species loss may be extremely high. More conservative predictions would be in the neighbourhood of 3–15 per cent.

manage this problem the first requirement is to understand the ecological and economic implications of biodiversity loss, and second, to design appropriate policy and management strategies to conserve sufficient biodiversity to avert the potential threats to human welfare, and possibly existence.

In this opening chapter, we introduce the main themes of the book by reviewing briefly the emergence of biodiversity loss as an important conservation and scientific issue, providing an overview of current indicators of the status and prospects of global biodiversity and, finally, summarizing the view and approach taken in this book.

BIODIVERSITY AS A CONSERVATION AND SCIENTIFIC ISSUE

The more we have learned about the diversity of life around us, the more we have become concerned over the implications of biodiversity loss. As our scientific inquiry has revealed more about the intricate workings of nature and its importance to us, the calls for conserving what is left of the truly 'natural' world have also increased. Equally, the more that 'conservationists' have questioned the rationale and the sense in humankind's continuing destruction of nature and its complex living systems, the more social and natural scientists of all persuasions have examined this rationale and motivation with renewed interest. Clearly, biodiversity as a focus of scientific study has always been linked to biodiversity as a conservation issue.

However, human behaviour being what it is, we seem to value collective action to avert catastrophe only when the threat appears to be imminent, sudden and cataclysmic, for example, war, droughts, famines, earthquakes and other tangible eruptions of human or natural-made 'disasters'. We seem to find it much more difficult to muster the collective motivation for coping with potentially disastrous future events, which have no historical precedents and, more importantly, appear to be unfolding through accelerating, intangible and complex processes of which we know very little. The cumulative impacts on climate from greenhouse gas emissions are one example of such an event. The ecological and economic implications of biodiversity loss are clearly another.

In responding to such events, we tend to veer from the rational 'risk averse' behaviour of most standard economic models of individual and social decision making in the face of uncertainty, and instead opt for the more myopic, or 'business as usual', strategy. In other words, like the foolish person who jumps from the top of the Empire State Building without a parachute, we exclaim, 'So far so good!,' as we pass the twelfth floor on the way down. Evidently, it is also our collective assumption that somewhere between the second and first floor we will 'develop' some miraculous technical solution to our predicament, to ensure a safe landing at the very last moment possible. The burden of proof appears to rest with scientists and conservationists to indicate that this behaviour is foolishly dangerous.

In observing the current global biodiversity crisis, concerned conservationists and scientists are alarmed by our ignorance and collective inertia. Another famous analogy – the classic 'rivet-popper' problem – explains their view on this crisis facing humanity (Ehrlich and Ehrlich 1981 and 1992): given the fail-safe designs on aeroplanes that include considerable redundancy, the removal of a single rivet from an aeroplane's wing is unlikely to cause a crash. However, the continuous removal of numerous rivets will sooner or later lead to disaster. The timing of the disaster is difficult to predict, as it depends both on only partially understood factors in the wing and on unpredictable future environmental events (for example, rough landings, turbulent flying conditions and so on). For similar reasons, the precise impacts of the loss of biodiversity in ecosystems are difficult to predict, but the eventual costs in terms of ecosystem malfunction, breakdown and ultimately disaster cannot be avoided if biodiversity loss continues unabated. Again, however, it is up to the concerned scientists and conservationists to demonstrate that such a process typifies the problem of global biodiversity loss today.

In this book, we hope to bring together the scientific analyses and arguments of some leading ecologists, economists and scholars from other disciplines to lend credence to the 'rivet-popper' view of current trends in biodiversity loss. At the very least, we suggest that, given the overwhelming importance of biodiversity to ecological and economic activity, and ultimately, human welfare, and given our current scientific uncertainty and ignorance over the implications and predictability of biodiversity loss, human society should be more cautious and less myopic in its exploitation of biological resources and habitats.

As stated in the preface, our views on the biodiversity problem as presented in this book will please neither the optimists nor the pessimists. The optimists will find our concern over the 'biodiversity crisis' to be overly alarmist. In their opinion, there is nothing inherently wrong with the 'business as usual' strategy. Humankind's capacity to improve human and technical skills will be able to overcome the biodiversity problem – which will gradually fade away as did past concerns over Malthusian population constraints in the nineteenth century and 'limits to growth' from resource exhaustion in the early 1970s. On the other hand, the pessimists would maintain that humankind is already on a dangerous path of biological destruction, that we are on the brink of ecological catastrophe or heading towards it inexorably, and that the only solution is drastic curtailment of present economic activities and resource use.

Obviously, just as there are many different definitions of biological diversity today, there are many different perceptions of the importance of biodiversity to human welfare. The debate is a critical one and we hope that this book will contribute to it. However, before elaborating further our views on the biodiversity problem and the contribution that we hope to make, it is useful to provide a brief background to current scientific and conservationist concerns over biodiversity loss.

Background to current concerns

The period of European imperial expansion and colonization of the globe during the sixteenth to late nineteenth century also corresponded with the 'golden age' of scientific discovery and knowledge of the natural world. One important development during this era was the birth and prominence of taxonomy – the science of classifying living organisms. As Western explorers, merchants, officials and soldiers busied themselves with discovery, trade and conquest in both the 'new' and ancient worlds, so their counterparts in the natural sciences collected, recorded and studied each new living specimen revealed by the 'opening up' of newly 'discovered' and exotic habitats.

Gradually, as the variety and complexity of organization and function among living organisms became apparent, as well as the sheer range of the biodiversity encountered, simple collection and classification of species gave way to new scientific methods that sought to both explain and explore the evolution of biodiversity, as well as life itself. For example, Wilson (1992) notes that a fundamental advance of eighteenth-century biology was the description of diversity by organizing species into clusters according to how closely they resemble one another, eventually developing the following hierarchy of classification: kingdom, phylum, class, order, family, genus and species. However, by the twentieth century, it became more appropriate to describe diversity by level of biological organization, which is arrayed in the following hierarchy: ecosystem, community, guild, species, organism and gene. Clearly, scientific thinking had evolved from exploring the similarities and dissimilarities between and among plants, animals and micro-organisms in isolation, to examining the basic functional relationships of living organisms at the various levels of biological organization in which they exist. As a consequence, two fundamentally important and related issues have emerged: how biodiversity is assembled by the creation of ecosystems; and, alternatively, how ecosystem functioning depends on the level of biodiversity.

Crucial to this transition in scientific thinking was the 'revolutionary' work of Charles Darwin, *On the Origin of Species*, in 1859. Darwin's insight was that variation within species leads to natural selection and permits evolution, and thus the emergence of new species, whereas earlier scientists followed the principle of seeking the common features that identify the group and ignoring the divergences (Cook 1991). In other words, the origin of species and thus biodiversity:

> is therefore simply evolution of some difference – any difference at all – that prevents the production of fertile hybrids between populations under natural conditions. … The origin of most biological diversity, in a phrase, is a side product of evolution. (Wilson 1992)

Just as natural scientists were exploring both the origins of biological diversity and its importance to the functioning of ecosystems, conservationists were noting, with great concern, the rapid disappearance of biological resources and their habitats. In the nineteenth century, many of the early conservationists such as Clements and Thoreau were also respected 'naturalists', who both recorded and were inspired by the diversity they encountered in the natural world (Magurran 1988). Some influential economists, too, such as John Stuart Mill, added their voices to the conservationists' concerns, in other words that there is not 'much satisfaction in contemplating the world with nothing left to the spontaneous activity of nature' (Mill 1862).

By the early twentieth century, conservationists were already organizing them-selves into politically influential 'movements', with a corresponding 'doctrine' of views on humankind's relationship with nature. One influential voice in the early American conservation movement was the nineteenth-century naturalist George Perkins Marsh, who argued that the fundamental characteristic of nature is its ecological complexity and diversity, which is continually undergoing change. Moreover, he viewed nature and humanity as an inseparable, inter-dependent unit – the 'nature-man continuum'. He maintained that 'man changes the natural complex and nature's changes, in turn, exert their major influence on man. The interaction is continuous' (Marsh 1865).

Marsh's views summarize what both conservationists and scientists in the second half of the twentieth century found intriguing – and important – about nature's diversity. During this period, the study of diversity and its measurement became a feature of the new discipline, ecology, that emerged to prominence as the study of the inter-relationships between living organisms and their environ-ment.[3] According to Magurran (1988), there are three reasons why biological diversity has become a central focus of ecology:

- the spatial and temporal variation in diversity which intrigued early biologists and naturalists still holds the fascination of the modern ecologist;
- measures of diversity have come to be viewed as indicators of the well-being of ecological systems;
- considerable debate continues to surround the measurement and definition of biological diversity, despite the extensive range of indices and models that have been developed for measuring diversity.

In fact, the increased scientific attention paid to biological diversity in recent years has convinced many that the concept 'is rather like an optical illusion. The more it is looked at, the less clearly defined it appears to be and viewing it from different angles can lead to different perceptions of what is involved' (Magurran 1988). Indeed, some scientists go so far as to dismiss the term as a 'non-concept' (Hurlbert 1971).

Despite the difficulties that modern science has had in formulating a consensus on the definition and measurement of biodiversity, there is more or less agree-ment on some general aspects of the term. Scientists basically agree that biologi-cal diversity refers to the range of variation or differences in living organisms and their environments, and that it can be distinguished by the three main levels of biological hierarchy: genes, species and ecosystems. This distinction between genetic, species and ecological diversity has in itself tended to cause confusion over definitions and measurement, but it does serve to illustrate the different levels of scientific concern over the biodiversity problem. For example, on one level, conservation of biodiversity has been characterized as ensuring sufficient variation in the genetic make-up of species. Alternatively, conservation of bio-logical diversity has also focused on reducing threats to species extinction and richness. Finally, at the broadest level, it is concerned with the conservation of

---

3 See pages 42–49 for more discussion of ecology and its various sub-disciplines.

natural ecosystems and their components in the face of conversion and modification from human activities.

Nevertheless, as the living world has traditionally been categorized in terms of species, conservation of biodiversity has generally been interpreted in terms of species diversity. This is usually defined as 'species richness', or the number of species in a site or habitat (WCMC 1992). Moreover, although the loss of biological diversity may take many forms, the extinction of species is usually taken to represent its most dramatic and irreversible manifestation.

Conservationists, in particular, have almost invariably translated biodiversity conservation in terms of conserving species richness. This is usually based on the rationale either that species have a right to exist or that they have an actual or potential economic benefit to humankind (IUCN/UNEP/WWF 1980 and 1991). However, conservationists have also been quick to point out that declines in species and genetic diversity are clearly inter-related. Continuing loss of species diversity – and certainly species extinction – implies a reduction in the overall pool of global genetic material as well, with profound significance for both natural evolutionary change and artificial selective breeding. Moreover, conservationists argue, the loss of both genetic and species diversity is mainly due to human activities. It occurs both directly through over-exploitation of species and sub-species via hunting, collection and persecution, and indirectly through the loss or modification of habitats and ecosystems. Conversion and alteration of habitats and ecosystems are by far the most important factors; consequently, conservationists have increasingly called for the preservation of 'species rich' habitats and ecosystems as the basic strategy for biodiversity conservation (Ehrlich and Ehrlich 1981 and 1992; McNeely et al 1990; Myers 1979; WWF 1989).

Some economists, too, have stated the need for habitat preservation to conserve endangered species. For example, more than 40 years ago, Ciriacy-Wantrup (1952) argued that, as a result of species extinction, future societies may discover that they have forgone significant benefits. In order to avoid species extinction and the corresponding loss in benefits, society today ought to preserve a minimum viable population of the species and its required supporting habitat. This approach was called the safe minimum standard strategy for avoiding extinction in day-to-day resource management decisions. Exceptions would occur only when the costs of avoiding extinction are intolerably large or that other social objectives must take precedence (see also Bishop 1993 and Chapter 9 of this book).

The modern conservationist argument for preserving habitats as a means to protecting threatened species and valuable genetic material has challenged the notion that ex situ conservation – the use of zoos, botanic gardens, breeding programmes, germ plasm 'laboratories', gene or seed banks, and other methods of maintaining species and genetic stocks away from their natural habitats – is sufficient for this purpose. Increasingly, scientists have come to the same conclusion. For example, Weissinger (1990) stresses the importance of ex situ conservation through germ plasm technologies in maintaining genetic diversity, but he also acknowledges that such methods cannot conserve the whole range of an organism's diversity; rather they preserve a sample of it. Moreover, this sample is necessarily incomplete. It represents only a portion of the population at the moment of its extraction. Similarly, in reviewing the recent developments in major ex situ conservation efforts over recent years, Wilson (1992) maintains that they may save a few species beyond hope, but the major source of biodiversity conservation must come from preservation of natural ecosystems and habitats.

More fundamentally, in recent years the conservationists' argument for biodiversity conservation and mounting scientific concerns over the implications of biodiversity loss has led to increased calls for a global biodiversity conservation strategy as being essential to ensuring 'sustainable' development (McNeely et al 1990; IUCN/UNEP/WWF 1980 and 1991). Although the 1972 United Nations Conference on the Human Environment, held in Stockholm, is usually credited with popularizing the concept of sustainable development, it was the 1987 report of the World Commission on Environment and Development (WCED) that propelled the concept on to the global policy agenda. Perhaps the most important contribution of the latter report was to provide a simple and comprehensive definition of sustainable development: 'development that meets the needs of present generations without compromising the ability of future generations to meet their own needs' (WCED 1987). Moreover, for the proponents of biodiversity conservation, it was a definition that was clearly suited to their arguments.

In fact, conservationists had long been calling attention to the need for a global strategy linking biodiversity conservation and sustainability of human societies. The First World Conservation Strategy argued that 'the maintenance of essential ecological processes and life-support systems, the preservation of genetic diversity, and the sustainable utilization of species and ecosystem' have the overall aim of achieving 'sustainable development through the conservation of living resources' (IUCN/UNEP/WWF 1980). By the Second World Conservation Strategy in 1991, the rationale for linking biodiversity and sustainable development were being justified on economic, as well as scientific and moral grounds:

> 'Biological diversity is the total variety of genetic strains, species and ecosystems. ... Human activities are now accelerating the depletion and extinction of species and changing the conditions for evolution and this is a matter of considerable concern. Biological diversity should be conserved as a matter of principle, because all species deserve respect regardless of their use to humanity ... and because they are all components of our life support system. Biological diversity also provides us with economic benefits and adds greatly to the quality of our lives. (IUCN/UNEP/WWF 1991)

By the time of the United Nations Conference on Environment and Development (UNCED) held in Rio de Janeiro in June 1992, the various arguments linking global biological diversity to sustainable development had resulted in international agreements on the establishment of a Global Environmental Facility (GEF) to fund projects that yield global benefits, such as biodiversity conservation, in developing countries and preliminary negotiations leading to an international agreement on global biodiversity conservation. The Convention on Biological Diversity was signed by 154 nations at UNCED. Since then, even more nations have signed.

Article 2 of the Convention distinguishes between biological resources, which are defined as including 'genetic resources, organisms or parts thereof, populations or any other biotic component of ecosystems with actual or potential use or value for humanity,' and biological diversity, which is defined as 'the variability among living organisms from all sources, including inter alia, terrestrial, marine and other aquatic ecosystems, and the ecological complexes of which they are a part: this includes diversity within species, between species and of ecosystems' (UNEP 1993). However, it is clear that the concerns over biodiversity loss as expressed in the Convention go much further than the traditional preoccupation with species extinction. The greater part of the biodiversity problem concerns the relation between biodiversity and the ecological services obtained from the biosphere by humanity. The primary service of biological diversity is to make available on a sustainable basis a wide array of biological resources (including genetic resources) and ecological functions through contributing to the productivity, or 'services', of natural ecosystems (UNEP 1993).

In short, the Convention not only provides important international recognition of and impetus to the need to conserve global biological diversity at all levels, but also poses a challenge to ecologists, economists and scholars from other disciplines to provide further insight into the fundamental economic and ecological role of biological diversity. It is this 'new thinking' that the Beijer Biodiversity Programme and this book hope to foster.

CURRENT STATUS AND PROSPECTS

Before summarizing the views and approach of this book, it is worth reviewing briefly the current scientific understanding of the status and prospects of global biodiversity. Most of the statistics focus on species loss, partly because of the limitations on data, partly because biodiversity has been traditionally equated with species diversity and partly because much attention has been focused on species extinction as a 'barometer' of the health of global biodiversity. As we shall discuss presently, current and projected trends in species loss is an important indicator of the status and prospects of biodiversity, but they do not convey adequately the implications of the problem of biodiversity loss for ecosystems and human welfare.

A recent and comprehensive compilation of global biodiversity status and trends has been undertaken by the Wildlife Conservation Monitoring Centre (WCMC 1992). Following established tradition, the study quantifies rates of species extinction to provide the most straightforward indicator of biodiversity status. Historical data on actual extinction rates are most readily available for birds, mammals and molluscs (see Table 1.1). Documented island extinctions began almost two centuries before continental extinctions. However, for all animals, extinctions increased rapidly from the early or mid-nineteenth century until the mid-tentieth century. The apparent decline in extinctions since 1960 is most probably attributable to the increase in conservation efforts.

Estimating rates of loss for habitat and ecosystems is much more difficult, as ecosystems are not easily delineated and habitat alteration hard to define. Usually,

Table 1.1 *Historical trends in animal extinctions*

Period	Molluscs	Birds	Mammals	Other	Total
1600–59	0	6	0	2	8
(% on islands)		(100%)		(100%)	(100%)
1660–1719	0	14	0	2	16
(% on islands)		(100%)		(100%)	(100%)
1720–79	0	14	1	0	15
(% on islands)		(100%)	(100%)		(100%)
1780–1839	0	11	3	5	19
(% on islands)		(91%)	(0%)	(100%)	(79%)
1840–99	69	27	12	9	117
(% on islands)	(100%)	(93%)	(42%)	(78%)	(91%)
1900–59	79	35	15	46	175
(% on islands)	(61%)	(83%)	(33%)	(52%)	(61%)
1960–	13	7	5	19	44
(% on islands)	(69%)	(71%)	(60%)	(37%)	(54%)
No date	30	1	22	37	90
(% on islands)	(83%)	(100%)	(91%)	(73%)	(81%)
TOTALS	191	115	58	120	484
(% on islands)	(79%)	(90%)	(59%)	(62%)	(63%)

Source: WCMC (1992).

fairly simplistic measures of land use change are employed. For example, Table 1.2(a) indicates that the area of cropland has expanded dramatically over the years 1700–1980, mainly at the expense of forests and woodlands. As indicated in Table 1.2(b), the most rapid land use change is currently the conversion of forests in tropical regions. Preliminary estimates from the United Nations Food and Agricultural Organization (FAO) suggest that the annual area of tropical deforestation during the 1980s was approximately 170,000 km^2, or a rate of around 0.9 per cent of the 1980 total forest area (FAO 1993).

Tropical deforestation is considered a significant factor in global biodiversity loss because the vast majority of terrestrial species occur in tropical moist forests. As a result, most predictions of global extinction rates – as opposed to historical rates – are usually projected on the basis of estimates of species richness in tropical forests, combined with actual and projected deforestation trends. Table 1.3 summarizes some of these recent estimates. As methods of estimation have improved, it appears that predictions of species loss have been revised somewhat downwards. Nevertheless, even the most conservative calculations would suggest a rate of species loss of around 1–5 per cent per decade.

However, Lugo, Parrotta and Brown (1993) suggest that estimations of species loss based on projections of deforestation through simplified species–area relationships are misleading. In particular, such models fail to take account of land use after forest clearing; they essentially assume that such uses involve little or no biological diversity. Although substantial biodiversity loss occurs due to forest clearing and degradation, certain land management practices, such as the estab-

Table 1.2   *Historical trends in land use*

(a) Global land use, 1700–1980[a]

Vegetation Types	Area (10^4 km^2)					Change 1700–1980	
	1700	1850	1920	1950	1980	Percentage	Area (10^6 km^2)
Forests and woodlands	6215	5965	5678	5389	5053	–18.7%	11.62
Grasslands and pasture	6860	6837	6748	6780	6788	–1.0%	0.72
Croplands	265	537	913	1170	1501	+466.4%	12.36

(b) Tropical forest area cleared (10^3 km^2), pre-1650–1990[b]

Region	Pre 1650	1650–1749	1750–1849	1850–1978	1980–90
Central America	12–18	30	40	200	135
Latin America	12–18	100	170	637	695
Asia	640–974	176–216	596–606	1220	360
Africa	96–226	24–80	16–42	469	503

Notes: [a] Original source Richards (1990).
[b] Original source FAO (1993) for 1980–90 and Williams (1990) for all other periods.

Source: WCMC (1992).

lishment of plantations and secondary forest, can restore a significant amount of biodiversity. Thus the development of better indicators of global species loss will require further research on the relationships between species diversity and forest clearance.[4]

Recent efforts to provide a framework for assessing conditions and trends in biodiversity status attempt to develop a set of 'multiple indicators' to assist conservation policy making. Rather than attempting to provide a universal indicator of biodiversity status and trends, such approaches acknowledge that the difficulty in 'capturing' a complex concept such as biodiversity in a single 'index' suggests that indicators must become more policy specific. That is, a different indicator should be used depending on the stated objective of conservation policy. For example, Reid et al (1993) argue that, if the objective is to minimize species extinction, then a useful indicator would be changes in the number of species over time; alternatively, if the objective is to minimize the loss of species 'diversity', then such an indicator is misleading as it says little about the 'distinctiveness' of each species. As shown in Table 1.4, the authors suggest a set of 22 alternative indicators of biodiversity based on three categories:

■   indicators used to measure the diversity of 'wild species' and genetic diversity;

---

4   See Chapter 5 of this book for further discussion of the arguments by Lugo, Parrotta and Brown (1993).

Table 1.3 *Estimated rates of extinction based on tropical deforestation*

Estimate	Percentage global loss per decade	Method of estimation	Reference
One million species between 1975 and 2000	4%	Extrapolation of past exponentially increasing trend	Myers (1979)
15–20% of species between 1980 and 2000	8–11%	Estimated species area curve; forest loss based on Global 2000 projections	Lovejoy (1980)
12% of plant species in neotropics; 15% of bird species in Amazon Basin	NA	Species curve (z = 0.25)	Simberloff (1986)
25% of species between 1985 and 2015	9%	Loss of half the species in area likely to be deforested by 2015	Raven (1988)
5–15% of forest species by 2020	2–5%	Species area curve (0.15 < z < 0.35); forest loss assumed twice rate projected for 1980–5	Reid and Miller (1989)
0.2–0.3% per year	2–3%	Species area curve (low z value); 1.8% forest loss per year	Ehrlich and Wilson (1991)
2–8% loss between 1990 and 2015	1–5%	Species area curve (0.15 < z < 0.35); range includes current rate of forest loss and 50% increase	Reid (1992)

Source: WCMC (1992) and references.

- indicators used to measure diversity at the community/habitat level;
- indicators used to assess domesticated species (the diversity of crops and livestock).

With a comprehensive set of multiple indicators at their disposal, it is then up to policy makers and planners to choose the right indicator or indicators to help set priorities for biodiversity conservation. Moreover, the choice of indicators should also depend on the scale of the decision making, whether it is at the local, national or global level, as well as on whether genetic, species or community diversity is being assessed (Reid et al 1993).

Developing multiple indicators to represent different priorities for biodiversity conservation may be one practical solution to the problem of the lack of scientific agreement over a precise definition and measurement of 'biological diversity'. It may also have some merit in that, through their choice of indicators, different decision makers and actors (such as non-governmental organizations, scientists and politicians) will 'reveal' their respective opinions on what 'matters' in biodiversity conservation. Once 'revealed', such objectives and views can then be open

Table 1.4 *A multiple set of indicators for biodiversity conservation*

Indicator	Biodiversity conservation concerns		
	Genetic diversity	Species diversity	Community diversity
Wild species and genetic diversity			
1. Species richness (number, number per unit area, number per habitat type)	X	X	
2. Species threatened with extinction (number or per cent)	X	X	
3. Species threatened with extirpation (number or per cent)	X	X	
4. Endemic species (number or per cent)	X	X	
5. Endemic species threatened with extinction (number or per cent)	X	X	
6. Species risk index	X	X	
7. Species with stable or increasing populations (number or per cent)	X	X	
8. Species with decreasing populations (number or per cent)	X	X	
9. Threatened species in protected areas (number or per cent)	X	X	
10. Endemic species in protected areas (number or per cent)	X	X	
11. Threatened species in ex situ collections (number or per cent)	X	X	
12. Threatened species with viable ex situ populations (number or per cent)	X	X	
13. Species used by local residents (number or per cent)	X	X	
Community diversity			
14. Percentage of area dominated by non-domesticated species		X	X
15. Rate of change from dominance of non-domesticated species to domesticated species		X	X
16. Percentages of area dominated by non-domesticated species occurring in patches greater than 1,000 km^2		X	X
17. Percentage of area in strictly protected status		X	X
Domesticated species diversity			
18. Accessions of crops and livestock in ex situ storage (number or per cent)	X		
19. Accessions of crops regenerated in the past decade (per cent)	X		
20. Crops (livestock) grown as a percentage of number 30 years before	X		
21. Varieties of crops/livestock grown as a percentage of number 30 years before	X		
22. Coefficient of kinship or parentage of crops	X		

Source: Reid et al (1993).

to public debate, and, hopefully, resolved into agreed and clearly stated priorities for conservation.

However, the danger of developing different indicators of diversity is that ultimately they may confuse conservation priorities by being based on inherently incomparable and inconsistent measures of biological diversity. As argued by Weitzman (1994), at some point we need to come up with 'a more-or-less consistent and usable measure of the value of diversity' – namely a 'value-of-diversity objective function' – in order to resolve real-world conservation choices. That is, if a value of diversity function can be meaningfully postulated, then it can, at least in principle, be made commensurate with other benefits and costs, and society will therefore be able to determine how much diversity ought to be 'preserved' at the expense of sacrificing other choices open to us. Moreover, as suggested by Weitzman, the diversity 'measurement' that constitutes the value of diversity of function should be sufficiently 'neutral' that it could be applied equally to any collection of biological 'units' – whether they be genetic material, sub-species, species, communities or ecosystems. One ought to be able to develop a 'criterion of distance' that reflects precisely those characteristics that define the 'difference' between the various biological 'units' comprising a given collection. Once such a criterion is defined, it can be used to determine what is valuable about maintaining the 'diversity' of the collection; consequently, a sequence of actions to minimize diversity loss can be constructed, and their relative costs and benefits calculated.

Weitzman (1994) illustrates conceptually the use of diversity function through the example of a collection of species, employing the criterion of genetic distance between species to construct a measure of diversity and, in some instances, using the probability of the extinction of species, along with their expected benefits, to construct the value of diversity function. Thus the 'expected diversity loss per preservation dollar' among species can be compared. Weitzman also examines the operational criteria for determining preservation site priorities of a US non-governmental organization, the Nature Conservancy. Their mandate is to purchase land in order to preserve rare or endangered species, or natural communities, which are ranked by how rare they are as well as the number of site occurrences. These criteria are used in turn to determine an overall biodiversity ranking of sites and to prioritize the acquisition of sites. The resulting biodiversity ranking system gives a site a higher value if it contains more endangered species and/or if the survival probability of the endangered species on that site is more greatly improved when the site is preserved. According to Weitzman, the ranking system corresponds very roughly to identifying sites whose preservation would cause a relatively large change in expected diversity. That is, given the values implied by their stated objectives, the Nature Conservancy have defined a method of selecting sites that more or less corresponds with Weitzman's own criteria for developing a value of diversity function.

At least conceptually, it may be possible to develop a single criterion for measuring diversity and thus determining a value of diversity function, but in practice we are clearly far from applying a universal approach. Development of any such criterion for measuring diversity in itself implies not only consensus on what we mean by 'diversity' and how it should be measured, but also that we agree on what it is about biological diversity that we value. Even if we are close to consensus on measuring the diversity of any given 'collection' of biological entities, we are far from agreement on what constitutes the ecological and economic implications of having more, as opposed to less, biological 'diversity'. One problem is that we currently use the term 'biological diversity' as a catch-all for distinctly different phenomena – genetic, species and ecosystem diversity. Analysis of the ecological and economic implications of biodiversity loss in terms of one of these levels of biological hierarchy does not necessarily yield the same results at another level (Perrings et al 1994).

However, even if we are concerned with diversity at only one level of biological hierarchy – say, species diversity – and we agree on a common measurement of diversity – say, the genetic difference among species – determining a value of species diversity may still have to be modified depending on the problem under consideration. That is, the 'diversity' as measured by the genetic differences between species may have a different value to us depending on what we perceive to be the economic and ecological implications of species diversity for human welfare.

For example, as argued by Perrings et al (1994), wild and domesticated grasses are genetically different, but depending on which of their uses we consider, they can be viewed as either substitutes or complements; this means that, on the one hand, both grasses can be used alternatively as fodder staples and, on the other, they both work together to maintain the ecological functioning and resilience of rangeland systems.[5] Because both wild and domesticated species have similar value in consumption as fodder, there is very little lost in the substitution of domesticated for wild grasses. If we consider the use of grasses for fodder only, then there may be little additional value to be gained from maintaining the diversity of grasses in rangelands. In contrast, both types of grasses are necessary for the maintenance of rangeland ecosystem functioning and resilience (see Chapter 8). As a consequence, in terms of ecological functioning, maintaining 'diversity', namely a mix of both grasses, is important. Focusing exclusively on the fodder value and not the ecological role of wild grasses can lead to the conclusion that diversity of grasses is not necessary in the rangeland system, whereas taking account of the latter ecological role will lead to the opposite conclusion.

Unfortunately, not only do current indicators and assessments of biodiversity status tend to focus predominantly on species diversity, but they also tend to emphasize only certain characteristics of species, such as their genetic properties, their relative abundance across sites, their endangered or threatened status, or whether they are 'wild' or 'domesticated' (for example, see Table 1.4). Such characteristics by themselves tell us very little about the ecological role of biological diversity, which is the role of living organisms in underpinning the functioning and resilience of ecosystems. It is this role, and its implications for human economic activity and welfare, that is the focus of this book.

---

5   In ecology, the term 'resilience' usually refers to the capacity of an ecosystem to recover in response to stress or shock, to absorb the perturbation. See also Chapter 2 of this book.

THE ECOLOGICAL ECONOMICS OF BIODIVERSITY

The views expressed in the Biodiversity Convention suggest that global concern over the overall loss of biodiversity, and its economic and ecological importance – whether focused at the genetic, species or ecosystem level – must ultimately come to terms with the need to conserve natural habitats and ecosystems, as well as individual species and genetic material (UNEP 1993). However, at the same time, the scientific world is undergoing a profound reassessment of what the ecological implications of biodiversity loss might be. The traditional focus has been on the problem of species loss and extinction, the implications for the availability of genetic material, and the potential impacts on human production and consumption activities. More recently, however, the focus has shifted to the role of biological diversity in maintaining the functioning and resilience of ecosystems, and the implications of any ecological disruptions resulting from biodiversity loss on human economic activity, welfare and, ultimately, existence. Although acknowledging that the traditional concern with biodiversity loss is of importance, in this book we highlight the implications of biodiversity loss from the second perspective.

There are several reasons why we are exploring the 'ecological role' of biodiversity in this book. First, the economic and ecological implications of this role appear to be extremely significant yet difficult to assess, and therefore require much more analysis by scientists and attention by policy makers than has been the case at present. Second, because our understanding of the problem is extremely limited, it is surrounded by a great deal of uncertainty and ignorance, which in turn should influence the development of appropriate research and policy responses to biodiversity conservation. Third, improvement in both the scientific and policy analysis of the implications of biodiversity loss for ecosystem functioning and resilience, as well as human welfare, will require the development of integrated approaches to analysing these implications that will involve ecologists, economists and scholars from other disciplines working together.

In the remaining chapters of Part I we will examine some of these arguments further. Here, we briefly summarize our views on biodiversity loss as emphasized in those chapters and throughout this book.

Although species extinction is the most fundamental and irreversible manifestation of biodiversity loss, the more profound implication is for ecological functioning and resilience. By ecological functioning, we mean those basic processes of ecosystems, such as nutrient cycling, biological productivity, hydrology and sedimentation, as well as the ability of ecosystems to support life. By ecological resilience, we mean the capacity of an ecosystem to recover from and thus absorb external shocks and stresses, whether they be natural (such as drought, fire or earthquakes) or human-induced (such as pollution or biomass removal). Some minimal level of biological diversity is necessary to maintain ecological functioning and resilience, which in turn are necessary for generating the biological resources (trees, fish, wildlife, crops and so on) and ecological 'services' (e.g. watershed protection, climate stabilization, erosion control, etc.) on which economic activity and human welfare depend. Unfortunately, in determining exactly what level of biodiversity loss is tolerable before the impacts on human welfare become severe, we are faced with the same 'rivet-popper' problem discussed on page 5: the precise impacts of the loss of biodiversity in ecosystems are difficult to predict, but the eventual costs in terms of ecosystem malfunction, breakdown and ultimately disaster cannot be avoided if biodiversity loss continues unabated.

At first the ecological and welfare impacts may be localized, but in many cases they generate wider national, regional or even global effects. Consequently, the biological resources and ecological 'services' available today may not be so abundant tomorrow. In short, the world will be experiencing greater ecological scarcity. Not only will this manifest itself through a growing 'relative' scarcity of essential environmental assets and ecological services on which human welfare depends, but, at the extreme, will also lead to irrevocable ecological damage and the potential collapse of ecosystems on which human livelihoods – and even existence – depend.[6]

Coping with ecological scarcity is not an easy task. Biodiversity loss can be irreversible, its consequences uncertain, and the environmental values that are lost are so difficult to assess and often unknown. This would suggest caution in our current efforts to convert and exploit natural resources – particularly as we do not know the preferences and technology of future generations whose welfare and even existence may be affected by the pace and scale of biodiversity loss today. However, caution in resource use is hardly an attribute of modern society today. Thus management of the current biodiversity crisis will require fundamental changes in our economic, environmental and social relationships. It is how we manage these changes which is one important theme of this book.

In short, the fundamental problem is to maintain that level of biodiversity which will guarantee the functioning and resilience of ecosystems on which not only human consumption and production but also existence also depend (Perrings, Folke and Mäler 1992). However, as argued above, preservation of natural habitats and ecosystems – or a sufficient store of global biological resources in general – from human modification and conversion is essential to ensuring this critical level of biodiversity conservation. The biodiversity problem therefore requires that we address the interaction between economic and ecological systems to determine the appropriate level of exploitation – as well as conservation – of our natural environment.

Unfortunately, as discussed on pages 23–41, our current indicators of global biodiversity status do not provide sufficient information to determine either the extent of biodiversity loss or the implications of current rates of biodiversity decline for guaranteeing the functioning and resilience of ecosystems. In other words, we cannot be sure how close we are to the critical level of biodiversity conservation for maintaining global welfare and existence, nor what that critical

---

6 The next two chapters will discuss the economic implications of and approaches to the problem of ecological scarcity in more detail. Drawing on recent advances in environmental and natural resource economics, Barbier (1989a) developed this concept of 'an increasing relative scarcity of essential environmental services and ecological functions' as an economic problem and called it an 'alternative view of natural resource scarcity'. For example, he argued that 'this alternative approach may be particularly applicable to cases where cumulative resource depletion and degradation through economic over-exploitation lead to severe ecological disruption and the collapse of livelihoods', ie 'conditions under which present patterns of resource exploitation have transgressed ecological thresholds'.

level might be. For all we know, we may be at that threshold already, or will be driven towards it inevitably, given current economic and demographic trends. Although incomplete, the existing indicators available to us do suggest a continuing, and perhaps accelerating, trend of biodiversity loss.

Improvements in indicators of global biodiversity loss are clearly necessary and urgent; nevertheless, this is not the main theme of this book. Rather, we believe that existing indicators are sufficient to suggest that a serious problem of global biodiversity loss exists – and is possibly getting worse.

Instead, our main concern is with the ecological economics of biodiversity loss. By this we mean how ecology, economics and possibly other disciplines can best work together to improve our understanding of the biodiversity problem and to help design strategies for tackling it. Figure 1.1 summarizes the biodiversity problem as we see it. Biodiversity and biological resources are fundamental to the functioning and resilience of ecosystems, which in turn supply essential ecological services and resources to support the production and consumption activities of the economic system, and, ultimately, human welfare and existence. However, the economic activities of production and consumption also lead to biodiversity loss, directly through over-exploitation of biological resources, and indirectly through habitat modification and destruction.

Consequently, as shown in Figure 1.1, through these inter-relationships the economic and ecological systems are not separate but fundamentally inter-connected. The two are essentially sub-systems integrated into a complete economic–environmental system. Because the problem of biodiversity loss can only be understood in full through analysing these ecological–economic inter-relationships, we believe that both economics and ecology will be required to work jointly and cooperatively to provide this analysis.

Figure 1.2 illustrates what would be the ideal framework for such policy analysis.[7] We believe that the ecological economics of biodiversity loss should be relevant to policy decisions concerning the exploitation of ecosystems and biodiversity. That is, what is needed are ecological–economic 'models' of biodiversity loss that can inform policy makers of the full implications of the various alternative policy and management options available to them, and, in particular, that indicate the costs and benefits of the different policy options relative to existing policy, namely the status quo.

For each policy option, the ideal ecological–economic model should be able to trace through the various economic–environmental linkages, as shown in Figure 1.1, to determine the various consequences for human welfare associated with that option. The evaluation of the different policy options may in turn depend, where possible, on valuation; that is to say, the quantification of the specific welfare impacts – or costs and benefits – of each policy option to facilitate comparison by decision makers. Where quantification of welfare impacts is not possible, then policy evaluation may be qualitative, which in itself presents no problem as long as the overall objective is the same: employing the results of

7 We are grateful to Karl-Göran Mäler for providing the basic idea for Figure 1.2.

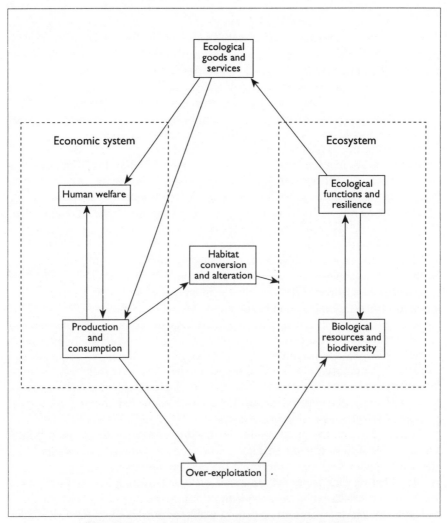

Figure 1.1 *Economic–environmental systems*

ecological–economic analysis to inform policy makers of the various welfare consequences of alternative policy options to control biodiversity loss.

Finally, evaluation of the available policy options relative to the status quo will inform decision makers about the choices available, and consideration of these alternatives may lead to adjustment in priorities, and even the development of new policy and management options. These in turn should be evaluated and the new questions for policy analysis may require further development of ecological–economic models for this purpose. Thus the process outlined in Figure 1.2 is never static but is dynamic, leading both to improvements in our methods of ecological economic policy analysis and, hopefully, to the policies to control biodiversity loss.

We wish that the ecological economics of biodiversity was sufficiently developed to provide such a comprehensive policy analysis. Unfortunately, it is not.

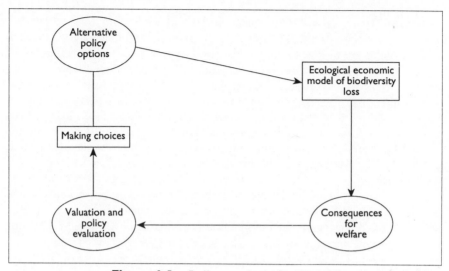

Figure 1.2 *Policy analysis framework*

For example, a major problem facing ecologists is a lack of knowledge of the role of biodiversity in supporting ecological functioning and resilience. This makes it extremely difficult to predict the ecological consequences of biodiversity loss, including whether there are significant 'threshold' effects at work. Such uncertainty also makes the task of economists assessing the potential welfare implications of biodiversity loss and evaluating appropriate policy responses equally problematic. Until relatively recently, these difficulties have been compounded by the reluctance of ecologists and economists to pool their knowledge in a concerted effort to analyse the economic–environmental linkages arising from biodiversity loss. It appears that we are not yet ready to make even a first 'loop' around the policy analysis framework indicated in Figure 1.2.

However, we do believe that ecologists and economists are at the early stages of developing such an analysis, as evidenced by the papers produced by the Beijer Biodiversity Programme. The remainder of this book is an attempt both to illustrate the progress in this analysis as represented by these papers and to indicate the challenges facing future progress in developing an ecological economics of biodiversity.

In the remaining chapters of Part I, we attempt to illustrate further the type of economic–environmental linkages associated with biodiversity loss as outlined in Figure 1.1. In the next chapter, we discuss current evidence of the role of biodiversity in ecosystem functioning and resilience, and thus in sustaining human welfare. In Chapter 3, we focus on how ecology and economics have approached the biodiversity problem to date, and how more recent efforts have raised questions as to whether a single-discipline approach is sufficient for analysing the problem. In Chapter 4 we review briefly the proximate causes of over-exploitation and habitat alteration, and the more complex driving forces underlying these factors.

Part II provides evidence from the Beijer Biodiversity Programme paper of progress in ecological economic policy analysis of biodiversity loss in four key systems: forests, wetlands, island and marine systems, and rangelands. For none of the systems are we able to provide the 'ideal' type of policy analysis framework for evaluating policy and management options as indicated in Figure 1.2. No suitable, comprehensive, ecological–economic model of biodiversity loss exists yet for this task. For example, so little is known about the ecological role of biological diversity in these systems, that we are unable to trace through fully even the basic economic–environmental linkages of biodiversity loss: the implications for ecosystem functioning and resilience; the resulting impacts on the provision of ecological goods and services; and thus the consequences for human welfare. Instead, we try to assemble as many of the pieces of the puzzle as possible, focusing in particular on the empirical evidence of the ecological role of biodiversity, and of the potential economic value of essential ecological goods and services. Nevertheless, by examining this evidence, we are able to draw out some important management and policy issues for each system, as well as some key challenges to be addressed.

The other side of policy analysis is the development of appropriate tools, institutions and management responses. A fundamental issue raised by the problem of global biodiversity loss is whether there are important lessons for management and policy to be learned. Or, more specifically, does even 'partial' ecological–economic policy analysis of selected systems, such as the analysis in Part II, reveal common weaknesses in the way we currently approach the use and management of our ecosystems and biodiversity? Do these weaknesses suggest that biodiversity conservation on a global scale will require new policy strategies, tools, institutions and management practices? Part III addresses these questions directly. In Chapter 9, we discuss existing policy instruments and tools for biodiversity conservation, and the need to develop more innovative measures where appropriate. In Chapter 10, we highlight the necessary policies and institutions required for global biodiversity conservation at the international, national and local level.

Finally, as argued throughout this book, we are at the beginning of an ecological economics 'learning curve'. In this chapter, we have tried to indicate with Figure 1.1 the basis of the biodiversity loss problem and with Figure 1.2 how an ecological–economic approach can contribute to policy analysis that will assist decision makers in formulating a solution to this problem. Most of this book is about current progress towards this goal; the final chapter, Chapter 11, overviews the challenges ahead if we are to attain it.

2

Ecological and Economic Implications of Biodiversity Loss

The previous chapter provided a brief background to and overview of the current concern over biodiversity loss. We noted that, while species extinction remains the most highly publicized aspect of the problem, recent scientific thinking – as expressed by participants in the Beijer Biodiversity programme – is focusing on the more fundamental role of biodiversity in supporting ecosystem functioning and resilience, and thus human welfare generally. In this chapter we elaborate on the latter concern by explaining further the important ecological and economic implications of biodiversity loss.

ECOLOGICAL IMPLICATIONS

Ecosystems generate ecological resources and services that are crucial for human welfare. Biodiversity at genetic, species, population and ecosystem levels contributes in maintaining these resources and services. In this section we will discuss the role of biodiversity in ecosystems and the implications of biodiversity loss for ecosystem sustainability.

The structure and organization of ecosystems

An ecosystem consists of biological communities which interact with the physical and chemical environment, with adjacent ecosystems and with the atmosphere. The structure and functioning of an ecosystem are sustained by synergistic feedbacks between organisms and their environment. For example, the physical environment puts constraints on the growth and development of biological subsystems which, in turn, modify their physical environment.

Each ecosystem is composed of a number of physical, biological and chemical components such as soil, water, plant and animal species, and nutrients. Processes among and within these components result in a specific type of ecosystem function or property such as nutrient cycling, biological productivity, hydrology and sedimentation. All such ecological functions are of importance in maintaining the overall performance and integrity of the ecosystem, in particular its fundamental role in supporting and sustaining the various living organisms dependent on it.

In this book, we are especially concerned with those components and functions of ecosystems that affect human welfare. Because of the complex inter-relationships that characterize ecosystems and the inter-connectedness across different systems, at the extreme it is possible to claim that all ecological components and functions ultimately influence human well-being. However, as will become clearer below, human use of ecological functions is more apparent for some than for others. From a purely anthropocentric perspective, we are particularly interested in those ecological functions that support and protect the human activities of production and consumption, or affect overall well-being in some way, thus impacting on human welfare. Throughout this book, we will refer to this special category of ecological functions as *ecological services*. Equally from an anthropocentric perspective, the key feature of an ecosystem is that it consists of and sustains a unique array of biotic, or 'living', components in the form of biological communities, many of which also support human production and consumption activities, or which have some other actual, or potential, use or value to humanity. We refer to this category of biological components as *ecological resources* – again to indicate their importance to human welfare.

Solar energy is the driving force of ecosystems, enabling the cyclic use of the materials and compounds required for system organization and maintenance. Ecosystems capture solar energy through photosynthesis by plants and algae. This is necessary for the conversion, recycling, and transfer to other systems of materials and critical chemicals that affect growth and production, namely biogeochemical cycling. Energy flow and biogeochemical cycling set an upper limit on the quantity and number of organisms, and on the level of organization that can exist in an ecosystem. This indirectly constrains the biodiversity of the biological community (Odum 1975; Holling et al 1994).

Ecosystems possess a capacity for self-organization. They develop and evolve in a dynamic fashion within the constraints set by energy flow and biogeochemical cycling. Ecosystems are formed in response to these fluxes, are maintained and developed by them, and will continuously respond to them through numerous feedbacks. Ecosystems often maintain an appearance of stability, but it is a very dynamic stability. Self-organization implies that species and their environments are connected by a complex web of inter-relations that are non-linear, contain lags and discontinuities, and thresholds and limits. These are attributes of complex systems that characterize the structure and organization of ecosystems (see, for example, Costanza et al 1993; Jørgensen 1993; and Kay 1991 for reviews).

The sustainability of ecosystems

The theory of ecological succession is well known in ecology. It describes the development of ecosystems from colonization to mature or so-called climax stages (Odum 1969). Holling (1986) has described ecosystem behaviour as the dynamic sequential interaction between four system functions: exploitation, conservation, release and reorganization. The first two are similar to ecological succession. Exploitation is represented by those ecosystem processes that are responsible for rapid colonization of disturbed ecosystems during which the species capture easily accessible resources. Conservation occurs when the slow resource accumulation takes place that builds and stores increasingly complex structures. Connectedness and stability in the ecosystem increase during the slow sequence from exploitation to conservation, and a 'capital' of nutrients and biomass is slowly accumulated. The next function is that of release or creative destruction. It takes place when the conservation phase has built elaborate and tightly bound structures that have become 'over-connected' so that a rapid change is triggered. The stored capital is then suddenly released and the tight organization is lost. The abrupt destruction is created internally but caused by an external disturbance such as fire, disease or grazing pressure. This process of change both destroys and releases opportunity for the fourth stage, reorganization, where released materials are mobilized to become available for the next exploitive phase. Figure 2.1 depicts the inter-relationship between these four system functions.

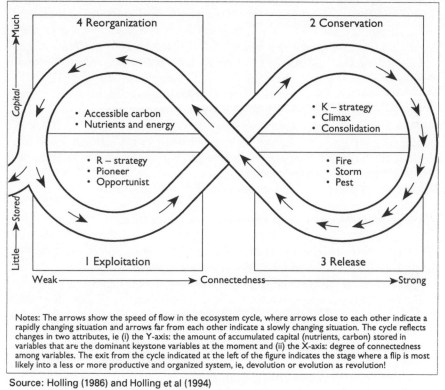

Notes: The arrows show the speed of flow in the ecosystem cycle, where arrows close to each other indicate a rapidly changing situation and arrows far from each other indicate a slowly changing situation. The cycle reflects changes in two attributes, ie (i) the Y-axis: the amount of accumulated capital (nutrients, carbon) stored in variables that are the dominant keystone variables at the moment and (ii) the X-axis: degree of connectedness among variables. The exit from the cycle indicated at the left of the figure indicates the stage where a flip is most likely into a less or more productive and organized system, ie devolution or evolution as revolution!

Source: Holling (1986) and Holling et al (1994)

Figure 2.1 *The four ecosystem functions and the flow of events between them*

The stability and productivity of the system is determined by the slow exploitation and conservation sequence. Resilience, that is the system's capacity to recover after a perturbation (disturbance), is determined by the effectiveness of the last two system functions.[1] Some natural disturbances, such as events trig-

---

1   The resilience of a system has been defined in two very different ways in the ecological literature. The more traditional way focuses on resilience in the context of the *efficiency* of function; that is, resistance to disturbance and speed of return to a near equilibrium steady state (for example Pimm 1991). The definition that is used here is based on Holling (1973) and focuses on resilience in the context of *existence* of function; that is, the amount of disturbance that can be sustained and absorbed before a change in system control or structure occurs (see also Kay 1991). In contrast to the first definition, the latter emphasizes conditions far from the equilibrium or near equilibrium steady state, where instabilities can flip a system into another regime of behaviour (Holling et al 1994).

gered by fire, wind and herbivores, are an inherent part of the internal dynamics of ecosystems and in many cases set the timing of successional cycles (Holling et al 1994). Hence, these natural perturbations are part of ecosystem development and evolution, and seem to be crucial for ecosystem resilience and integrity (Costanza, Kemp and Boynton 1993). If they are not allowed to enter the ecosystem, it will become even more over-connected, and thereby even larger perturbations will be invited with the risk of massive and widespread destruction.

For example, small fires in a forest ecosystem release nutrients stored in the trees and support a spurt of new growth without destroying all the old growth. Sub-systems in the forest are affected but the forest remains. If small fires are blocked out from a forest ecosystem, forest biomass will build up to high levels and when the fire does come it will wipe out the whole forest. Such events may flip the system to a totally new system that will not generate the same level of ecological functions and services as before – as was the case with Yellowstone National Park in the US, where the policy of 'natural burn' management of the modified forest system culminated in catrastrophic forest fires.

Human societies are dependent on ecological services for welfare and ultimately for existence. These services are generated by the proper functioning of ecosystems. A proper functioning is sustained when its sub-systems are allowed continuously to renew themselves, develop and evolve. Ecosystem integrity and sustainability are maintained when the system is resilient to change. Biodiversity plays an important role in this respect, to which we now turn.

The role of biodiversity in ecosystem sustainability

It has long been understood by the discipline of ecology that for an ecological function to be sustained, a minimum amount of species is required to develop the cyclic relations between producers (plants), consumers (animals) and decomposers (micro-organisms). However, ecologists still have insufficient knowledge of the role of particular species, or groups of species, over time, in the generation of ecological functions (Ehrlich and Daily 1993; Perrings, Folke and Mäler 1992). In particular, further research is required to investigate critical thresholds of diversity and the conditions or time scales over which diversity is particularly important (Schulze and Mooney 1993a). In addition, further research is required into the range of interaction strengths within biological communities and the generality of trends across communities (Mills, Soulé and Doak 1993).

Although there is much to learn about the role of plant and animal diversity, even less is known about micro-organisms. We know that a main function of microbial activity is to complete the cycling of nutrients and other essential compounds through individual ecosystems and the biosphere as a whole. This role is crucial to the persistence of life on earth. However, as stated by Meyer (1993), it is amazing how little we know of the number, functions and activities of individual species of micro-organisms in their natural habitat, and the role of changes and dynamics in species composition for ecosystem functioning. This is not surprising given that the abundance of micro-organisms is enormous. One gram of fertile agricultural soil may contain over 2.5 billion bacteria, 400,000 fungi, 50,000 algae and 30,000 protozoa (Ehrlich and Ehrlich 1992). Yet it is not the sheer number of plants, animals and micro-organisms that make them important; it is the key roles that they play in ecosystems.

Hence, a major issue to be addressed by ecologists is how critical the mix of species of plants, animals and micro-organisms is in maintaining the ecosystem functional properties of production, and energy and material circulation and storage, that is, in preserving the functional performance of the system. A further issue concerns the role of species in mechanisms that permit the persistence of an ecosystem through time in a constantly changing environment, ie, the species role in system resilience (Solbrig 1993; Walker 1992). Resilience is again taken here to be the same as defined by Holling (1973 and 1986) and discussed above. It is the capacity of the system to recover from perturbations, shocks and surprises, thus absorbing them. That is, the self-organizing ability of the system, or more particularly the resilience of that self-organization, determines its capacity to respond to the stresses and shocks imposed by predation or pollution from external sources.

The principal ecological importance of biodiversity must therefore be its role in preserving ecosystem resilience. This occurs in two ways. First, biodiversity provides the units through which energy and material flow, giving the system its functional properties. Second, it provides the system with the resilience to respond to unpredictable surprises (Solbrig 1993). The challenge of biodiversity management and conservation is to sustain ecosystem functions that generate ecological services and maintain the resilience of the ecosystem to change.

Genetic variability within a species is important for its own long-term survival, enabling the species to recuperate from shocks. Ehrlich and Daily (1993) emphasize that the genetic variability represented by geographically disparate populations helps assure the ability of the entire species to adapt to environmental change. Hence, a species with many populations (with inter-population genetic variation) is more likely to include individuals that are suited to new conditions, than a single local population. In the northern latitudes and the seasonal tropics (wet–dry seasons) a relatively small percentage of the total number of species are often abundant or dominant (represented by, for example, a large number of individuals, biomass or productivity), and a large percentage are rare in the sense that they have small importance values for the functioning of the ecosystem. In the wet tropics with unchanging seasons, one usually finds many species that have low relative abundance (Odum 1983).

In natural systems species diversity tends to increase with the size of area, and from high latitudes to the equator, but the geographic range of each species appears to decrease. The average range of temperate zone species is between two and three times larger than that of their tropical counterparts, which implies that there are almost certainly more populations per animal species in temperate, subarctic and arctic regions than in the tropics (Ehrlich and Daily 1993). Loss of species and the continued depletion of populations can be paralleled to rivets in an aeroplane wing. Some species are more critical than others in maintaining the present functions of the system, but the continued depletion of populations, like the prising of rivets from a wing, will at some stage reach the critical threshold and eventually lead to collapse (Ehrlich and Daily 1993).

Generally, species which have been listed as endangered are already highly

vulnerable to natural variations in climate, disease outbreaks and human disturbances, but also to inbreeding depression and genetic drift. What is not clear is
how diversity of genes, genotypes, species and communities influences ecosystem
function, or what are the optimal levels of diversity in communities and ecosystems, and the factors that control them (Solbrig 1991). However, it is clear that
some sub-groups of species are crucial to maintaining the organization and
diversity of their ecological communities. These are often referred to as keystone
species (Paine 1969), a concept in ecology that has drawn attention to differing
strengths of interaction in community food webs. The range of the effects of
keystone species on their communities has been categorized as keystone predator,
prey, herbivores, mutualists, competitors, hosts, pathogens, earth movers and
modifiers (Bond 1993; Mills, Soulé and Doak 1993).

Furthermore, empirical studies suggest that, in the short term, full ecosystem
functioning in most systems can be maintained and controlled by a small number
of processes and a reduced number of species (for example, Schindler 1990). It
seems that some species (or groups of species) are driving the critical processes
necessary for ecosystem functioning (Johnson and Mayeux 1992; Lawton and
Brown 1993). These species can be referred to as keystone process species
(Costanza, Kemp and Boynton 1993; Holling 1992; Walker 1992). By focusing
on the processes which maintain the critical ecosystem functions, it may be
possible to determine the keystone process species which are required to maintain
ecosystem functioning – at least in the short term (Perrings, Folke and Mäler
1992).

Although keystone process species are necessary for ecosystem functioning,
they may not be sufficient for ecosystem sustainability. The remaining species
that depend on the niches formed by keystone process species are also important
for maintaining the resilience of ecosystems. The former are often referred to in
the literature as passenger species, but this term may be misleading (Holling
1992; Holling et al 1994; Walker 1992).[2] The loss of such species and their role
as a buffer to rare or unusually extreme events may be detrimental for the survival
of the ecosystem and its capacity to generate ecological services – it implies a loss
of ecosystem plasticity (Ehrlich and Daily 1993). Furthermore, unoccupied
niches lay the ecosystem open to invasion and possibly to disruption, as has been
the case when alien invaders totally changed the functions of ecosystems (Woodward 1993). In addition, in the evolution of the ecosystem over time, species that
at present are not critical for functional performance may transform into keystone
process species through the internal reorganization of the ecosystem.

Consequently, the role of 'passenger' species in ecosystem resilience and their
potential conversion to keystone process species should not be ignored (Schulze
and Mooney 1993b). 'Passenger' species can be viewed as natural insurance
capital for securing the generation of ecological services in the future. We
therefore prefer to call them life insurance species to emphasize this critical role.
The 'life insurance' aspect includes the reservoirs of genetic material necessary

---

2 Passenger species have also been referred to as redundant species (Holling et al 1994; Walker 1992). However, due to
   their role in ecosystem resilience and potential role as keystone process species, the term 'redundant' species appears
   to be even more misleading. As will be made clear below, we prefer the term life insurance species.

for evolution of microbial, plant, animal and human life. This may be particularly important on a global scale, if we are to manage successfully planetary or climatic stresses to our biosphere in the coming decades. Thus, over the long term, it is important to conserve not only keystone process species but also life insurance species to ensure the functioning of ecosystems, and the ability of species, populations and communities to respond to ecosystem stresses and shocks.

There exist several inter-dependent diversities at different organizational or hierarchical levels (see Figure 2.2). The hierarchical approach in ecology makes it possible to shift the focus from preservation of single species to protect the resilience of socially important ecological processes or functions, and the services they generate, and of which biodiversity is the crucial part (Norton and Ulanowicz 1992). For example, species diversity is dependent on the interactions between ecosystems. Functional diversity is enhanced by the topography of an area, as well as the occurrence of varied geological, climatic and meteorological features that give rise to a spatial and temporal diversity (Hammer, Jansson and Jansson 1993). Spatial diversity encompasses a mosaic of ecosystems in the landscape which provides opportunities for a larger number of species than do monotonous environments.

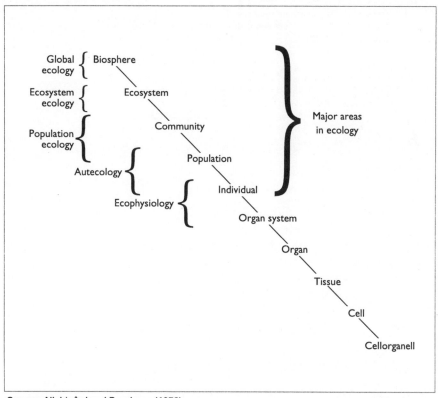

Source: Nichlgård and Rundgren (1978)

Figure 2.2   *Organizational levels in biology and major areas in ecology*

A diverse mix of species that can change in proportions and distribution has a much better chance of maintaining ecosystem function than a monoculture (Ehrlich and Daily 1993). Diversity tends to be reduced in stressed biological communities, at least among 'visible' organisms such as plants and animals. The impacts on micro-organisms are still largely unknown. The effects of stress on ecosystem structure and function have been discussed by Odum (1985), and these characteristics have been compared with those of monocultures by Folke and Kautsky (1992) (see Table 2.1). Hence, land and water uses that reduce the diversity of the landscape, and with it communities, populations and species, are likely to be less resilient to change in the long run.

Table 2.1 *Similarities between stressed ecosystems and intensive monocultures*

High dependence on extra energy
Short residence time of energy
Increase in exported or unused primary production
Increase in nutrient turnover
Increase in nutrient loss
Decrease in resource use efficiency
Increase in growth-strategy species
Increase in parasitism, diseases and other negative interactions
Increase in horizontal one-way transport
Decrease in vertical cycling
Few, simple, rapid, open (leaky) cycles
Shortening of food chains
Network with low average mutual information
Simple structures with few hierarchical levels
Low complexity, low diversity, low system efficiency
Throughput-based systems due to reduced internal cycling

Source: Odum (1985); Folke and Kautsky (1992)

ECONOMIC IMPLICATIONS

In the previous section we described how biodiversity loss affects the functioning and resilience of ecosystems. If this occurs, then ecosystems cannot provide the biological resources and ecological 'services' that are needed to support human production and consumption, and, ultimately, human welfare and existence. In this section we discuss these linkages in terms of the impacts on the economic system, including its sustainability, as depicted in Figure 1.1.

In short, the economic implications of biodiversity loss are concerned with the impacts on human welfare. These arise in a number of important ways:

- the welfare of existing generations may be affected by any current impacts on biological resources and ecological services due to declining biodiversity today;
- there may also be additional implications for current welfare from biodiversity loss if individuals are uncertain about their future demand for biological resources and ecological services, and/or their availability in the future;

- further complications also arise from ignorance, in that individuals today may not be aware of or recognize the full implications of biodiversity loss;
- there may also be concerns both for intra-generational equity, or how biodiversity loss today affects different individuals, countries and regions, and for inter-generational equity, or how biodiversity may affect the welfare of future as opposed to current generations;
- finally, concerns over inter-generational equity are also linked to the overall problem of how biodiversity loss impacts on the sustainability of production and consumption activities, and, ultimately, welfare and even existence.

The analytical framework and approach that economics employs in assessing these welfare implications are examined further on pages 49–56. Here, we will simply indicate and discuss briefly each implication in turn.

Welfare of current generations

The first two welfare impacts listed above suggest that individuals today can be made 'worse off' through the ecological disruption resulting from biodiversity loss. That is, certain economic benefits or values provided by ecosystems may be lost when they are altered or modified. The values of most concern are those ecological functions and components that affect human welfare, namely the economic value that individuals may derive from the ecological resources and services of ecosystems in terms of contributions to human consumption, production and overall well-being.

As noted on pages 23–30, the ecological consequences of decisions to reduce biodiversity today will affect the amount of ecological resources and services available to current generations. An important role of economics is to employ valuation as a tool to quantify the resulting impacts on the welfare of individuals today, as a way of informing them whether their decisions to deplete biodiversity – compared to other options – should be pursued. To give some idea of what the economic implications for current generations of biodiversity loss might be, it is worth discussing briefly the different types of welfare effects that may arise from any resulting impacts on ecological goods and services.

Probably the most tangible effects of any ecological disruption caused by biodiversity loss would be on the various ecological resources that are extracted and exploited by humans, such as fish, fuelwood, agricultural products and meat. However, extraction or exploitation of resources is not the only way in which individuals benefit from direct interaction with ecosystems. Many individuals also attach value to activities like recreation (such as bird watching), water transport (such as the use of natural waterways) and education (such as field visits).[3] One would expect that all such values that arise through direct human interaction with ecosystems would be the most visibly affected through the

---

3 Using standard distinctions in the economics literature, Brown (1990) refers to these latter benefits as (direct) non-consumptive values to distinguish them from the former category of direct consumptive values that are derived from the extraction or exploitation of resources. However, in a comment, Hanemann (1990) points out that distinguishing between whether an individual's level of enjoyment of an ecological resource is a consumptive or non-consumptive value is not always necessary, particularly if the main concern is with the more general issue of whether the availability of ecological resources affects the consumer's choice and welfare.

impacts of biodiversity loss on ecosystem functioning and resilience. As suggested by Aylward and Barbier (1992), most empirical economic studies of natural ecosystem modification and alteration tend to start with such welfare impacts first, as they are generally the most straightforward to value.

The welfare of individuals is also affected by the natural functioning of ecosystems – even if the individuals do not appear to interact directly with these systems. Certain ecological functions, such as flood control, storm prevention, external support (such as mangrove habitats for off-shore fisheries) and ground-water recharge, may support or protect economic activity and property. Because of the ecological linkages across natural and human-modified ecosystems, the economic activity and property supported and protected may be far removed from the ecosystems generating these functions. As a consequence, their economic importance is often difficult to discern. For example, Holling et al (1994) discuss the role of boreal forests in protecting freshwater lakes and thus their fisheries from wind exposure. Barbier (1994b and 1994c) describes many examples of the indirect benefits provided through the regulatory ecological functions of tropical wetlands, such as the external support and storm prevention functions of mangroves, and the groundwater recharge of floodplains. Dixon, Scura and van't Hof (1994) indicate that coral reef systems in the Bonaire Marine Park in the Caribbean support various fishing activities.[4] As indicated at the beginning of this chapter, we refer to this special category of ecological functions as ecological services in order to highlight their important – but often intangible – economic value.[5]

On pages 23–30 we noted how the loss of biodiversity can disturb severely the regulatory functions of an ecosystem and its capacity for resilience. To the extent that economic activities and property are protected or supported by these functions, then human welfare will also be affected by such disturbances. Unfortunately, the linkages between these regulatory ecological functions and the generation of key ecological services by the ecosystem are often not well understood. Equally, economists have generally overlooked the implications of the loss of ecological services for economic activity and human welfare – although mounting empirical evidence suggests that such impacts may be significant (Aylward and Barbier 1992; Barbier 1994b and 1994c; Perrings, Folke and Mäler 1992).

As a consequence, we may feel the impacts of disruptions to ecological functions and services arising from biodiversity loss, but we may not be able to demonstrate that biodiversity loss is the principal factor behind the problem. For example, declining cod stocks and changes in the composition of nearshore fisheries in the Baltic may have been observed in recent years, but it is more difficult to discern the underlying problem of disruptions to basic regulatory

---

4   Individual species living in ecosystems can also support and protect economic activity or property. For example, Narain and Fisher (1994) estimate the value of the Anolis lizard of the Greater and Lesser Antilles in terms of supporting and protecting the production of sugar cane, banana and cocoa through eliminating crop pests.

5   To highlight the special role of ecological services in supporting economic activity and welfare without involving direct human interaction with the ecosystem, Barbier (1994b and 1994c) refers to these benefits as indirect use values. Similarly, Brown (1990) refers to genetic resources that have the same characteristics, for example, through predator–prey relationships or other natural inter-species production relationships, as generating indirect productive value. However, as noted above, the same caveat raised by Hanemann (1990) also applies to whether it is necessary to classify ecological services in this way.

functions and ecological services as a result of increased nutrient load from agricultural runoff, municipal sources and atmospheric fallout (see Box 2.1).

Box 2.1
The economic implications of the loss of ecological functions and services in the Baltic Sea

The Baltic Sea is surrounded by industrialized countries and is close to the major sources of air pollution in Northern and Eastern Europe. Thus it is subject to eutrophication from human activities in the Baltic Drainage Basin. Although over-fishing is clearly a major problem, decline in cod stocks and changes in the composition of nearshore fisheries can also be linked to this eutrophication process, and its effects on regulatory ecological functions and the services they generate.

Increased nutrient load from agricultural runoff, municipal sources and atmospheric fallout has increased phytoplankton primary production by some 30 per cent, which has broadened the base of the trophic pyramid. The resulting sedimentation of organic matter has depleted oxygen and benthic fauna below the halocline, whereas the animal biomass on bottoms less than 50 m deep has increased four times since the 1920s. One implication is the significant decline in the isopod *Saduria entomon* which was once a staple food for cod in the northern Baltic. The more direct impacts of the eutrophication process on cod and other fish populations are mixed. Primary production and fish yields tend to increase when primary production increases, as was the case with the large increase in cod stocks in the first part of the 1980s. However, loss of spawning areas counteracts the positive effects of greater primary production. The fertilization and hatching of the cod's pelagic eggs are dependent on a minimum salinity of 11 per cent. Due to low oxygen conditions in the deep water layers where the salinity is high enough, the cod can now reproduce successfully only in a very restricted part of the Baltic Sea.

The increase in primary production on the rocky bottoms without a corresponding increase in decomposition has led to accumulation of sediments, oxygen depletion and a successive transformation of diverse hard bottoms to soft bottoms with lower species diversity. The rich brown algae (*Fucus vesiculosus*) community has decreased in depth distribution due to decreasing light in the more turbid water. The extensive growth of filamentous algae replacing *Fucus* has become a great problem for the nearshore fisheries because fishing nets are clogged by drifting algae. Also, the balance within the fish community has changed. Carp fishes like bream and roach have increased at the expense of fishes like whitefish, pike and perch.

In addition to the eutrophication is the widespread release of toxins and pollutants that accumulate in the sediments and in the food web. Sea mammals, sea birds and Baltic fish species have been particularly affected, and some animals, such as the grey seal and the sea eagle, are threatened with extinction.

Source: based on Hammer, Jansson and Jansson (1993).

Because biodiversity loss may make individuals more uncertain about their future demand for biological resources and ecological services, and/or their availability, individuals may adjust their current production and consumption patterns to reflect this uncertainty. Essentially, to the extent that the threat of ecological disruptions resulting from biodiversity loss increases this uncertainty, the more individuals would see themselves benefiting from the 'option' of preserving ecological resources and services for future use.[6] In other words, the value to individuals of this 'preservation option' increases with the uncertainty surrounding the ecological impacts of biodiversity loss; as a consequence, as this value increases, society may begin allocating more of its resources to activities that promote conservation of biodiversity as opposed to activities that contribute to biodiversity loss.

At the very least, the uncertainty of individuals about the future value of ecological resources and services, or whether current rates of biodiversity depletion may be irreversible and threaten the availability of these resources and services, may also mean that individuals would prefer that biodiversity loss is delayed until further information is learned about such threats. That is, there may be value derived from conserving biodiversity today if we learn more about its role in generating essential ecological resources and services in the future. This benefit is simply the expected value of information derived from delaying excessive, irreversible biodiversity loss.[7] Consequently, as the threats to biodiversity and ecosystems increase, so does the expected value of this information.

The potential welfare implications of the enormous uncertainty surrounding ecological disruptions may be substantial. As argued by Perrings and Pearce (1994), the main source of uncertainty is our ignorance of the functions and structure of ecosystems. On pages 23–30 we discussed how the functioning and resilience of ecosystems is affected by biodiversity loss. However, it is clear that our understanding of these relationships is basic at best.

A more intractable source of uncertainty is the existence of discontinuities or threshold effects in ecosystems (Perrings and Pearce 1994). These thresholds are defined by critical values for either populations of organisms or biogeochemical cycles. At these levels the ecosystem begins losing resilience and thus self-organization (see also pages 23–30). Uncertainty as to whether ecosystems are being driven close to their critical values therefore has important welfare implications as, once these thresholds are crossed, wholesale disruption to and perhaps even collapse of ecosystems can occur. In other words, ecological change is discontinuous, and there could be dramatic impacts on biological resources and ecological services. This would suggest that, to the extent individuals are concerned with the uncertainty surrounding ecological disruptions, their welfare would be especially sensitive to threshold effects and to the uncertainty associated with such effects.

So far, we have discussed the potential welfare implications arising from the impacts of biodiversity loss on individuals who 'use' or plan to use the ecosystem in some way – even if they are not fully aware of the benefits they derive. However, there are individuals who do not currently make use of certain ecosys-

---

6   As a consequence, the benefits of preserving such options in the face of uncertainty are often referred to as option values in the economics literature. See, for example, Smith (1993) and Freeman (1984).

7   The expected value of information from postponing biodiversity loss, given uncertainty by individuals today over its potential importance, is often referred to as quasi-option value in the economics literature. See, for example, Fisher and Hanemann (1987).

tems, species and genetic resources, nor want to retain the 'option' of using them in the future, but who nevertheless may wish to see biodiversity preserved 'in its own right'. Just knowing that ecosystems, habitats and the biodiversity they contain continue to exist is valued by these individuals.[8] It is a form of value that is extremely intangible and difficult to measure – precisely because existence values involve subjective valuations by individuals unrelated to either their own or others' use of biodiversity, whether current or future. To the extent that some individuals in society perceive such a value in conserving biodiversity, then its loss is detrimental to welfare.

Additionally, individuals may place a high value on preserving biodiversity not necessarily for their own future use but for future generations, including perhaps their own progeny.[9] This may be particularly significant for populations local to an ecosystem or natural environment who currently enjoy many of its benefits, and would like to see their way of life or intimate association with the ecosystem passed on to their heirs and future generations in general. Such values are also very intangible and difficult to assess, but they may also be an important component of welfare that is affected by ecosystem loss and disruption arising through biodiversity depletion.

Intra-generational and inter-generational equity

Up to now, we have been assuming that the welfare impacts of biodiversity loss and ecological disruption are distributed equally. However, this is not the case. The implications for various groups in society, and even across regions or countries, may be different. Similarly, because the loss of biodiversity and its ecological consequences may be irreversible, it is not just current generations but also future generations that must live with the consequences. In fact it may be that future generations are made disproportionately worse off. Consequently, biodiversity loss also raises issues of intra-generational and inter-generational equity.

Barbier (1994a) provides evidence that it is both the poorest countries of the world and the poorest populations that are the most at risk from environmental degradation and the ecological disruptions arising from biodiversity loss. Many low and lower middle income developing countries display a high degree of resource dependency. Many of these economies are directly dependent on natural resource products for the overwhelming majority of their exports, and on natural resource systems for their economic development and employment generation in general (see Box 2.2). In most cases, export earnings are dominated by one or two commodities. Resource dependency has been a feature of these economies

---

8 Such an 'intrinsic' value is often referred to as existence value in the economics literature; it is generally classified as a 'non-use value' in the sense that it is unrelated to the individual's current or future use of an ecological resource or service. See, for example, Barbier (1994b) and Munasinghe (1992).

9 Consequently, such values are often referred to as bequest values in the economics literature. See, for example, Barbier (1994b) and Munasinghe (1992). Although also classified as a type of 'non-use value', bequest values should be distinguished from existence values. However, it is importatnt to note that as both existence and bequest values are in some sense 'preservation values' – namely, they derive from preserving ecosystems and biodiversity – then like the other 'use' values discussed previously they may also be affected by the uncertainty surrounding threshold effects and ecological disruptions.

over the past 25 years and, for most low income countries, has remained a persistent feature since the mid-1960s. More of the lower middle income economies have reduced their resource dependency with time, but this is clearly a long term process. For most low income economies, careful management of the natural resource base may be necessary to maintain the 'natural' capital required for this transition and to achieve long term development goals.

Box 2.2
Resource dependency in India

Gadgil (1993) describes the extent of resource dependency across the population and communities of India. Over two-thirds of India's 850 million people depend on agriculture for their subsistence. Annually they gather some 150 million tonnes of fuelwood for domestic use and free-range grazing by their livestock amounts to a fodder demand of over 500 million tonnes. Around two thirds of Indian communities are also reported to use indigenous herbal medicines. In a recent survey of the 2600 ethnic communities comprising India's population, at least 5 per cent are engaged in hunter-gathering, 7 per cent in fishing, 2 per cent in trapping birds, 2 per cent in wood work, 7 per cent in basket and mat weaving, 3.5 per cent in shifting cultivation, 20 per cent in animal husbandry and 50 per cent in settled cultivation.

A further survey of 82 villages in semi-arid districts of seven Indian states suggests that biomass harvests from common lands furnish 14–23 per cent of household income from all sources. Furthermore, the poorer households derive a larger fraction of their income from such lands. Over an area of just 1000 km^2 in south India 58 different plant species were used to make some 66 different kinds of articles, including brooms, ropes, baskets, mats, various kinds of fishing and agricultural implements, furniture and decorative articles.

Thus a significant proportion of India's large population depends on a diversity of products of living organisms. The majority of these people gather the plant and animal material with their own labour from the immediate vicinity. Some 35–40 per cent of the Indian population reportedly earns just enough to feed itself and has no purchasing power to meet other needs from the market place. Fully half of the ethnic communities making up the Indian population report dependence on state-sponsored rural employment programmes, which provide wages that meet only basic nutritional requirements. Consequently, a third or more Indian people behave as 'ecosystem' people – households whose quality of life is intimately linked to the productivity and diversity of living organisms in their own restricted resource catchments.

However, the resource base in poor, resource dependent economies is far from static. Although comparison of land classifications across countries is fraught with difficulties, the most notable change over the last 15 years in the majority of economies is the decline in forest area and the increase in cropland (Barbier 1994a; see also Chapters 1 and 5 of this book). Much of the forest land has presumably been lost to agricultural conversion, with fuelwood and fodder gathering a factor in some areas, and depletion for timber operations important in major producing countries.

A further worrying trend in developing economies is the concentration of the poorest groups in 'ecologically fragile' zones – areas where environmental degradation or severe environmental hazards constrain and even threaten economic welfare. As indicated by Leonard (1989) around 470 million, or 60 per cent of the developing world's poorest people, live in rural or urban areas that can be classified as 'ecologically fragile'.[10] Around 370 million of the developing world's poorest people live in 'marginal' agricultural areas. These less favourable agricultural lands, with lower productivity potential, poorer soils and physical characteristics, and more variable and often inadequate rainfall, are easily prone to land degradation due to overcropping, poor farming practices and inadequate conservation measures.

The result is that the economic livelihoods and welfare of the poorest income groups in low potential areas are at greater risk from increasing environmental degradation and biodiversity loss. As these ecosystems are more 'fragile' – that is to say, less resilient and stable as discussed on pages 23–30 – then the problems of threshold effects, ecosystem collapse and scarce resources may be particularly severe for these poor households.[11]

However, it is also clear that any change in biodiversity that affects ecological functioning and resilience has implications not just for present but also future generations. Although the preferences of future generations are unknown to us today, we must assume that the biodiversity management problem is the same for all generations – to maintain that level of biodiversity which will guarantee the functioning and resilience of ecosystems on which not only human consumption and production but also existence depend (Perrings, Folke and Mäler 1992). Unfortunately, the conversion and modification of ecosystems that are occurring today may actually mean 'less' biodiversity available for future generations. That is, by our actions today that convert and modify ecosystems, we may be pushing future generations inevitably towards that 'minimum' or 'threshold' level of biodiversity necessary to maintain welfare and even existence.

This is the heart of the inter-generational equity problem surrounding biodiversity loss. By choosing a development path today that results in large scale biodiversity losses and ecological disruptions, the current generation may be making future generations unavoidably worse off. Conversion and modifications to ecosystems today may be reducing the economic opportunities available to generations in the future. This may be occurring in several ways.

First, as argued so far in this book, although species extinction is the most fundamental and irreversible manifestation of biodiversity loss, the more profound implication is for ecological functioning and resilience. These latter impacts are generally localized, but in many cases they generate wider national,

---

10 The 'poorest people' are defined by Leonard (1989) as the poorest 20 per cent of the population in developing countries. In commenting on the data presented by Leonard, Kates (1990) argues that it is too simplistic to equate all land of low agricultural potential and squatter settlements with 'areas of high ecologically vulnerability'. Thus 'while there is good reason to expect an increasing geographic segregation of the poor onto the threatened environments, both the purported distribution of the hungry and the actual state of environmental degradation needs to be examined much more carefully.'

11 Further examples of the linkages between environmental degradation, ecological disruption and collapse, and economic activity in 'fragile' areas are discussed throughout this book.

regional or even global effects. Consequently, the biological resources and eco-logical 'services' available today may not be so abundant tomorrow.

In short, the world will be experiencing greater ecological scarcity. Not only will this manifest itself through a growing 'relative' scarcity of essential environ-mental assets and ecological services on which human welfare depend, but, at the extreme, will also lead to irrevocable ecological damage and the collapse of ecosystems on which human livelihoods depend.[12]

In addition, it may cost future generations more to maintain the resilience and functioning of ecosystems than it does today. As the world moves towards the minimum levels of biodiversity necessary to sustain ecosystems and thus welfare, it may become more imperative not to cross the remaining critical ecological thresholds. The options for environmental management may become more con-strained and expensive. In other words, future generations may have little choice but to allocate increasing economic resources to avoiding further ecological disruptions, as these may lead to major environmental catastrophes. Given the uncertainties surrounding ecological disruptions and threshold effects, then ab-solute constraints on economic activity as a means to preserving ecosystems may become a necessary and more frequently invoked strategy.

Sustainable development

The inter-generational equity considerations raised by the biodiversity problem ultimately point to fundamental concerns over sustainable development. The WCED defined sustainable development as 'development that meets the needs of the present without compromising the ability of future generations to meet their own needs' (WCED 1987). This suggests that an increase in welfare today should not have as its consequence a reduction in welfare tomorrow. That is, the welfare of society should not be declining over time (Pezzey 1989). As indicated in Box 2.3, this concern with sustainability is somewhat different, but related, to the problem of achieving economic efficiency.

By depleting the world's stock of biological wealth and biodiversity, the development path chosen today will have detrimental implications for the welfare of future generations. In other words, current economic development is essen-tially unsustainable. This is inevitable, as long as current generations fail to compensate future generations for the welfare implications arising from the irreversible loss of 'natural' capital today. As argued by Mäler (1994), the crucial issue is whether we can compensate future generations for the current resource consumption and, if that is the case, with how much should the future genera-tions be compensated.

This is not an easy issue to resolve, as we are really interested in ensuring that the well-being of individuals in the future is not detrimentally affected, yet we have no idea what their preferences are. As a result, the best we can do is to ensure that future generations have the same economic opportunities available to

---

12 Detailed discussion of this 'new' or 'alternative' economic view of ecological scarcity can be found in Barbier (1989a), which explains through both theoretical and empirical examples how this problem differs fundamentally from more 'conventional' natural resource scarcity problems of resource depletion and pollution. For a further review of these issues, see Common and Perrings (1992).

Box 2.3
Economic efficiency and sustainability

Economists define an outcome as efficient if there is no change in the allocation of inputs (natural resources, labour and capital) or outputs (intermediate products, and final goods and services) that makes one individual in society better off without making any other individual worse off. Well-functioning markets generally promote efficiency by providing opportunities for individuals to achieve mutually agreeable gains from trade.

However, underlying any state of the economy is what economists call initial endowments. Each member of the economy holds some share of the total natural, labour and capital resources with which to enter the market and trade so that an efficient final outcome can be achieved. Including time and multiple generations involves numerous complications. Today's initial resource endowments and institutions will result in future time paths for endowments of natural resources, capital and labour, which are used to produce flows of goods and services over time. Depending on how complicated one wants to make the analysis, technological progress can be added, affecting the productivity of inputs over time and the degree to which they are substitutable.

Under ideal conditions, efficiency can still be achieved. Each possible time path for endowments would lead, through market trade, towards a different inter-generationally efficient time path for the economic well-being of each member of society. There are an infinite number of such outcomes, each of which is intergenerationally efficient in the sense that there would be no way to reallocate inputs or outputs to make one or more individuals better off without making others, either of the same or of different generations, worse off. Under some time paths for endowments, the generations may enjoy relatively egalitarian economic circumstances, while under others some generations may be quite rich while others will not have the capital and natural resources to live above poverty levels.

Although sustainability is more difficult for economists to define, we might say that it is achieved if an economy is on a time path where future generations have economic opportunities that are at least as large as those of earlier generations. Each generation's endowment may be taken to include its own labour. Whether an economy is sustainable or not depends on the time paths of natural resource and capital endowments and technological progress, all broadly defined. Time paths of endowments and technology that lead to constant or increasing economic opportunities over the indefinite future are taken as sustainable. Time paths where earlier generations leave later generations such poor endowments of resources and capital that economic opportunities decline over time would be said to be unsustainable.

Thus, theoretically, there are potentially an infinite number of efficient time paths, only some of which are sustainable. Efficiency does not guarantee sustainability. Some efficient paths are not sustainable. At the same time, there is no reason in theory why an economy could not be both efficient and sustainable.

However, suppose that an economy is on an unsustainable path and that it is desirable to achieve sustainability. Taken literally, theory would suggest that inter-generational endowments be reallocated in the direction of future generations. Once reallocation is accomplished, market trade and the usual steps to eradicate market failures could be used to guide the economy along an efficient and sustainable path. However, problems of uncertainty over the preferences of future generations, 'missing' markets linking present and future generations, and environmental valuation all make it difficult to reallocate endowments – particularly the natural resource endowments – successfully to future generations. To achieve sustainability, policies should be considered that constrain the day-to-day operations of the economy in ways that enhance the natural resource endowments of future generations, but with an eye towards the economic implications of specific steps to implement such policies.

Source: Bishop (1993).

them as the current generation. Given the difficulty in grappling with the issue of sustainability, it is not surprising that economists have approached this problem from different perspectives. The different approaches are discussed further on pages 49–56. However, a clear consensus is emerging that, given the uncertainty and irreversibilities surrounding the biodiversity problem and increasing ecological scarcity, society should be cautious in making decisions that affect the economic opportunities for future generations through continued ecological disruption.

Finally, it is important to realize that current development efforts may be sustainable, but this does not necessarily imply that they will also be equitable. In other words, achieving inter-generational equity does not necessarily imply intra-generational equity. For example, if sustainable development requires conserving more of the world's natural resources and biological diversity today, then a large share of the burden for conservation may fall on developing countries that contain a large share of these resources. For these countries, conservation may imply forgoing many development opportunities today to ensure more biodiversity and resources for all future generations of the world. It could be argued that the wealthier countries of the world should compensate the developing countries for their inequitable share of the burden of ensuring the sustainability of global welfare and existence. These and other issues concerning sustainability and management of the biodiversity problem, are discussed further in Part III.

SUMMARY AND CONCLUSIONS: IMPLICATIONS FOR SUSTAINABILITY

Biodiversity at genetic, species, population and ecosystem levels all contributes in generating ecological functions and services. The ecological implications of biodiversity loss include:

- the loss of genetic variability through reductions of populations and extinction of species;
- the breakdown and loss of functional performance and ecosystem resilience.

The first aspect has been largely dealt with in the literature and in policy. The second has received less attention. It is the focus of this book. Since the levels of biodiversity are nested, from cells, to organisms, to ecosystems, a functional and resilient system is dependent on its genes, genotypes, species and communities as well as its relations to adjacent ecosystems and their role in the overall global system. The question is how the mix of biodiversity keeps ecosystems sustainable. How critical are various species in maintaining the functional performance of the ecosystem, and what is the role of species in mechanisms that permit the persistence of an ecosystem through time in a constantly changing environment?

As discussed earlier in this chapter, some species (or groups of species) drive the critical processes for ecosystem functioning, structure ecosystems, entrain other variables and set the rhythm of ecosystem dynamics. They are crucial for maintaining the functional performance and can be described as keystone process species. The remaining species depend on the niches formed by keystone process species, but do not affect the critical structure and functioning of the ecosystem under normal conditions. They have an important ecological role in enabling the system to be resilient to perturbations which challenge its structure, and can be viewed as natural insurance capital for securing the generation of ecological services in the future. They can be described as life insurance species.

Loss of species, and the continued depletion of populations and simplification of habitats, will at some stage reach the critical threshold and eventually lead to breakdown of ecological function and resilience, and thereby cause ecosystem collapse. Human societies are dependent on healthy ecosystems, since they generate essential ecological resources and services (see pages 42–49). A major challenge for biodiversity conservation is to sustain ecosystem functioning and maintain the resilience of ecosystems to change.

A further challenge is to understand the full economic implications of biodiversity loss in terms of the welfare of both current and future generations. As noted throughout this chapter, this is a complicated task given:

■   our basic ignorance concerning the role of biodiversity in ecosystem functioning, and the generation of valuable ecological resources and services;
■   many important values associated with ecological resources and services are not 'captured' through markets or other institutions, are essentially intangible and extremely difficult to quantify and estimate;
■   the threat of ecological disruption and threshold effects posed by continued biodiversity loss also raises the possibility of increased uncertainty, which carries additional implications for individuals' choice and welfare; and
■   as biodiversity loss increases the problem of ecological scarcity human society will be confronted with problems of intra-generational and inter-generational equity, given that essential ecological resources and services are neither evenly distributed nor sustainably managed.

Consequently, the need to sustain ecosystem function and maintain the resilience of ecosystems to change through biodiversity conservation is also necessary to sustain essential ecological resources and services, and thus human welfare. Biodiversity conservation, ecological sustainability and economic sustainability are inexorably linked; uncontrolled and irreversible biodiversity loss ruptures this link and puts the sustainability of our basic economic–environmental system at risk.

The ecological and economic implications of biodiversity loss highlighted and discussed in this chapter are important themes to which we will return throughout this book. In the next chapter, we discuss how ecology and economics in turn approach the analysis of these implications, and we ask the important question whether analysis based on a single discipline alone is adequate for both illuminating the problems posed by biodiversity loss and formulating the appropriate policy responses.

3

Ecological and Economic Perspectives: Convergence or Divergence?

In this chapter we examine how the two disciplines, ecology and economics, have traditionally approached the biodiversity problem. We first look at each discipline in turn, particularly recent developments that would suggest a convergence in approach. We then address the issue of whether a single-disciplinary approach is sufficient for tackling the biodiversity problem. We suggest that it is not. What is required is that ecology, economics and other disciplines begin applying their specialized knowledge and analytical methods collectively to extend beyond the current frontiers of their respective disciplines. Only through this approach can we be sure of the appropriate diagnosis and remedy for the global biodiversity problem. The result is what we call the ecological economics of biodiversity.

HOW ECOLOGY APPROACHES THE PROBLEM

Ecology is the study of individual organisms, populations, communities and systems of plants, animals and micro-organisms, and their relations to each other and their changing physical environments. Much of ecology is devoted to studying interactions between biotic (living) and abiotic (non-living) entities with a focus on the effects of such interactions on individuals, populations or communities of organisms. Within this branch you find evolutionary ecology, population ecology and community ecology (Pianka 1986; Pimm 1991).

Ecosystem ecology studies these interactions from the viewpoint of their effect on both the biotic and abiotic entities, and within the context of the system. This branch of ecology aims to provide an understanding of the organisation and operation of ecosystems, and how they respond to changes in internal and external factors (Pomeroy and Alberts 1988; Likens 1992). This helps us to understand the implications of biodiversity loss from an ecological perspective and plays an important role in determining appropriate policies for biological conservation.

Until recently, the two major streams of ecology, namely population or community ecology and ecosystem ecology, have been developed independently. Population and community ecology studies the local assemblage of species population without specific regard for the physical environment. The biological community is seen as a unit that is readily distinguishable from the ecosystem (Krebs 1985). Population and community ecology have emerged from basic studies where generalized patterns were sought in the natural interactions among organisms, with the goal to deduce general and simple theory. A major thrust of ecosystem studies has been to understand, in an integrated way, the response of communities to their environment and how this results in the resilience shown by many ecosystems (Pomeroy, Hargrove and Alberts 1988). A description of an ecosystem is an organized, and more or less formalized, model of structure and function of a complex system. Ecosystem models are complex, generally descriptive and heuristic. The understanding of ecosystem dynamics has emerged from specific applied problems where both biotic and abiotic, as well as human disturbances, transformed ecosystem function (Holling et al 1994).

These sub-disciplines have now matured substantially and are becoming integrated (Roughgarden, May and Levin 1989). Community and population ecologists have begun to address applied problems, such as the problem of species loss (Orians and Kunin 1990), and ecosystem ecologists have become active in formulating theory by utilizing applied studies to provide focus and relevance (Cole, Lovett and Findlay 1991). The integration is reflected in the recognition that animals not only passively adapt to but also shape their ecosystems, and that species dynamics can be more sensitive to ecosystem stress than the continuous functioning of the ecosystem (Odum 1983).

In the past, many ecologists, whether community or ecosystem scientists, have in their work often assumed that the human system is exogenous to their populations or their ecosystems. In recent years, however, a larger part of the ecological profession have started to emphasize the necessary role of ecological science in the wise management of the earth's resources and life-support systems, as reflected in the Sustainable Biosphere Initiative (SBI) research agenda of the Ecological Society of America. In the SBI it is stressed that:

> [E]cologists will be challenged over the coming decades to evaluate the functional significance of genetic diversity, species diversity, and ecosystem diversity ... [and] the SBI calls for new research programs that focus on the role of biological diversity in controlling ecological processes, and the complex suite of ecological processes that shape patterns of diversity (Lubchenco et al 1991).

This book focuses on biodiversity conservation at the level of ecosystems emphasizing functional diversity (see also pages 23–30). The systems approach to ecology has emerged from biology as an essentially new integrative discipline that links physical and biological processes, and forms a bridge between the natural and the social sciences. In particular we stress that a major reason for conserving biodiversity is the role that the mix of micro-organisms, plants and animals plays in ecological systems in generating the natural resources and ecological services that underpin the world's economy (Perrings, Folke and Mäler 1992).

Life-support systems, and ecological resources and services

Ecological resources and services of value to humans are produced and sustained by ecosystems. Biodiversity plays an important role in this context. Ecological resources and services are generated by the continuous interactions between organisms, populations, communities, and their physical and chemical environment. The life-supporting ecosystem is the functional term for these interactions (Odum 1989).

Ecologists have noted that many of the ecological resources and services generated by the life-support functions of ecosystems are indispensable, and of fundamental value since they sustain human societies. This value is associated with a wide range of ecological services and resources derived from ecosystems, such as supply of drinking water, production and provision of food and other renewable resources, maintenance of a genetic library, soil preservation and generation, operation of the hydrological cycle, local precipitation, recycling of nutrients, flood control, filtering of pollutants and waste assimilation, pollination of crops and maintenance of the gaseous composition of the atmosphere. Box 3.1 lists the key life support functions of ecosystems, and the important ecological resources and services they generate.

The role of biodiversity in ecosystem functioning was discussed on pages 23–30. In the context of biodiversity conservation and human welfare a major challenge is to sustain the amount of biodiversity that will ensure the resilience of ecosystems, and thereby the flow of crucial renewable resources and ecological services to human societies (Barbier 1989; Perrings, Folke and Mäler 1992). A sustainable use of biodiversity and ecological services thus implies avoiding thresholds, and keeping within ecological limits. Otherwise the system may lose its resilience and flip to a totally new one.

In ecology, the notion of ecological limits is generally linked to the system's carrying capacity. Carrying capacity is the maximal population size of a given species that an area can support without reducing its ability to support the same species in the future, and is a function of characteristics of both the area and the organisms (Daily and Ehrlich 1992).

Carrying capacity is never stable, because of the continuous evolution of systems. In the theory of ecological succession the early stages of ecosystem development are characterized by rapid colonization of recently disturbed areas and consequently with the major part of the energy flow diverted to exponential growth. When the system reaches its more mature stages the energy flow is mainly used for maintenance of the system, with a slow accumulation and storage of energy and material. Hence, the biomass and standing crop of organic matter increases throughout the succession and stabilizes at the mature stages.

Species diversity increases initially, then becomes stabilized or declines in the later stages of ecosystem development. The highest species diversity often occurs in the intermediate stages of the succession. In very general terms, species found in the early stages often exhibit high reproductive rates and have simple life histories (called r strategies), whereas species with longer and more complex life histories, specialized niches and more cooperation among species (called k strategies) often tend to be more dominant in the later stages of development. Hence, during succession the ecosystem generally becomes more complex, in the sense that it develops interactions and a diffuse network of sub-system feedbacks that increase the system's ability to accumulate and store energy and materials, its information content and its ability to survive perturbations. This is a consequence of the self-organizing capacity of living systems.

Box 3.1

Life-support systems and the generation of ecological resources and services

A life supporting ecosystem is the functional term for the continuous interactions between organisms, populations, communities, and their physical and chemical environment. These interactions, or life support functions, generate many ecological resources and services that are of fundamental value as they sustain human societies and existence. They include supply of drinking water, production and provision of food and other renewable resources, maintenance of a genetic library, soil preservation and generation, operation of the hydrological cycle, local precipitation, recycling of nutrients, flood control, filtering of pollutants and waste assimilation, pollination of crops and amelioration of the gaseous composition of the atmosphere. Many key ecological resources and services can be traced to specific life support functions of ecosystems. Some are indicated below, under the categories of regulation, production, carrier and information functions.

Table 3.1 *Life support functions of ecosystems*

Regulation functions	Production functions	Carrier functions	Information functions
Providing support for economic activity and human welfare through:	Providing basic resources, such as:	Providing space and a suitable substrate inter alia for:	Providing aesthetic, cultural and scientific benefits through:
■ protection against harmful cosmic influences ■ climate regulation ■ watershed protection and catchment ■ erosion prevention and soil protection ■ storage and recycling of industrial and human waste ■ storage and recycling of organic matter and mineral nutrients ■ maintenance of biological and genetic diversity ■ biological control ■ providing a migratory, nursery and feeding habitat.	■ oxygen food, drinking water and nutrition ■ water for industry, households etc ■ clothing and fabrics ■ building, construction and manufacturing materials ■ energy and fuel ■ minerals ■ medicinal resources ■ biochemical resources ■ genetic resources ■ ornamental resources.	■ habitation ■ agriculture, forestry, fishery, aquaculture ■ industry ■ engineering projects such as dams and roads ■ recreation ■ nature conservation.	■ aesthetic information ■ spiritual and religious information ■ cultural and artistic inspiration ■ educational and scientific information ■ potential information.

Sources: de Groot (1992); Ehrlich and Ehrlich (1992); Folke (1991); and Odum (1975).

The initial view of ecosystem succession of a highly ordered sequence of species assemblages moving towards a sustained, steady-state climax has been considerably revised through empirical research over the last decade. Holling et al (1994) state that the revision includes four principal points (see pages 23–30):

■ both early and late successional species can be present continuously;
■ large and small disturbances triggered by events such as fire, wind and herbivores are an inherent part of the internal dynamics and in many cases set the timing of successional cycles;
■ the species that invade after disturbance and during succession can be highly variable and determined by chance events; and
■ some disturbances can carry the ecosystem into a quite different development path, for example mixed grass and tree savannahs can shift into shrub dominated semi-deserts.

This implies that there are thresholds in ecosystems and that disturbances can flip the system into a new one. Hence, there seems to be more than one possible climax state in ecosystem development (Kay 1991; Walker 1993).

Preserving any system 'as it is' is therefore impossible. Natural disturbance seems to be part of ecosystem development. Ecological sub-systems should be allowed to go through the dynamic sequence proposed by Holling (1986) and discussed on pages 23–30. Policies and management that apply fixed rules for achieving constant yields, for example fixed carrying capacity of cattle or wildlife, or fixed sustainable yield of fish, wood or other products, lead to ecological systems that lack resilience.[1] That is, the resulting resource and ecosystem management regimes are of the type that may suddenly break down in response to disturbances that previously could be absorbed (Holling et al 1994).

The challenge is therefore to manage the resilience of systems, that is to conserve the possibility for a system to recover after it has been perturbed. In the context of biodiversity conservation this is a very difficult task, due to the complexity in the functioning of ecosystems and their biota, and because of the dynamics and uncertainty of system behaviour (Costanza et al 1993). In addition, the widespread fragmentation of the landscape in many areas of the world makes it even more difficult to conserve the functioning of ecosystems, particularly the ability to recover from and absorb disturbances. The fragmentation may be so extensive that the capacity to reorganize into similar ecosystems may be lost, and with it the species and populations dependent on the habitats contained within these systems.

How ecology approaches the problem of biodiversity conservation

Ecology is applied in resource management, environmental impact assessment, monitoring, risk assessment, ecotoxicology, ecotechnology, restoration of nature and so on. However, as stressed in the first part of this section, ecology as a

---

1 For various examples of different resource and ecosystem management regimes, see Folke and Kautsky (1992); Hammer, Jansson and Jansson (1993); Holling et al (1994); Perrings and Walker (1994); Reiger and Baskerville (1986); Trenbath, Conway and Craig (1990); and Walker (1993). See also the discussion of selected ecosystems in Part II.

science is often divided into two major branches. Biodiversity conservation, up until recently, has largely been approached from the branch of genetic, species, population and community levels (Simberloff 1988). In reality the levels from evolutionary, population, community, ecosystems, landscape to global ecology are inter-connected, in both space and time (see Allen and Hoekstra 1992 and Figure 2.3 of this book).

The perspective taken here is that to be able to deal effectively with conservation of biodiversity we need to recognize the inter-connectedness of these levels. According to Nelson and Serafin (1992) biodiversity so far has been viewed from a relatively narrow biological perspective to the neglect of a broader ecosystem perspective which would also include the activities and influences of humans. Efforts to conserve biodiversity should therefore focus increasingly also at the ecosystem and landscape levels. It is the resilience of the self-organizing ability of the system, and not only of its species and populations, which determines its capacity to respond to stresses imposed by predation or pollution from external sources, human influences included (Perrings, Folke and Mäler 1992). Understanding and managing the habitats, as well as the landscape matrix of ecosystems – including greenways and corridors to counteract habitat fragmentation – is therefore likely to be more effective than focusing on species and populations alone, and it has been argued that in order to sustain biodiversity over multiple human generations biodiversity policy should in fact be set at the landscape level of the ecosystem.[2] Furthermore, to be able to conserve biodiversity effectively it must be understood dynamically, in terms of process and function, rather than as maintenance of current elements of the ecosystem (Norton and Ulanowicz 1992).

This is emphasized by Walker (1993) in relation to rangeland management (see also Chapter 8). Every rangeland, at whatever scale one chooses to examine it, is spatially heterogeneous, the pattern of development is dynamic and changes in the species composition are commonly episodic, occurring in response to rare and extreme events or, more commonly, particular sequences of events such as a very dry year followed by a very wet year, two successive years of drought, a rare frost etc. In between such events production will vary from year to year in response to variation in rainfall, but the composition of the rangeland remains essentially the same and changes little in response to management. But the level of grazing does, however, affect the physiological status of the plants, and therefore influences the response and resilience of the rangeland during the next event.

Ludwig, Hilborn and Walters (1993) argue that harvesting natural resources is subject to a 'ratchet' effect. During relatively stable periods, harvesting rates tend to stabilize at positions predicted by management, through, for example, estimates of maximum sustainable yields. The sequence of good years generally encourages investments in further exploitation and infrastructure, whether in fisheries, forestry, agriculture or aquaculture. But in periods of disturbance and

---

2 See for example, Franklin (1993); Hudson (1991); Norton and Ulanowicz (1992); and Turner and Gardner (1991).

change the exploitive pattern generally continues.[3] The ratchet effect is caused by the lack of inhibition on investment during good periods, along with strong pressure in management and policy not to disinvest during poor periods. To use species and ecosystems sustainably, management should instead favour actions that are robust to uncertainties, informative and reversible, and update assessments and modify policy accordingly. This is often referred to as adaptive management (Walker 1993; Walters 1986).

For adaptive management to be effective, ecologists wrestle with identifying indicators of ecosystem integrity and health (Costanza, Norton and Haskell 1992; Kelly and Harwell 1990). Ecosystem health is defined in terms of four major characteristics applicable to any complex system. These are sustainability, which in turn is a function of activity, organization and resilience of the ecosystem and its species (Costanza, Norton and Haskell 1992).

Ecological indicators of ecosystem health and resilience are helpful in the efforts to avoid thresholds, limits and system collapses. For the same reason ecologists also engage in estimates of ecological limits and carrying capacity. For example, Vitousek et al (1986) estimated that 40 per cent of the capacity of global terrestrial ecosystems to support life on the planet is diverted or forgone as a consequence of human activity.

Estimates of limits to expansion have also been made for the salmon farming industry, for various fisheries and for shrimp farming in mangrove areas.[4] These analyses reveal the high dependence of such activities on widespread ecosystems. For example, to produce salmon in a cage a surface area from marine ecosystems of about 50,000 times the surface area of the cages is required to produce the fish that are fed to the salmon (Folke 1988). Similarly the 'ecological footprint' for a semi-intensive shrimp farm ranges from 35 to 190 times the surface area of the farm (Larsson, Folke and Kautsky 1994). When such activities use resources in a manner that degrades the function and resilience of life-support ecosystems, the ecological carrying capacity will be more rapidly approached.

To avoid such behaviour ecologists have started to quantify the functional aspects of ecosystems, with the purpose of illuminating their role in supporting human society (de Groot 1992). In this vein Ehrlich and Ehrlich (1992) classify the values of biodiversity in four major categories (see also Box 3.1, above):

- Humans have an ethical, stewardship responsibility towards their only known companions in the universe.
- Biodiversity has aesthetic values.
- Humanity has derived many direct benefits from biodiversity in the form of ecological resources, including food, many medicines and industrial products. The use and potential of the genetic library for providing these benefits is often emphasized in relation to biodiversity conservation.
- Most important from the anthropocentric perspective, biodiversity helps to

---

3   See, for example, Folke and Kautsky (1989); Hammer, Jansson and Jansson (1993); Reiger and Baskerville (1986); and Trenbath, Conway and Craig (1990).
4   See, for example, Folke and Kautsky (1989); Folke, Hammer and Jansson (1991); Hammer (1991); and Larson, Folke and Kautsky (1994). See also Chapter 7.

supply humans with an array of free ecological functions and services that support and maintain human activity, and even existence.

The first three categories are those that have been dealt with in biodiversity conservation and management, including management of parks and reserves. The fourth is the main focus of this book.

The field of ecological engineering also touches on this fourth issue. Sub-sets of ecological engineering include ecosystem rehabilitation, restoration ecology, synthetic ecology, sustainable agroecology, integrated aquaculture, habitat reconstruction, and river and wetland restoration (Jordan, Gilpin and Aber 1987; Soule and Piper 1992; Wisniewski and Lugo 1992). These approaches are concerned with the design of human society in relation to its natural environment for the benefit of both. The technology developed depends on the self-designing capability of ecosystems, with biological species as key components (Mitsch and Jörgensen 1989). Appropriate ecosystem management is compatible with sustainable land use, energy conservation and conservation of biodiversity. For example, Lugo, Parrotta and Brown (1993) emphasize the opportunity to couple natural processes with management to reduce species extinction and restore species richness in degraded lands. They show how tropical monoculture tree plantations can foster diverse native forests in areas previously deforested (see also Chapter 5). Hence, ecological engineering is not biodiversity conservation per se, but it is important for designing economic–environmental systems that foster biodiversity conservation and sustainable use of ecosystems.

HOW ECONOMICS APPROACHES THE PROBLEM

In Chapter 1 we suggested that the fundamental biodiversity management problem is to maintain that level of biological diversity which will guarantee the functioning and resilience of ecosystems on which not only human production and consumption but also existence depends (Perrings, Folke and Mäler 1992). The failure to do so will result in greater ecological scarcity – an increasing 'relative' scarcity of essential environmental assets and ecological services on which human welfare depends and, at the extreme, irrevocable damage to and collapse of ecosystems and their life-support services (Barbier 1989a).

As modern economics is principally concerned with the allocation of scarce resources to meet human needs, then economics can provide an important perspective on the biodiversity problem. It is this perspective which is the focus of the following section.

Instrumental values

As argued by Randall (1991), economics approaches the biodiversity problem through an anthropocentric perspective. In this book we argue that the most immediate reasons for caring about biodiversity are instrumental and utilitarian.

A diversity of species in a variety of viable ecosystems serves as an instrument for people seeking to satisfy their needs and preferences.

Consequently, from an economic perspective, the most important anthropocentric reason for conserving biological diversity is rooted in its fundamental instrumental value: the role that the mix of micro-organisms, plants and animals plays in providing ecological services and resources of value to humanity (Perrings, Folke and Mäler 1992). In Chapter 2, we discussed the various values that derive from biological diversity and ecosystem functioning. Biodiversity loss and ecological disruption affects human welfare directly through impacting on these values. In turn, it is these welfare impacts that provide the motivation for doing something about the biodiversity problem. That is, the economic implications of biodiversity loss for human welfare – of both current and future generations – are a powerful incentive for human society to develop strategies today for managing the biodiversity problem.

However, as long as the value of biodiversity is judged in terms of human preferences or needs, then this value is always relative. That is, biodiversity is just one of many things that individuals might want. In a finite world, in order for individuals to have 'more' biodiversity, they have to 'give up' the opportunity to satisfy their other preferences or needs. Thus the instrumental value of biodiversity is not absolute but can always be compared to the other 'good' things that people may want. This implies that the value of biodiversity can be compared to the value of other commodities that people may want; consequently, more biodiversity will be conserved if people are 'willing to pay' through adjusting society's production and consumption patterns so as to have more biodiversity and less of other goods.

Some economists have recognized that the instrumental value of biodiversity may not be sufficient to provide safeguards against the consequences of biodiversity loss.[5] As argued by Randall (1991), without resorting to the other extreme of according biodiversity preservation absolute or pre-eminent value over all other human moral obligations, it is possible to develop moral principles that would ensure that humans should make some, but not unlimited, sacrifices for biodiversity. For example, one approach might be to accept the principle of a safe minimum standard – a sufficient area of habitat should be preserved to ensure the generation of ecological services and the survival of species, sub-species or ecosystems, unless the costs of doing so are intolerably high (Bishop 1993; Perrings and Pearce 1994). Others argue the case for applications of a precautionary principle – in its broadest sense this implies that the opportunity set for future generations can only be assured if the level of biodiversity they inherit is no less than that available to present generations (Pearce and Perrings 1994; Perrings 1991). We will return to these arguments again in Chapter 9 when we consider the appropriate policy responses for biodiversity conservation.

---

5 See, for example, Bishop (1993); Common and Perrings (1992) Daly and Cobb (1990); Pearce and Perrings (1994); Perrings and Pearce (1994); and Randall (1991). See also the discussion in Chapter 9.

Natural resource and ecological scarcity

Economic approaches that view biodiversity loss as a problem of ecological scarcity are relatively new. However, economists have been analysing natural resource and environmental problems for some time. To a large extent, recent economic analyses of the biodiversity problem have evolved from the more 'conventional' economic approaches to natural resource scarcity. As this 'evolution' in economic thinking has been mainly a response to the increasing concern for global environmental issues and ecological processes, there are important insights that can be gained from examining the development in approach.

Barbier (1989a) provides an overview of the historical evolution of economic approaches to natural resource scarcity. We briefly summarize this overview here.

Natural resource scarcity was a major preoccupation of the early or 'classical' economists, such as Adam Smith, Thomas Malthus and David Ricardo, in the late eighteenth and early nineteenth centuries. During this important period of rapid agricultural development and industrial take-off, the early economists became concerned with the scarcity of fertile land relative to the demands of an expanding population as a possible constraint on economic growth. However, as the classical economists generally underestimated the potential of technological change in agriculture and in industrial development, and over-exaggerated the influence of population growth, fertile land as a constraint on growth never materialized.

Thus, by the late nineteenth and early twentieth centuries, economists were generally less preoccupied with natural resource constraints on growth and more interested in the efficiency of market systems in allocating scarce economic resources – including specific natural resources such as coal, oil, timber, fish and so forth.[6] They recognized that some of these specific natural resources could become relatively scarce, but the resulting increase in resource prices would generally encourage substitution and greater efficiency in use. As long as markets worked efficiently to generate these price signals, then increasing relative scarcity of specific exhaustible and renewable resources would not act as a constraint on overall economic activity and welfare. Thus in modern economics, the sub-discipline of resource economics emerged, which became concerned with the optimal depletion or management of exhaustible and renewable resources so as to maximize human welfare, both currently and in the future.

However, modern economists also began recognizing that the waste by-products of production and consumption may also have a negative impact on human welfare, particularly when such pollution interferes with the health, amenity and recreational benefits provided by the natural environment. Moreover, it was acknowledged that such costs are often afflicted externally to the market mechanism. In other words the external costs of pollution are an example of market failure. Certain individuals gain from the production and consumption of a

---

6 This is not to say that the work of this period was not important to the development of environmental and resource economics. For example, there were the pioneering contributions of Hotelling (1931) to the economics of exhaustible resources, Faustmann (1849) to the economics of forestry and Pigou (1920) to the economics of market 'externalities' such as pollution.

waste-generating commodity, but the rest of society suffers from the resulting pollution without any compensation. Thus environmental economics became concerned with determining optimal levels of pollution that would ensure that the marginal (social) benefits of reducing pollution would just equal the marginal (private) costs of doing so, and the appropriate economic and regulatory policies for achieving such pollution levels.

In the 1960s and 1970s, increased public awareness of global environmental and resource problems sparked renewed interest in economic approaches to these problems. Conventional approaches to resource depletion and pollution advanced considerably, and the global limits on the physical availability of many strategically important resources – such as fossil fuels and timber – and the increased pollution of industrialized societies also became a major social issue.[7]

In addition, however, environmental and resource economics began considering newer problems, such as the preservation of natural environments. An important focus was on the transformation and loss of whole environments as the result of economic activity, in particular irreversible development or conversion decisions. Several important considerations emerged.

■ There are few adequate substitutes for rare natural environments. While the value of these areas appreciates with increased demand, their fixed – and often diminishing – supply precludes an increase in their availability. Thus the economic value of natural areas is expected to increase over time.

■ There is often asymmetry between alternative uses of natural environments. Although they can either be preserved or developed, the development decision is irreversible. In contrast, if the natural environment is preserved initially, both preservation and development remain open as options.

■ Technical change is also asymmetric. That is, it results in expanded capacity to produce ordinary goods and services, but it can do little to replicate the ecological biophysical and geographical characteristics of natural environments.[8]

The likely result is that unique natural environments, and the ecological services and biological resources they yield, will increase in value relative to the ordinary goods and services produced by the irreversible development of these environments. In addition, economists noted an important market failure aspect to the problem: because most of the economic values of natural environments are not automatically reflected in markets, their increasing 'relative' scarcity is not readily captured by price signals.[9] Although natural environments, and their ecological services and resources, may be growing increasingly scarce, allocative choices based on market criteria alone that ignore the external social costs of this

7 Of course, the conclusions of most economic analyses did not alter: as long as markets operate efficiently, then increasing relative scarcity of specific exhaustible and renewable resources would not act as a constraint on overall economic activity and welfare. See Barbier (1989) for specific references and further discussion.

8 See, for example, Krutilla and Fisher (1985); and Miller and Menz (1979). For further references and discussion, see Barbier (1989).

9 A major reason that many economic values associated with the environment are not reflected in markets is the difficulty in assigning property rights to many environmental goods and services. Another important inter-disciplinary research programme launched by the Beijer Institute is concerned specifically with the critical role of property rights and security of access in natural resource and environmental management.

increasing scarcity will be biased towards appropriating natural environments for development. Only the costs of preservation – the opportunity cost of forgoing these development options – will be recognized as 'real' costs.

Economists also began exploring further the economic value of natural ecosystems in terms of the ecological services and biological resources they provide. As a result, a very substantial body of empirical estimates of environmental benefits has been assembled.[10] In addition, economists began distinguishing between three important economic functions performed by scarce environmental assets: not only does the environment provide useful material and energy inputs to the economic process and absorb any resulting waste, but the environment also provides important ecological functions or services that support production and consumption, and thus human welfare. These services range from recreational, health, cultural, educational, scientific and aesthetic services to the maintenance of essential climatic, hydrological, biogeochemical, and ecological cycles and functions (see pages 30–40).

As a consequence, there has been a growing appreciation in economics that the 'new' natural resource scarcity problem is fundamentally concerned with the problem of increased ecological scarcity. As discussed in Chapters 1 and 2, this scarcity problem is clearly linked to the continuing loss of global biological wealth and biodiversity, the underlying causes of which are extremely complex, and lie at the heart of our approach to economic and social development.

Natural capital

The recognition of the biodiversity and ecological scarcity problem as an important new challenge for economics has been coupled with a fundamental 'rethinking' of the environment as a form of natural capital that supports economic activity. Following this thinking, economists have begun to consider the conditions under which 'depletion' of the natural capital stock is consistent with 'sustaining' economic development.

Environmental resources are seen to be like other 'assets' in the economy. That is, they have the potential to contribute to long-run economic productivity and welfare. Thus the value of a natural resource as an economic asset depends on the present value of its income, or welfare, potential. However, in any growing economy there will be other assets, or forms of wealth, that yield income. Any decision to 'hang on' to natural capital therefore implies an opportunity cost in terms of forgoing the chance to invest in alternative income-yielding assets, such as human-made, or 'reproducible', capital. The latter can take the form of investments in 'physical' capital, such as factory plants, machinery, buildings, and so forth, or it can even be investment in the potential earning power of 'human' capital, through education, job training and other forms of skills development. Investments in other forms of 'wealth', whether they are art treasures,

---

10 For accessible overviews of these studies for both industrialized and developing countries, see Munasinghe (1992); Pearce and Markandya (1989); and Pearce and Warford (1992).

financial assets or even wine, could also be considered alternative economic assets to natural resources.

If natural resources are to be an 'efficient' form of holding on to wealth, then they must yield a rate of return that is comparable to or greater than that of other forms of wealth. In other words, natural resource depletion is justified up to the point where the comparative returns to 'holding on' to the remaining natural capital stock equal the returns to alternative investments in the economy. If the latter always exceeds the former, then in the long run even complete depletion of natural capital is economically 'optimal'. The only economic problem remaining is similar to the conventional problem of resource depletion described above: the process of depletion of natural capital and its transformation into other economic assets must be done in the most efficient manner possible.

The idea that economic well-being, or welfare, may not be affected and may even be enhanced if the rents derived from depleting natural capital, such as forests, wetlands, marine resources, energy, minerals and even soils, are reinvested in reproducible capital has been around for some time in the theoretical economics literature. For example, what is now known as the 'Hartwick-Solow rule' states that reinvestment of the rents derived from the intertemporally efficient use of exhaustible natural resources are reinvested in reproducible, and hence non-exhaustible, capital will secure a constant stream of consumption over time (Solow 1974 and 1986; Hartwick 1977). Similarly, basic renewable resource economic theory suggests that, for slow growing resources such as tropical forests, it may, under certain conditions, be more economically optimal to harvest the resource as quickly and efficiently as possible, and reinvest the rents in other assets that increase much faster in value. Equally, if the harvesting costs are low, or the value of a harvested unit is high, then the resource may also not be worth holding on to today (Clark 1976; Smith 1977).

Such 'rules' for natural capital depletion offer an important perspective on sustainable development. Economists generally consider development to be sustainable if it leads to non-decreasing welfare over time – so future generations are left no worse off than present generations (see pages 23–30). However, the conventional 'rules' for natural capital depletion described above suggest it is possible that such depletion can occur and welfare stay the same or even increase. For exhaustible resources, depletion must occur; otherwise, it is inefficient to use them. Such depletion is none the less consistent with sustaining economic welfare. As long as the natural capital that is being depleted is replaced with even more valuable human-made capital, then the value of the aggregate stock – comprising both human-made and the remaining natural capital – is increasing over time.[11] Conservation of aggregate capital alone is sufficient to attain sustainable development. Such 'rules' for depleting natural capital that emphasize this condition have been referred to as weak sustainability by some authors (Pearce, Markandya and Barbier 1989).

---

11 As pointed out by Pearce and Perrings (1994), rapid population growth may imply that the value of the per capita aggregate capital stock is declining even if the total value stays the same. Moreover, even if the per capita value of the asset base were maintained, it may not imply non-declining welfare of the majority of the people. These considerations also hold for the 'strong sustainability' arguments discussed below. Other population and distributional implications are discussed in more detail elsewhere in the book.

However, some economists have questioned whether such rules and conditions always hold for all environmental decisions – in particular the assumption that there is sufficient substitutability between reproducible (human-made) and natural capital over time such that they effectively comprise a single 'homogeneous' stock. As discussed above, economic analyses of natural environments and the ecological services they provide now question whether such substitution possibilities exist for many ecological services and resources. Further complications for welfare arise through the failure to consider the economic consequences of the loss in 'resilience' – the ability of ecosystems to cope with random shocks and prolonged stress – that results from natural capital depletion (see Chapter 2).

Moreover, the 'weak sustainability' rules for 'optimal' depletion of natural capital assume that all economic values are reflected in the 'prices' of resources, markets are undistorted, resource extraction is efficient and rents are reinvested in other assets in the economy. If any uncertainty exists, 'weak sustainability' rules can still hold as long as there are markets for contingent claims that allow for such uncertainty. As will be discussed further in the next chapter, the presence of pervasive market and policy failures affecting environmental decisions – as well as the difficulty of fully valuing natural capital – means that such perfect economic incentives do not exist currently.

As a consequence, more recent theories now stress the limits to 'substitution' between many forms of natural and human-made capital, and instead suggest caution in development decisions that lead to the continued 'drawing down' of natural capital in favour of investing in other economic assets.[12] In contrast with 'weak sustainability', such rules that stress the special features of natural capital that limit substitution possibilities between natural and human-made capital are often dubbed strong sustainability (Pearce, Markandya and Barbier 1989).[13]

According to this view, it is very likely that choosing a development path today that leads to the depletion of 'natural' capital – including our stocks of biological wealth and biodiversity – will have detrimental implications for the welfare of future generations. In other words, current economic development is essentially unsustainable. This is inevitable, as long as current generations fail to compensate future generations for the welfare implications arising from the irreversible loss of 'natural' capital today. Moreover, 'strong sustainability' arguments stress the uncertainty of compensating future generations.

If it is difficult to determine whether we can compensate the future generations and how much compensation they require, then the best we can do is to ensure that future generations have the same economic opportunities available to them as the current generation. Given the limits to substitution between natural and other forms of capital, as well as the problems of irreversibility, uncertainty of threshold effects and the potential scale of social costs associated with loss of environmental assets, 'strong' sustainability suggests that it is difficult to ensure

---

12 See, for example, Barbier (1989a); Barbier and Markandya (1990); Common and Perrings (1992); Mäler (1994); Pearce and Perrings (1994); and Perrings and Pearce (1994).

13 See Turner (1993) for further discussion of the differences between weak and strong sustainability. He suggests that a further classification of theories in terms of 'very weak' and 'very strong' sustainability is also possible. The latter is not necessary for the purposes of this book.

that future economic opportunities are maintained without imposing some conditions on the depletion of natural capital. As discussed above, a major problem is increasing ecological scarcity – as natural environments disappear the essential ecological services and resources they provide will increase in value relative to the ordinary goods and services in the economy produced by human-made capital. The value of these 'ecological' components of natural capital will continue to rise relative to that of human-made capital. That is, maintaining the value of the entire asset base comprising both human-made and natural capital will in turn require maintaining those ecological services and resources of increasing value to human welfare.[14]

Consequently, according to strong sustainability, the only way to ensure that the value of the entire capital stock is maintained or increasing, and thus sustainable development assured, is to prevent irrevocable disruptions to ecosystem functions and resilience through biodiversity loss. That is, the economic opportunities available to future generations can only be maintained if the level of biodiversity available to future generations is no less than that available to present generations (Pearce and Perrings 1994).

THE PROS AND CONS OF A SINGLE-DISCIPLINE APPROACH

The previous two sections described the different approaches developed by ecology and economics in response to the biodiversity problem. Given the vast size and complexity of this problem, it is often questioned whether economics, ecology or any other scientific discipline on its own is capable of grasping the full implications of biodiversity loss. In this section, we briefly discuss why a single-discipline approach may not be adequate, and thus the need for ecology, economics and other disciplines to work collectively to develop additional approaches to this problem.

Specialization and scientific disciplines

As the previous sections have illustrated, one of the advantages of modern scientific thinking is that it has allowed specialization of intellectual methods and tools. Thus, various and different approaches are developed by economists, ecologists and other scientists to deal with the multitude of 'scientific' problems that confront us in the modern world, and each discipline quickly develops an expertise in analysing and indeed even 'solving' the particular set of problems with which it is confronted.

As a consequence, our scientific method has become highly specialized, with each discipline rapidly developing analytical 'tool kits' best suited to its particular speciality. The degree of specialization even within disciplines is quite striking.

---

14 As noted above, there are obviously important considerations concerning population growth and welfare distribution when it comes to maintaining even the value of essential ecological resources and services. The implications of these factors are discussed elsewhere in the book.

For example, on pages 42–49 some of the important differences in approach between population and systems ecology were noted. Economics as well is renowned for its sub-disciplines, and even further sub-divisions. For example, 'macro' economists are concerned with the investment, consumption and government policy decisions that affect the entire economy, whereas 'micro' economists are more concerned with allocation decisions made at the household, firm or industry level. Traditionally, environmental and resource economics has been considered a part of the 'microeconomics' approach.

The advantage of such specialization is that it allows a great deal of effort to be concentrated on extremely specific and 'acute' problems of scientific interest. Highly sophisticated techniques can be applied and developed to advance our understanding of such problems, and in devising specific solutions. An analogy can be made with modern medicine. If you have a heart problem, you will eventually be referred to a specialist, such as a cardiologist. A slipped disc or a pinched nerve may require a neurologist; a broken bone or knee injury may require an orthopaedist; mental illness a psychiatrist, and so on.

The danger of such specialization is of course that it can be overly reductionist and partial when faced with an extremely complex and multi-faceted scientific problem. Each discipline is concerned with reducing a problem to a level it feels comfortable with. Alternatively, each discipline will only approach that part of the problem which it feels is most suitable for its specialized analytical approach.

A further problem arises in that each scientific discipline has become specialized to the degree that it becomes very difficult for scientists in one field to communicate with each other. It is as if they are speaking two different languages. The academic tendency is to be so highly trained in the analytical approaches and techniques of a single discipline – or even sub-discipline – to the extent that we are totally unfamiliar with the approaches and perspectives of other disciplines. Frequently, scientists from different disciplines may be working on the same type of general problem, such as biodiversity conservation, and yet have little to share with each other in advancing our collective knowledge of the problem.

As a consequence, the tendency is to become extremely rigid in our individual disciplinary perspectives. Our ignorance of other disciplines tends to make us less tolerant of their different perspectives and analytical approaches. More importantly, we fail to realize any potential mutual gain from working together on common or overlapping problems. Finally, society itself may potentially lose, as there may simply be a class of problems that are beyond the capacity of a single discipline to analyse and solve by itself.

Science and the biodiversity problem

We believe that the biodiversity problem as defined in this book may be one important issue facing humankind that requires more than the standard single-disciplinary approach. The capacity of either ecology or economics alone to grapple with this problem may simply be insufficient. However, both disciplines – and indeed others – are clearly needed in developing the analytical methods and techniques necessary to understand the full implications for human welfare, and the entire biosphere of the continuing loss of biodiversity.

At the same time, the highly specialized analytical techniques and approaches that ecologists, economists and other scientists are currently using and developing further are extremely important 'tools' for this task. Each discipline may discover some of its 'tools' to be more appropriate than others and new 'tools' may have to be forged through the various disciplines working together to develop common analytical approaches to the biodiversity problem. However, progress also requires each discipline to contribute through its own specialized skill; advances cannot be made if scientists show up with an empty 'tool kit'. In short, a single-discipline approach may not be sufficient for tackling the current biodiversity problem, but the specialized scientific benefits offered by the specialized skills of each discipline are necessary for the task.

Again, an analogy can be made with medicine. The biodiversity problem is similar to that of a seriously ill patient, whose symptoms are mysterious but becoming increasingly apparent, the exact causes of the illness complex and difficult to fathom, and the critical condition uncertain but possibly terminal. Several specialists may be called in to deal with the patient, because they have skills that are relevant to the apparent symptoms and to determining the diagnosis. However, not one specialist alone is capable of diagnosing the malady or suggesting the remedy. All the specialists have to combine their skills together to make the diagnosis and decide on the appropriate cure. Other specialists may have to be called in if other skills are required. More importantly, all of them may, through their combined effort, have to climb a collective 'learning curve' before the full implications of the illness can be determined and a remedy proposed.

Finally, the specialists will also have to learn to communicate better with generalists, such as policy makers, educators, the media and others who are both responsible for seeing the situation 'as a whole', and who must also respond to and interact with the public at large. After all, it is the public who must become better informed of what the true situation and its likely consequences are.

This analogy perhaps best describes the collective approach that we mean by the term the ecological economics of biodiversity loss. We do not imply that a new and alternative discipline needs to be forged out of ecology and economics in order to deal with the current biodiversity problem. We believe that the skills available in ecology, economics and other disciplines should be used to tackle this problem, and new skills can be forged to meet this challenge as the need arises.

Rather, what is required is that ecology, economics and other disciplines begin applying their specialized knowledge and analytical methods collectively to extend beyond the current frontiers of their respective disciplines, so that we can be sure of the appropriate diagnosis and remedy for the global biodiversity problem. Ecological economics is not a new discipline as such, but a new category of analysis for approaching problems of economic–environmental interaction where a single-discipline approach will not suffice. As stressed in this book, the depletion of the world's biological wealth and biodiversity is perhaps the most pressing example of this 'new class' of environmental problem that we are facing today.

The next chapter illustrates more fully why biodiversity loss is such a complicated, but pressing, issue today by examining in more detail the proximate and underlying causes of the problem. The rest of this book is concerned with further discussion of empirical case studies, analytical methods and policy responses that are relevant to the ecological economics of biodiversity loss.

4

Driving Forces for Biodiversity Loss

Previous chapters have described the nature of the biodiversity loss problem, the ecological and economic implications of this loss, and recent developments in how ecology and economics approach the problem. This chapter completes our introduction to these issues by looking at the factors causing biodiversity loss. We begin by making a basic distinction between proximate and underlying causes of the problem, and then discuss in more detail key issues of population and scale, culture and ethics, economic incentives and institutions.[1]

PROXIMATE AND UNDERLYING CAUSES: AN OVERVIEW

The main driving forces behind biodiversity loss arise from human activities, and can be distinguished in terms of proximate and underlying causes.

- Proximate causes refer to the direct over-exploitation of species (for example, through hunting, fishing, collection and persecution) and the indirect impact of ecosystem degradation or destruction that leads to species loss (for example, through habitat alteration and conversion).
- Underlying causes refer to the economic, social and cultural factors that lie behind the economic activities that lead to the direct depletion of species, and the destruction and degradation of their habitat. These underlying causes include the scale and growth of human population, culture and ethics, economic incentives and institutions.

Such driving forces, or proximate and underlying causes, are illustrated and discussed throughout this book. In this chapter, we seek simply to describe very briefly and in general terms how each of these driving forces contribute to the problem of biodiversity loss.

Proximate causes

In Chapter 1 we provided a brief overview of the statistical evidence of biodiversity loss. It is clear that the major threat for species extinction arises from habitat destruction and alteration, and to a lesser extent from direct exploitation.

The direct impact of exploitation (and over-exploitation) of species populations is fairly well documented by the biological sciences and economics, in terms of

---

1 The distinction between proximate and underlying causes in this chapter draws heavily on Perrings, Folke and Mäler (1992).

the relationship between species stock levels, growth functions, harvest rates and effort, and resource output. However, much less is known about the role of biodiversity in natural resource management, which has often resulted in the failure to take ecosystem functioning and resilience into account in natural resource management strategies.[2]

A few case studies also explore the role of biodiversity in natural resource management, and provide essential insights into ecosystem functioning and resilience, and appropriate natural resource management schemes. For example, Hammer, Jansson and Jansson (1993) describe how over-exploitation by Sweden's highly specialized fishery industry has contributed to the depletion of fish stocks in the Baltic Sea (see also Box 2.1). Current concern for fish stock depletion has led to questions being raised about the problems of over-harvesting and diversity loss. The predominant management regime for offshore fisheries aims to smooth out the natural fluctuations in fish production in order to achieve a stable economic output. Given the declining stock of highly demanded fish, a steady supply has been achieved by increasing effort and by releasing more fish from hatcheries.

Ecological research shows that fisheries display complex dynamic patterns, for example a rapid turnover of dominant species, changes in species abundance distribution and wide year-to-year fluctuations. As a result, current management strategies tend to create or enhance ecological instability, and may actually undermine the functioning of the ecological life support system and its capacity to sustain fish production. The key fisheries management problem to be addressed is not just the preservation and production of a particular fish species that is currently threatened by extinction, but rather the maintenance of the resilience and ecological functions of those ecosystems on which fish production depends.[3]

The forces for conversion, substitution, specialization and globalization have encouraged the current trends in worldwide homogenization of species and ecosystems for production of economic goods and services (Swanson 1992a and 1992b). For example, of the estimated 250,000 species of flowering plants, only around 3000 have been regarded as a food source, around 200 have been domesticated for food and of these about 15–20 are crops of major economic importance (WCMC 1992). In fact, the four major carbohydrate crops (wheat, maize, rice and potatoes) feed more people than the next 26 crops combined. Similarly, a handful of domesticated species provide nearly all the terrestrial sources of protein for the majority of the population. Land under the few domesticated crops and animal species has been increasing steadily at the expense of natural habitats.

On a global level, the apparent recent decline in extinction rates reflects a substantial increase in conservation efforts over the past 30 years (WCMC 1992; see also Table 1.1 of this book). Conservation has generally been focused on

---

2 In recent work, Brown and Roughgarden (1994) develop an inter-disciplinary ecological–economic approach to natural resource harvesting.
3 See Chapter 7 for a more detailed discussion of estuarine and marine ecosystems, and Chapters 9 and 10 for discussion of appropriate policies and institutions to manage natural resource problems arising from biodiversity loss.

saving well-known species that are under imminent threat of extinction. Several projects have targeted severely endangered wild species by taking them into captivity, building up the populations and then releasing them back into the wild when environmental conditions are suitable. This direct manipulative intervention has led to the survival – at least in the short to medium term – of numerous species that were extremely vulnerable to extinction. However, while we have become adept at ensuring individual species conservation, the more pressing problem of how to control habitat destruction still remains. Indeed, the success of targeting individual threatened species through 'capture, support and conservation' programmes depends directly upon having a suitable habitat for the species to return to. This is similar to the fisheries management problem described above. While the challenge of conserving key threatened species will undoubtedly remain, the problem of managing habitat conservation to ensure the long term survival of species within functioning and resilient ecosystems is the really crucial issue.[4]

Habitat change by humans is caused directly through land-use changes, urbanization, infrastructure development and agricultural expansion. Habitat change is also caused indirectly through environmental effects caused by the use and extraction of resources from the environment, and the introduction of species to new areas. Biodiversity loss is also affected by the discharge of wastes to air, soil and water, and by the global climatic changes due to fossil fuel burning, and emission of greenhouse and ozone depleting gases. The ecological impact of habitat degradation on biodiversity loss is fairly well understood. For example, Box 4.1 provides a discussion of proximate causes of biodiversity loss in Australia. However, the resulting implications for ecological function and resilience are less well known (see Chapter 2).

Resource and environmental management practices that attempt to maintain highly managed domesticated ecosystems run the risk of developing systems that are less resilient. Although domesticated ecosystems are heavily supported by a variety of exogenous inputs such as irrigation, industrial energy, fertilizers, pesticides and so on, they may still be susceptible to unexpected shocks and stresses. In addition, highly managed ecosystems also tend to be characterized by their lack of diversity which, as we discussed in Chapter 2, may also affect their resilience. As a result, the impact of an unexpected shock on a managed system can be the collapse of the system, and thus the loss of production, on a large scale. Box 4.2 shows that even those ecosystems with high productivity may be susceptible to stress and shocks, for example ecosystems that are adapted to employ green revolution monocultures.

A key problem for ecologists is to assess when ecosystems are likely to lose their capacity to absorb stresses or shocks directly incurred by species exploitation and indirectly through habitat degradation. It is also important to determine when these pressures will lead to a reduction in biodiversity and when the loss

---

4 Lugo, Parrotta and Brown (1993) discuss how traditional models of deforestation and species loss may overestimate the rates of species extinctions due to natural resilience. Opportunities exist to couple natural process with management practices to reduce species extinction and restore species richness to previously degraded land. For example, in Puerto Rico species rich understories develop inside monoculture tree plantations.

Box 4.1

Proximate causes of biodiversity loss in Australia

Species extinction has been mainly confined to medium sized mammals in Australia – mostly native marsupials. There are several proximate causes for the loss of these species. First, the difficult environment for medium sized herbivorous mammals, with its highly patterned productivity, and variable and drought prone climate, exposes them to frequent local disappearance. This makes these mammals particularly susceptible to the external threats. The introduction of exotic species, especially the rabbit with its high reproductive capacity and later the fox which preys on medium sized mammals, led to the widespread destruction of habitats and species.

The introduction of exotic plant species accidentally for agricultural, ornamental and scientific purposes has also led to the invasion of exotic plants into the Australian ecosystem. Land management practices have encouraged the spread of introduced plants, through clearing native vegetation for agriculture, timber harvesting and urban development. Also, fertilizer use, modified fire regimes and habitat fragmentation have assisted the progress of introduced species. Finally, around urban areas, the dispersal of exotic plants is assisted by the disposal of garden refuse and over wider areas by tourism.

A further proximate cause of habitat destruction and biodiversity loss in Australia is related to the displacement of Aborigines. Aboriginal displacement led to reduced and modified burning patterns that further contributed to habitat change. In addition, over-stocking with introduced domestic animals during favourable climatic periods, combined with a reluctance to run down herd sizes during less favourable periods, was an important factor in habitat modification in many areas.

Source: Common and Norton (1992)

---

of biodiversity signals the irreversible collapse of the system or a process of creative destruction within the system. The choice of system boundaries – both spatial and temporal – are obviously important factors determining whether ecosystem shocks and biodiversity loss are perceived to lead to an irreversible collapse or creative destruction. As we shall discuss in more detail in Chapter 9, the decision over spatial and temporal boundaries often depends on a range of ecological, economic, social and political factors.

A further issue to be considered when discussing the impact of habitat loss on biodiversity is the effect of ecosystem scale and distribution. The geographical patterns of extinction indicate that 75 per cent of all recorded animal extinctions recorded since 1600 have occurred on islands (see Table 1.1). One important reason for this is that island species tend to be constrained by the scale of their range. Typically, island birds, animals and plants have a small range that contains a relatively small number of potential habitats. Therefore, when an island habitat is degraded or destroyed there are few, if any, alternative habitats for the species to find refuge in. In comparison, continental species often have much greater access to alternative habitats. The small scale of their range and low availability

Box 4.2
The green revolution and sustainability

Beginning in the 1950s there was an increasing concern with the problem of feeding a rapidly growing world population. The goal of achieving rising per capita food productivity was to be achieved through the 'green revolution'. The green revolution focused on three inter-related areas:

- breeding programmes for staple cereals that produced early maturing, day-length insensitive and high-yielding varieties (HYVs);
- the organization and distribution of packages of high pay-off inputs, such as fertilizers, pesticides and water regulation;
- implementation of these techniqual innovations in the most favourable agro-climatic regions and for those classes of farmers with the best expectations of realizing the potential yields.

Its impact in the Third World, particularly on wheat and rice production, has been phenomenal. Between one-third and one-half of the rice areas in the developing world are planted with HYVs. In the eight Asian countries that produce 85 per cent of Asia's rice (Bangladesh, Burma, China, India, Indonesia, Philippines, Sri Lanka and Thailand), HYVs add 27 million tonnes (mn tn) annually to production, fertilizers another 29 mn tn and irrigation 34 mn tn. Estimates of the contribution of new HYVs to increased wheat production in developing countries vary from 7 to 27 mn tn. Per capita food production in the developing countries has risen by 7 per cent since the mid-1960s, with an increase of over 27 per cent in Asia. Only in Africa has there been a decline.

Post green revolution problems

Although these results are very impressive, they have been associated with various problems of equity, stability and sustainability. For instance, while producers have widely adopted the HYVs irrespective of farm size and tenure, factors such as soil quality, access to irrigation water and other biophysical–agroclimatic conditions have been formidable barriers to adoption. Farmers without access to the better-endowed environments have tended not to benefit from the new technologies, which partly accounts for the relative lack of impact of the green revolution in Africa. But even under favourable conditions in Asia or Latin America, a significant gap persists between performance on the agricultural research station and in the farmers' fields.

The higher productivity of rice and wheat, relative to other crops for which no green revolution has yet occurred, has led many farmers to substitute these cereals for other staples and for more traditional mixed patterns of cropping. The resulting widescale monocropping has been associated with increased output variability, as crop yields grown with the new technologies may be more sensitive to year-to-year fluctuations in input use arising from shortages or price changes. For example, although the modern varieties are more responsive to fertilizers than traditional varieties, farmers have to apply higher levels of fertilizer to the modern varieties if they are to get the full benefits. Thus, the gap between actual and potential yields is highly sensitive to the price of rice relative to that of fertilizer. Evidence from the Philippines, Thailand, Indonesia, Sri Lanka and Taiwan reveals that where it takes less than 0.8 kg of rice to buy 1 kg of urea, the gap attributed to fertilizer is over 0.5 tonnes per hectare (tn/ha) or less. But where it takes over 1.5 kg of rice to buy 1 kg of urea, the gap yield generally exceeds 1 tn/ha.

Intensive monocropping with genotypically similar varieties has also led to increased incidence of pest, disease and weed problems, sometimes aggravated by pesticide use. Severe outbreaks of the brown planthopper occurred on rice in the1970s with losses in Indonesia of around 2 mn tn. Planthoppers are naturally controlled by wolf-spiders, and a variety of other natural predators and parasites which are destroyed by many of the pesticides commonly used on rice.

There are now signs of diminishing returns to the HYVs and high pay-off inputs in intensive production. Perhaps, more importantly, the experience on the less well-endowed farms, particularly in Africa, suggests that there are real limits to replicating the 'successes' of current green revolution technologies and packages in more marginal agricultural areas.

Source: Conway and Barbier (1990).

of alternative habitats puts island species under extreme threat from habitat destruction and degradation.

The patterns of habitat loss and extinctions of island species have important implications for worldwide biodiversity loss. That is, the loss and fragmentation of habitats leads directly to species extinctions. In addition, this process reduces the total supply and accessibility of habitats. The gradual depletion and fragmentation of natural habitats on a global scale places a further indirect pressure on species survival. The consequence is that there are fewer alternative habitats for threatened species to find refuge in. One serious concern is that it is extremely difficult to assess how close we are to a global crisis of habitat loss; even assessing more localized problems has proved difficult.

Underlying causes

The key driving forces behind the proximate causes of biodiversity loss discussed above are the joint effect of human population numbers and human behaviour in relation to the natural environment. Such underlying causes of biodiversity loss include factors as diverse as population pressure, economic incentives, institutions, and culture and ethics. Because they are so wide ranging, these underlying causes are not summarized here. Instead, each is briefly reviewed in the remaining sections of this chapter.

POPULATION PRESSURE

Human population pressure is considered an important underlying cause of species over-exploitation, and habitat destruction and degradation, which in turn leads to biodiversity loss. However, the role of human population pressure on biodiversity loss is not straightforward. Three important issues are:

- the scale of the human population relative to the carrying and assimilative capacity of the environment;

■   human population growth as a function of social, economic and political factors; and

■   the patterns of production and consumption undertaken by the human population and their effect on ecosystem sustainability.

Population scale

The scale, or size, of the human population can be an important source of stress on an ecosystem's sustainability, either directly or indirectly through reducing biodiversity. The resilience of an ecosystem depends upon its internal capacity to deal with stress, and the level and type of stress to which it is subjected. There are, of course, numerous other factors that may increase or reduce stress on ecosystems and its ability to cope with stress, for example, human behaviour, technology, ecosystem maturity and natural external shocks.

The carrying and assimilative capacity of an ecosystem is an indirect measure of the maximum level of stress that the ecosystem can maintain. Too much stress and the ecosystem may exceed its carrying or assimilative capacity. This can lead to a loss in the resilience of the ecosystem. If the ecosystem experiences further stresses or shocks it may collapse.

Holding all other factors constant (for example, human behaviour, technology, ecosystem capacity, natural external shocks), population growth implies increasing stress on the ecosystem. At some scale of population, the level of stress imposed on the ecosystem will become intolerable, and the associated loss of biodiversity and ecosystem resilience will lead to ecosystem collapse. At the same time, it is important to note that the sustainability of an ecological system does not imply a unique equilibrium level of human population (Perrings, Folke and Mäler 1992).

Localized human population expansions have placed increasing, and sometimes intolerable, stress on ecosystems. Box 4.3 provides an example from Bangladesh of increasing food demand from a rapidly expanding population putting excessive pressure on the agricultural land resources available, thus leading to soil erosion and land degradation. Excessive ecosystem stress may be offset to some extent by technological improvements, changes in production and consumption patterns, or reduced economic activity through out-migration. However, these adjustments are often undertaken only after irreversible damage has been imposed on the ecosystem, and severe economic and social costs incurred by the local and wider population.

It is often suggested that the rate of growth of the human population on a global scale is leading to a population expansion that exceeds the carrying and assimilative capacity of the entire world. Technological improvements and changes in production and consumption patterns may offset the stress imposed on the global ecosystem to some extent, as we will discuss below. However, a real concern is that these solutions will arrive too late and be insufficient to prevent the collapse of the global ecosystem.

Ehrlich and Ehrlich (1992) describe the role of population in the global biodiversity problem in terms of human impact on the planet's total supply of energy captured in photosynthesis, namely global net primary production. Net

---

Box 4.3

Population pressure, food production and land degradation

The high rate of population growth in Bangladesh is leading to projected levels of food demand that exceed food production potential. As Table 4.1 shows, while achievable foodgrain production is projected to outstrip food requirement narrowly up until 2010, food grain demand (reflecting estimated increases in income per capita) is expected to exceed achievable production. Increasing demand for food could be met, to some extent, by increasing cropping intensity and irrigated land, introducing modern varieties of crops and increasing yields (through fertilizers, drought management, farm management and so on). However, it will be extremely difficult to achieve this without further degradation of the agricultural resource base. In addition, regional climatic conditions (including floods, droughts, cyclones, winds and tidal surges) place additional shocks and stress on the local ecosystem and its productive capacity.

Land and soils are currently suffering from problems of degradation due to over-use and mis-use of agricultural resources. The hilly slopes are losing topsoil as a result of inappropriate farming practices and inadequate conservation measures, and as much as 1.74 million hectares (mn ha) of sloping land is currently under severe threat of erosion. In the active floodplains and 'char-land' (ie land that recently emerged from a river), severe loss of land resources is underway due to changes in river courses. Poor watershed management practices have resulted in siltation and soil deterioration.

The growing intensity and cultivation of modern crop varieties have increased the net removal of nutrients – approximately 4.5 mn ha of cultivated land is sulphur deficient and 1.75 mn ha zinc deficient. Furthermore, soil organic matter content is being reduced by the acute biomass crisis and use of crop residues and cow dung as fuel – more than 60 per cent of cultivatable lands have less than 1.5 per cent organic matter content.

In Bangladesh, the population pressure is already affecting the sustainability of agricultural development. The threshold limit may be reached in the next 10-20 years unless: i) population growth is controlled more effectively; ii) depleted agricultural resources need to be regenerated and augmented; and ii) agricultural technology and its adoption need to be improved.

Table 4.1   *Projected foodgrain requirement, demand and production potential (mn tonnes)*

Food items	Production	Food requirement		Food demand		Achievable production		Production potential	
	1990	2000	2010	2000	2010	2000	2010	2000	2010
Food-grain	18,450	24,530	29,720	26,810	35,660	25,520	31,950	35,120	42,120

Source: Mahtab and Zarim (1992)

---

primary production (NPP) is the energy fixed by photosynthesis, minus that required by plants themselves for their life processes. NPP is equivalent to the total supply of food to all animals and decomposers. Humans use NPP directly through consumption, divert NPP to their own use through alteration of natural ecosystems and change the potential for NPP through changing the productive capacity of natural ecosystems. Humans currently consume, divert or forgo almost 40 per cent of all NPP generated on land. While our impact on oceanic NPP is very small (about 2 per cent), in total we account for around 25 per cent of global NPP. Humankind's appropriation and loss of terrestrial NPP has contributed to the extinction problem through reducing the amount of NPP available for other species. It has been estimated that given the current levels of NPP available for non-human species, 3–9 per cent of earth's species may be extinct or endangered by the year 2000.[5]

The amount of terrestrial NPP available to accommodate future human population growth is therefore not substantial. Although more efficient use of terrestrial and oceanic NPP may occur alongside population growth, this is unlikely to offset the effect of projected high rates of population growth on NPP use. In addition, increased economic activity is anticipated to accompany future population growth, thus creating further demand for NPP and stress on the ecosystem. The implications of increased use, diversion and loss of terrestrial NPP through population and economic activity expansion are extremely significant – high rates of biodiversity loss, a breakdown of ecosystem resilience, and the potential collapse of the global ecosystem.

Causes of population growth

The causes of population growth are complex, and depend upon a range of social, economic and political factors. However, the extreme poverty of resource users in many degraded environments has itself encouraged population growth. Treating human population growth as if it is determined exogenously to the environment upon which it depends is therefore not appropriate. Nor is it possible to reduce fertility rates, and thus population growth, without first addressing the motivations determining high rates of fertility.

Dasgupta (1992) has recently explored the incentives that lie behind human population trends through the economic theory of resource allocation, as applied to rural households in poor countries. He suggests that the population problem in many developing countries is related to poverty and possibly also to degradation of the local natural resource base. One of the many incentives for poor households to have more children is for their income generating potential (for example, collecting fuelwood, dung and fodder, herding animals, fetching water, household chores and working on the farm). In areas that are poor in resources, the private benefits from a productive asset (that is to say, a child) may be perceived to outweigh the private costs incurred for their maintenance, including any environmental degradation that the child incurs. This may especially be the case if the natural resources are managed under a system of open access and the private decision maker (that is to say, the household head) fails to take the full social costs of environmental degradation into account.

---

5   This estimate of extinction by Wright (1990) is based on human impacts on energy flows through natural ecosystems. The estimate is not out of line with other estimates of extinction provided in Chapter 1.

Policies to deal with the population problem have traditionally focused on improving and providing more information on reproduction and contraception, and increasing the costs of having children (for example, through family planning programmes, increased female education and outside work opportunities). However, policies aimed at reducing the benefits of reproduction need also to be considered as a means of lowering excessive rates of population growth. Methods to achieve this may include alleviating poverty (for example, through improved credit and savings markets or alternative income opportunities), increasing the availability of basic household needs (for example, water, food and fuel) and ensuring households take into account more fully the costs of environmental degradation.

Patterns of production and consumption

The impact of the human population on the environment depends not only on the scale of the population but also on the level and type of economic activity, and the manner in which economic goods and services are produced and consumed – including the technology that is used for resource production and consumption. Box 4.4 provides an example from Korea where reduced family size was combined with rising incomes, which led to changes in the lifestyle and consumption patterns of Koreans. Although the gains from a slower population growth partially offset the greater demand for natural resources from increased economic activity, this was not sufficient to prevent severe environmental degradation problems, especially water and air pollution, arising in Korea.

Population growth clearly puts pressure on global resources. However, we should be cautious in attributing all the blame for biodiversity loss on population growth. First, as discussed above, high fertility rates, and thus population growth, are in part determined by poverty and environmental degradation. In addition, while the scale of the population is important, the consumptive patterns of the population are crucial. Table 4.2 shows that the developed countries, with only 26 per cent of the world's population, consume a disproportionate share of the global resources. To bring developing countries' energy consumption up to developed country levels by 2050 would require increasing global energy use by a factor of five. In terms of industrialization, a five to tenfold increase in manufacturing output – and therefore an inevitable rise in resource demand – would be required just to raise consumption of manufactured goods by the developing world to industrialized world levels. A crucial question is whether the global resource base – including its assimilative capacity – can sustain these increased demands as long as the advanced economies continue to hang on to their disproportionate share.

ECONOMIC INCENTIVES

Those factors that determine the behaviour of individuals and governments are the ultimate driving forces behind biodiversity loss. One of the most important

Box 4.4

Demographic transition, economic activity and environmental degradation in the Republic of Korea

The Republic of Korea, with its rapid decline in population growth rate and high levels of economic growth, represents a unique case study of the inter-relationship between population growth, economic expansion and natural resource use. Since 1960, Korea has experienced spectacular economic growth reflected by an annual average rate of growth of gross national product (GNP) of 10 per cent. This has been accompanied by a dramatic decline in mortality and fertility (the numbers of children per woman has fallen from 6.1 to 1.6 between the period 1955–60 and the year 1990). As a result, population growth rates have also declined rapidly from 3.1 per cent between 1955–60 to 1 per cent between 1985–90. A major factor contributing to these trends has been the substantial government support for family planning (for example, government programmes including target setting and the use of mothers' clubs), combined with a high degree of motivation by young couples for small families. In addition, Korea experienced a rapid transition from a largely rural population and agricultural economy, to a predominantly urban and industrial nation.

A slower population growth is generally expected to contribute to a more sustainable use of natural resources. However, in Korea the slower population growth was accompanied by rapid economic growth and led to a more wasteful resource consumption pattern. In fact, the low rates of population growth may have contributed to the high rates of economic development and thereby indirectly encouraged higher levels of environmental degradation. For example, per capita energy consumption increased sixfold over 20 years, from 238 kg (oil equivalent) in 1965 to 1475 kg in 1987. High levels of energy consumption led to serious problems of industrial waste and air pollution. A recent assessment by World Resources Institute indicates that the net annual atmospheric increase of emissions of carbon dioxide amounted to 21 million tonnes (mn tn) and methane 160,000 tn. Water pollution is also reaching an alarming level as a result of increased economic activity. In 1988, the daily production of household sewage was 1 mn tn and industrial waste over 450,000 tn. Only 28 per cent of this waste was treated before being discharged into rivers.

In short, slower population growth in Korea has generally not led to a more conservative use of natural resources. Instead, it has supported rapid economic development through industrialization and urbanization. The rapid changes in economic activities and patterns of resource use accompanying Korea's period of economic development have resulted in severe environmental problems, including air and water pollution. One lesson learned from the Korean experience is that countries cannot expect reduced population pressure alone to necessarily lead to more resource consumption. Population control needs to be accompanied by economic policies and institutions that ensure that economic development is undertaken in a sustainable manner.

Source: Kim and van den Oever (1992).

Table 4.2 *Distribution of world consumption, averages for 1980–2*

Commodity	Units of per capita consumption	Developed countries share in world consumption	Developed countries per capita consumption (1)	Developing countries share in world consumption	Developing countries per capita consumption (1)	Relative consumption (1) ÷ (2)
Food:						
calories	kcal/day	34	3395	66	2389	1.42
protein	gm/day	38	99	62	58	1.71
fat	gm/day	53	127	47	40	3.17
Paper	kg/year	85	123	15	8	15.38
Steel	kg/year	79	455	21	43	10.58
Other metals	kg/year	86	26	14	2	13.00
Commercial energy	mtce/year	80	5.8	20	0.5	11.60

Source: World Commission on Environment and Development (1987).

factors influencing the use of the natural environment is the pattern of economic incentives that prevail in society, which can either encourage or discourarge behaviour leading to conservation of biological diversity.

The pattern of economic incentives is often very complex and generally arises from a combination of other important driving forces in society, such as institutional and legal factors, and culture and ethics – which we will discuss further in subsequent sections of this chapter – and from the specific 'characteristics' of individuals, households and communities, such as:

- their level of income, wealth, education and skills;
- their access to resources and markets; and
- their overall status and influence in society.

For example, in the previous section we saw that, for poor rural households in low income countries, the economic incentives to have an additional child are great, because the benefits to the household of that child's production outweigh the potential costs, including degradation of the environment (Dasgupta 1992).

Understanding the pattern of economic incentives influencing biodiversity loss is a key component of any ecological economic analysis of the problem. Consequently, Parts II and III contain many examples of the role of economic incentives in the management of key ecosystems and biodiversity conservation. In the rest of this section, we review the main arguments briefly, focusing on market and policy failures, and biodiversity conservation projects.

Market and policy failures

As discussed in Chapter 2, the failure to appreciate and assess the economic value of biodiversity can result in a distortion of economic incentives. The implication of biodiversity values not being fully recognized and integrated into decision making processes may be an excessive loss of biodiversity.

As argued by Barbier (1993b), this problem is characteristic of most problems of environmental degradation, particularly over-exploitation of ecological resources and habitat conversion. That is, much excessive degradation of the environment and natural resources is thought to result from individuals in the market place, and by governments not fully recognizing and integrating environmental values into decision making process. If markets fail to reflect environmental values adequately, market failure is said to exist. Where government decisions or policies do not fully reflect these values there is policy or government failure.

In the case of the biodiversity problem the following can be said.

■ Market failure occurs if markets fail fully to reflect biodiversity values. This may result from the presence of open access resource exploitation and public environmental goods, externalities (for example, non-marketed environmental services), incomplete markets, uncertainty, the distribution of income and assets, and imperfect competition.

■ Government or policy failure occurs when the policy interventions necessary to correct market failures are not taken. It also arises when government decisions or policies are themselves responsible for worsening allocation failures that lead to excessive biodiversity loss.[6]

Market failures limit the effectiveness of markets and market prices to reflect the full social benefits (and costs) of biodiversity. While decisions by individuals may be privately rational, given the institutional set-up and the information available to the decision maker, it is unlikely that these decisions represent the best outcome for society.

Panayotou (1994) notes that if land owners are profit (or 'rent') maximizers, privately held land will only be set aside for biodiversity conservation if it is in the direct economic interests of the landowner to do so. However, setting aside land for biodiversity conservation has opportunity costs in terms of alternative uses. Therefore, land will only be allocated to conservation if this option maximizes the net present value of rents accruing to the land (discounted at the landowner's discount rate). Given that most of the benefits from biodiversity conservation and habitat protection are public rather than private, insufficient land will be allocated to conservation from society's point of view. Thus governments are required to intervene in land use decisions, through regulations, economic incentives or outright purchase of the land, to ensure that sufficient land is allocated for conservation. The implications of this for policy are discussed further in Part III.

However, governments often fail to take the appropriate action to solve the 'public good' aspect of the wider values of biodiversity and other market failures contributing to excessive biodiversity loss. What is more, poorly formulated economic and regulatory policies often exacerbate prevailing market failures. At worst, the direct private costs of biodiversity using activities are subsidized, further encouraging excessive depletion of biodiversity.

---

6 As we will see in a moment, the latter condition is characterized by economists as a policy failure problem of the 'second best', which was formulated by Lipsey and Lancaster (1956). We are grateful to Karl-Göran Mäler for clarifying this point and contributing to the discussion of this 'second best' problem, below.

For example, McNeely (1993) cites the case of Botswana where a combination of high export prices for beef (offered by the European Economic Community), veterinary services provided at low cost, subsidized veterinary cordon fences, development of bore holes to provide water to cattle, low land rents and improvements to trek routes have exacerbated the problem of excessive cattle production through uncontrolled grazing of 'open access' rangelands.[7] This in turn has led to degradation of the savannah, resulting in a reduction in the long term productivity of Botswana's biological resources.

The case studies of selected systems presented in Part II provide many additional examples of where market and policy failures have contributed to excessive natural resource degradation, biodiversity loss and ecological disruption. The standard 'textbook' solution is to 'correct' market failures or to end government interventions, such as subsidies, that are designed explicitly to reduce the private costs of over-exploitation of biological resources or habitat conversion. As will be discussed in Part III, removal of government subsidies and other interventions that reduce the incentives of individuals to conserve biodiversity can often be implemented fairly easily – provided there is sufficient 'political will'. Similarly, the use of additional economic and regulatory instruments to 'internalize' environmental values, including the 'public good' aspect of biodiversity, may be relatively straightforward to implement.[8]

However, there may exist many cases in which correcting market failures is not always·possible. For example, as will be discussed later in this chapter, the root of the problem of market failure may lie in cultural and ethical norms that are difficult to change. Equally, prevailing institutional structures, such as the system of property and resource use rights, are also extremely intractable to modification, yet may lie at the heart of the problem of perverse economic incentives for biodiversity conservation. In such circumstances, it is conceivable that – in the short run at least – the gains from correcting the sources of market failure may not exceed the costs to society of doing so. Careful analysis of the causes of the problem and alternative solutions is required.

As indicated in Figure 4.1, an additional problem is that there are many ways in which government policies can influence the use of the environment, including biodiversity. Many macroeconomic policies that are designed for other purposes, such as monetary, fiscal or trade policies, can have as their unintended side effects further deleterious impacts on the environment. The problem is that the policies may be designed to 'improve' the overall macroeconomic performance in the economy, but because of the presence of market failures with regard to the environment – such as inappropriate property rights or the lack of prices for environmental goods and services – the result may be incentive effects that worsen environmental degradation and biodiversity loss. Economists generally refer to this as the problem of the 'second best', as it occurs as the result of, say, policies designed with the intention of correcting or improving fiscal, monetary

---

7 As defined in the next section, an open access management regime means that access for resource use is effectively unrestricted; it is free and open to all.

8 However, as mentioned above and will be discussed in greater detail in Chapters 9 and 10 respectively, the biodiversity problem presents further challenges for policy, such as the protection of ecological 'thresholds', and the need to develop and coordinate incentives at the local, national and international level.

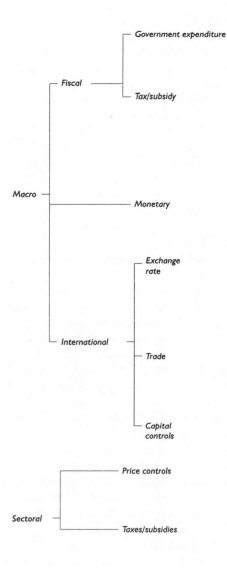

		Government expenditure	Publicly funded agencies can protect biologically unique areas; public infrastructure (roads and dams) may encourage land uses that degrade fragile areas.
	Fiscal	Tax/subsidy	Multi-sector instruments can alter general demand conditions and thus use of resources; for example, income tax breaks may encourage speculation in land and/or unnecessary conversion of natural areas; 'polluter pays' taxes and user fees can reduce waste and air/water pollution.
Macro		Monetary	Tied-credit analogous to subsidies; credit rationing and interest rate hikes may reduce demand, but can also discourage conservation investment.
		Exchange rate	Devaluation increases prices of imported inputs (pesticides, logging equipment), while increasing profitability of exports (crops and timber); environmental impacts will depend on the nature of the resource and product affected.
	International	Trade	Import/export taxes and quotas have effects similar to devaluation but on selected commodities only; may alter relative returns to environmentally destructive versus benign products.
			When used to prop up over-valued currency, similar to revaluation of exchange rate.
		Capital controls	May stimulate or retard environmentally damaging production; depends on nature of resource and products affected.
Sectoral		Price controls	Usually indirect impact via changes in demand, but may alter choice of inputs/outputs: for example, subsidies to livestock production may promote deforestation; fertilizer subsidies may retard adoption of soil conservation; pesticide subsidies may increase negative health effects of agro-chemical runoff etc.
		Taxes/subsidies	

Source: Bishop, Aylward and Barbier (1991).

Figure 4.1 *Economic policy and potential environmental impacts*

or trade 'imbalances' inadvertently exacerbating another allocative failure, such as the presence of market failures with regard to the environment and biodiversity values.

For example, in the case of Botswana discussed above, if the government chose to expand monetary supply to reduce interest rates generally in the economy, the result could increase unintentionally the incentives to over-graze. Lower interest rates make it easier to increase all investments in the economy, including purchasing and holding more cattle. However, because of 'open access' grazing, cattle owners do not face the full costs of stocking more herds on the land; hence, over-grazing and rangeland degradation occurs. Although there is a linkage between monetary policy, and environmental deterioration and biodiversity loss, the root of the problem lies in the 'market failure' of an inappropriate property rights regime. If there were instead enforceable private property rights for rangeland or, alternatively, communal ownership with strict control of grazing rights and access, then each cattle owner would take into account environmental damage to the rangeland in his or her decision to stock more cattle on the land.

Again, the obvious solution to such policy failures is to try to eliminate those market failures that lie at the heart of the 'second best' outcomes where problems of environmental degradation and biodiversity loss are unintentionally worsened through 'macro-economic' interventions. In the Botswana example discussed above, improving rangeland ownership and grazing rights regimes would be the natural starting point. As we noted earlier, however, these and many other sources of market failures with regard to the environment are often difficult to correct. Moreover, very rarely is the problem of biodiversity loss attributable solely to one kind of market failure alone – such as open access resource exploitation – usually several other 'failures' are also present – such as environmental externalities, the public good aspects of biodiversity and imperfect markets.

Faced with such complications, the role of policy analysis is to 'disentangle' the various linkages between policy and market failures, as well as the resulting implications for the economic incentives to conserve biodiversity. The first step is to design methods of analysis that improve our understanding of the linkages between, say, changes in macro-economic policies and biodiversity loss through environmental degradation. For example, in Chapter 8, we discuss a case study that develops the use of computerized general equilibrium analysis, as applied to Botswana, as a means for understanding the links between economic policy and rangeland degradation (see also Unemo 1994). If such methods of analysis reveal a significant linkage, then it is important that the macro-economic policies are designed to account for their potential effects on the environment and biodiversity loss. Once these effects are included, then it is possible to compare alternative policy scenarios to determine whether it is worth correcting the market failures and other underlying factors behind the problems of environmental degradation and biodiversity loss.

Biodiversity conservation projects

The economic incentives for biodiversity conservation can also be influenced more directly by publicly funded investment projects.

Biodiversity conservation projects have progressed throughout the years. However, getting the incentives right for biodiversity conservation still continues to remain a significant challenge. Too often in the past, attempts to encourage habitat and biodiversity conservation have actually resulted in perverse incentives for resource over-exploitation. One of the key constraints has been the lack of appropriate management regimes, which has resulted in conflicts over rights of access to resource use, and disputes over the distribution of the costs and benefits of biodiversity conservation.

Early approaches to biodiversity conservation focused on habitat protection – that is, demarcating land as state parks which are protected from use through policing and anti-poaching methods. These have often been unsuccessful due to conflicts over resource access between park managers and local populations, who have restricted access to cultivation, grazing, settlement and fuelwood gathering. In addition, protected parks are often unmanageable due to inadequate staffing and funding, which undermines their viability in the long run. An important lesson learned from habitat protection projects is that 'conservation measures are likely to be most successful when they provide real and immediate benefits to the local people' (McNeely 1993).

More recent approaches to biodiversity conservation tend to have a 'people-oriented' perspective. For example, the Integrated Conservation-Development Projects (ICDPs) aim to achieve their conservation goals by promoting development and providing local people with alternative income sources which sustain, rather than threaten, the flora and fauna in natural habitats. These projects include biosphere reserves, multiple-use areas and a variety of rural initiatives on the boundaries of national parks (including buffer zones), as well as regional land use schemes with protected area components (Munasinghe 1992; Wells and Brandon 1992).

In Chapter 10, we discuss in more detail the need for appropriate management incentives in the development of biodiversity conservation, including ICDPs. However, while the design of project-level incentives remains crucial to the success of conservation efforts, it is also important to look at the broader economic influences on incentives for efficient resource use and management, including the benefits of overall improvements in agricultural productivity and meeting basic human needs (Southgate and Clark 1992).

Finally, the success of biodiversity conservation projects in terms of encouraging appropriate economic incentives will require greater understanding of the overall institutional context in which the project is being implemented. It is to this role of institutions that we now turn.

INSTITUTIONS

The institutional framework of society is an important influence on individuals' decisions, concerning the use of resources and thus the incentives for biodiversity conservation. The term institutions refers to the rules and conventions of society that facilitate coordination among people regarding their behaviour, and includes both formal and informal, governmental and non-governmental rules and conventions (Bromley 1989; North 1989).

There are numerous levels at which institutions function, for example locally, regionally, nationally and internationally. Households, for example, are an important institutional 'unit' and, depending on the society, it may be the norm or convention for households to consist of primarily the nuclear family, the immediate extended family or a multi-household 'compound' of several related families.

Analagous to the problems of market and policy failure, institutional 'failure' may also be an important underlying cause of excessive biodiversity loss. More generally, institutional failure may occur where:

■ institutions are inadequately designed, and are unable to adapt to meet changing conditions and requirements;
■ institutions do not coordinate with other institutions, both within and across levels;
■ institutions fail to exist.

In Chapter 10, we provide several examples of how such institutional failures at the international, national and local level can contribute to the problem of biodiversity loss. Institutional failures on all three levels need to be assessed and corrected if this problem is to be adequately controlled. In the remainder of this section, we outline briefly the need for appropriate institutional structures for biodiversity conservation.

Property rights and management regimes

Property rights are among the most important institutions. Property rights are a bundle of entitlements defining the owner's rights, privileges and limitations to use of a resource (Eggertsson 1993). Broadly, four types of property rights regimes exist – although these rights tend to overlap and there is also variation within each category:

■ *private property*   resource rights and ownership are conferred on an individual, group of individuals or a corporation, in other words, the owner has the right to exclude others from use of the resource and to regulate its use;
■ *state property*   resource ownership is vested exclusively in the government, which determines and controls access, and regulates use;
■ *common property*   resource ownership and management is in the hands of an identifiable community of individuals, who can exclude others and regulate use of the resource;

■   *open access*   access for resource use is effectively unrestricted, in other words, it is free and open to all.

A frequent misperception is that common property leads to over-exploitation by individuals – the 'tragedy of the commons' – and should be replaced by state or private ownership of resources. However, many common property regimes traditionally have involved the sustainable use of resources, but may break down due to over-population, policy failures, and the expropriation of resource ownership and rights. This often occurs in the case of wildlife and natural habitats, where community management of the wild resources consists mainly of important social rules and rituals governing traditional 'rights of access' and harvesting. These rules and rituals are often informal and seldom legalized; consequently, they are easily undermined by external forces of change.

Open access exploitation increases the risks of rapid resource degradation of species and their habitats. As exclusion (or control of access) of users is problematic, each individual has the incentive to exploit the resource as quickly as possible. Each individual will therefore ignore any user costs of exploitation. That is, the concern will be with maximizing returns today – before they are lost to somebody else – rather than with the loss of future income due to resource depletion. Perversely, the presence of surplus profit, or excess economic rent, will also encourage over-exploitation – particularly under conditions of open access.[9]

If large profits are available from resource exploitation but they accrue exclusively, say, to a single individual or the government, then the single resource owner can sustain the income earned indefinitely by limiting over-exploitation. However, if it is impossible to exclude others from exploiting the resource as well, then the existence of excess economic rents will be an incentive for many individuals to undertake this activity or alternatively for the individuals already exploiting the resource to expand their activities. The result is that any profits will be quickly dissipated, as returns become rapidly dispersed over a growing number of individuals, none of whom will have any incentive to conserve the resource. Unfortunately, these conditions are characteristic of the exploitation of many of the world's remaining 'wild' areas and resources, which are rich in biodiversity (Barbier 1992b). In many developing countries, government policies – fiscal incentives, pricing policies, regulations and land titling – often exacerbate these tendencies by reducing or distorting the direct costs of rapid resource exploitation and conversion. Once again, market, policy and institutional failures interact as the driving forces for biodiversity loss.

In the context of biodiversity conservation, it is important to address such driving forces, and to define appropriate property rights to ensure the efficient and sustainable use of biodiversity and ecological services. The structure of property rights will strongly influence the success or failure of biodiversity management, which will vary from one institutional design to another. The

---

9   In economics, rent is the difference between the total value of selling a commodity and the costs of supplying it. Thus rent can in principle be determined by deducting from the gross income earned the costs of labour, material and capital inputs (including the costs of paying a normal return, or profit, to capital). The existence of rent therefore implies more remuneration than is required to keep an activity in operation – hence the term surplus profit.

choice of management regime itself could be anything from no action at all (laissez-faire) to market regulation and instruments, to communal, state or international governance. In the remaining parts of this section, we look into communal governance in terms of local institutions for biodiversity conservation, and into state and international governance. These issues are also explored further in Chapter 10.

Local institutions and biodiversity conservation

In many biodiversity-rich developing countries, local institutions – or social structures – play an extremely important role in resource allocation and use decisions. Social structures are often developed over a long period of time, and display unique traditions and rites that bond society together. A concept of 'social sustainability' can be used to look at how local institutions respond to changing social demands and resource supply, and their impact on the sustainable use of natural resources (Githinji and Perrings 1993).

The term 'social sustainability' reflects the similarity between human societies and ecological systems in terms of their resilience. The resilience of human societies is their ability to continue functioning in the face of shocks or stress. There are several organizational similarities between human societies and ecological systems. First, human societies are organized into tightly knit groups and looser associations at different levels, for example, families, communities, nations and so on. Second, the loose structure between the sub-systems gives society flexibility and the capacity to adjust in the face of exogenous shocks.

If these adjustments are consistent with the self-organization of the system, then they will also be within the culture and traditions of society. If the adjustments are not consistent with the self-organisation of the system, then society will experience either fundamental (catastrophic) institutional change or extinction (Berkes, Folke and Gadgil 1994). Thus societies which are unable to adapt become extinct, while societies which have lost resilience undergo fundamental institutional change. It may, of course, be possible to sustain social and economic systems through external intervention. However, the costs of maintaining current institutional conditions which enable the functioning of society at the status quo should not be ignored.

The relevance of social sustainability to biodiversity conservation is illustrated by the role of rural institutions in farmers' decision making in Kenya (see Box 4.5). According to Ghitinji and Perrings (1993), the literature on decision making by traditional livestock and arable farmers throughout sub-Saharan Africa is split between two approaches.

One approach assumes that rural households behave like profit maximizing farming firms. In this approach, the size of the family labour is contingent on production decisions. The firms hires labour and other inputs to meet the needs of a particular production target. This production target is a function of market and technological conditions. In addition, the production and consumption decisions of a household are separated.

Another approach assumes that rural households are qualitatively different from profit maximizing firms. In this approach, the size of the labour force is

Box 4.5

Cattle and social institutions in Kenya

Pastoralism is a traditional and significant economic activity in Kenya. While Kenya has attempted to increase livestock production during the last decade, there has also been rising concern for the environmental costs of over-grazing. This has been attributed, as elsewhere in sub-Saharan Africa, to the persistence of traditional land tenure regimes and methods of production. There are relatively few political and ideological constraints on the development of land markets in Kenya. However, rural land markets have failed to develop, even though there appear to be clear benefits to their establishment, for example in terms of natural resources, labour and insurance. Therefore, it could be asserted that the costs of establishment (for example, transaction costs) outweigh the benefits. However, a more significant factor may be the forgone opportunity cost of the existing land tenure structure, in terms of assuring social sustainability.

The Kenya Livestock Development Plan led to the formation of group and individual livestock ranches. Individual ranches were built on the concept of private property. On the group ranches, the land ownership title was made out to the group, although individuals owned the livestock. Individual members were expected to be constrained in the stocking decision by the fact that it was in the group interest to limit herd densities to the capacity of the ranch. However, this resulted in severe problems of range over-grazing and poverty. The problems arose due to several factors: individual herd ownership created incentives for individuals to hold as many cattle as possible on the group land; individuals with private ranches also registered for group participation; there was no effective collective regulation of individual behaviour; most group ranches were not ecologically viable units, in that few straddled both wet and dry season grazing; and even though actual herd sizes exceeded the carrying capacity of the ranches, they were still insufficient for individual family biological subsistence.

In addition to the biological subsistence needs, the cattle are extremely important for meeting social requirements. The viability of the continuity of a community may depend on their access to sufficient livestock for social functions. For example, a household within the Rendille people of Northern Kenya requires a minimum of eight animals to meet minimum subsistence needs. However, to meet the social obligations required by the Rendille, household animal requirement is increased by 200 per cent. Social uses of livestock include: marriage and associated ceremonies; age-set ceremonies; births; family festival; wealth and prestige.

As a result of the substantial number of non-market livestock requirements, which are largely independent of the market price of livestock, livestock ranchers have not responded as expected to changes in property rights and other factors. However, while traditional social obligations may have been ecologically sustainable prior to the introduction of group ranches, this is no longer the case. The costs to a society of changing the requirement of the social rites may include the loss of social authority among the institutions that have traditionally protected the resilience of the social system. The loss of the social support structure may reduce the income security of the group. Among risk averse people, this is a high price to pay.

Source: Githinji and Perrings (1993)

taken to be more or less independent of the process of production since it is based on a set of previously existing social relationships. It may be argued that the objectives of the peasant household not only extend beyond economic (production) goals, but also that such economic goals may also be a strictly subsidiary part of household objectives.

The different approaches affect the way in which institutions are considered. If the profit maximizing firm approach is adopted, one would expect to be able to anticipate the influence of price changes on demand and supply. However, empirical studies have shown that predicted prices responses are rare in sub-Saharan Africa. That is, increases in producer prices do not necessarily lead to increases in production output and increases in input prices do not necessarily lead to falls in the quantity demanded. The explanation offered for this phenomenon by advocates of the profit maximizing approach is the existence of institutional failures. For example, the main constraints on price responsiveness are thought to be the structure of property rights and the absence of markets for scarce resources. Political and ideological factors are believed to constrain the removal of communal property and the creation of markets, and thus inhibit the incentives for resource conservation.

The alternative model of rural household decision making provides a different perspective of institutions. For example, the objective of rural households may be to select the least risky option from a set of 'survival algorithms' – that is a risk minimizing strategy (Lipton 1968). Peasants may be faced with a choice of: (a) crops that are robust in poor rain, but have a low average yearly yield and are suitable for direct consumption; and (b) cash crops with higher yield but more vulnerable to poor rains. Peasants would be expected to select the former option to ensure acceptable levels of environmental and market risks. The model of risk minimization thus appears to anticipate limited farmer responses to relative price changes. Therefore, it is not appropriate to assume that institutional factors are constraining farmer responsiveness to market prices in this case.

Even if existing institutional structures are determined endogenously, and if they meet the perceived needs of the community, they may still have an impact on natural resource use. For example, traditional resource use and access rights may be passed on to all children equally. This can lead to the parcelling of land into sub-optimal holdings – both in terms of size and ecological characteristics (for example, strips on a slope). This in turn may encourage mis-use and over-use of land resources, resulting in lower productivity and land degradation. The allocation of land based on ancestral rights, rather than those who have the capacity to use it, can also lead to inefficient land use. The lack of land rental markets in Africa reinforces this land allocation inefficiency. A further problem for the conservation of biodiversity arises from the non-excludability of users with rights derived from their membership of the family, clan or ethnic group (in the case of rangeland) or the non-excludability of heirs (in the case of arable land). Under these conditions, the communal property rights system tends towards an open access system. As discussed above, open access resource use encourages individuals to ignore the 'user' costs of resource use, and thus over-exploit and degrade the land.

From a profit maximizing approach, given the high costs of preserving the traditional social structure and its requirements, it would appear that there is an institutional failure. However, as the case study of Kenya in Box 4.5 shows, the benefits of stability and support derived from maintaining the traditional social structure should not be ignored. Furthermore, when looked at from the 'survival algorithm' approach, the cost of the loss of social authority that traditionally protects the resilience of the social system may be even more significant. The loss of the social support structure may reduce the income security of the group – and among risk averse people, this is a high price to pay (Ghitinji and Perrings 1993).

National and international institutions and biodiversity conservation

The national and international institutional and legal framework also has an important role to play in biodiversity conservation. As discussed earlier in this chapter, market and policy failures can lead to excessive biodiversity loss. Therefore appropriate policy responses need to be developed to correct these problems. However, even carefully designed policies are unlikely to achieve their objective unless they are founded on effective institutions capable of implementing, monitoring, enforcing and assessing these policies, whether at a national or international level.

In recent decades, numerous international institutions have been established to support natural resource and environmental conservation at a global level. A key issue that is being debated in the international arena is the way in which to 'capture' the wider values of biodiversity conservation (often expressed in developed countries) and transfer 'compensation payments' to developing countries for their conservation activities. Various schemes have been proposed, and some implemented, to achieve this, for example, the creation of tradeable development rights, international franchise agreements, offset agreements, global environment facility investments, debt-for-nature swaps and so on.[10] Again, the success of all such schemes critically depends upon the institutional framework within which they operate.

Institutions can also provide a link among local groups, provide information networks, coordinate activities for the environment, and represent the views of local groups to government and vice versa. Historically, the role of institutions in biodiversity conservation has tended to be marred by inappropriate design, coordination and integration, although substantial efforts are being made to reduce these problems.

In Chapter 10 we discuss further the development of appropriate national and international institutions, alongside local institutions, for biodiversity conservation.

---

10 See, for example, Barrett (1994), CSERGE (1993), Panayatou (1994) and Swanson (1992a and 1994). See also Chapter 10 for further discussion of these international institutions and mechanisms.

CULTURE AND ETHICS

The factors affecting the natural resource use decisions taken by individuals and societies are the underlying causes of biodiversity loss, such as culture and ethics, economic incentives and institutions. In this section we discuss the role of culture and ethics in natural resource use decision making. We will address several issues:

- the ethics of valuing of natural resources;
- the ethics of the current generation's responsibility for future generations; and
- the cultural relationship between individuals, local societies and the global society, and biodiversity loss.

Values

We discussed economic valuation of natural resources in Chapter 2. However, we return to the issue of valuation here because of ethical questions that are raised about the assumptions underlying this approach when applied to biodiversity loss. One objection to the approach taken by economists to valuation is that it is rooted in an anthropocentric framework. That is, only values that humans perceive to exist are taken into account. For example, intrinsic value theorists argue that natural objects have value entirely independent of human consciousness. 'Intrinsic value' in this sense can be defined as a function of the objective characteristics of objects, entirely independent of human perception, cognition or valuation of them.

While the theory of intrinsic value may be appealing, there are certain problems with this approach as well. First, an intrinsic value cannot exist without a conscious valuer. In addition, attempts by humans to take intrinsic values into account are constrained by the universal values of nature. As defined above, intrinsic values are inherent in the object itself, independent of their functioning as viewed by the evaluator and are not conditioned by time or circumstance. Therefore, it is extremely difficult, if not impossible, for humans to take these values into account, and to 'balance' them with human needs and desires. However, the intrinsic value theorists do provide certain insights for valuation, in particular that human valuations of objects are not merely subjective, but are also imposed upon us by natural elements over which we have little or no control (Norton 1993).

Economists would add that they do recognize that intrinsic values exist. The benefits that individuals derive from just knowing that ecosystems are preserved 'in their own right' are usually described as existence values. However, as discussed in Chapter 2, existence values are extremely intangible and difficult to measure, precisely because they are subjective and unrelated to human use.

Inter-generational equity

A further ethical issue arises in the problem of biodiversity loss over the responsibility that current generations bear for future generations. It is generally accepted that, if sustainable development is a social objective, then current generations will be responsible for ensuring that the natural resource base is not destroyed or degraded to the extent that economic opportunities for future generations are reduced (see Chapters 2 and 3).

The question of inter-generational equity has focused on economists' use of discount rates. Discount rates implicitly involve ethical judgements about the inter-generational allocation of resources, and thus inter-generational equity. However, concern does not strictly lie with the use of discount rates per se. Rather, it lies with the choice of the rate of discount.

For example, it has been argued that if the current population has an ethical responsibility for future generations, then the costs of environmental degradation should not be discounted. Under this scenario, discount rates would effectively be zero. However, in recent years these arguments for removing or reducing high rates of discount have largely been refuted. A low discount rate may be insufficient to avoid imposing environmental costs on future generations. Low discount rates may in fact lead to investments in natural resource using and unsustainable activities. Thus lowering the discount rate does not necessarily imply reducing the rate of environmental degradation. Instead, as argued in Chapter 3, in order to ensure inter-generational 'fairness' the appropriate rate of discount should be based on the return to the total stock of capital, including natural capital. Only at this rate of discount is it possible to maintain or increase the 'value' of the total capital stock, thus 'sustaining' the economic opportunities available to future generations (Mäler 1994). To suggest that arbitrarily setting the rate of discount to zero would reflect an equal ethical concern between the welfare of current and future generations is therefore a false assumption.[11]

Recent proposals to deal with the effects of high discount rates have focused more on inter-generational transfers than manipulation of the discount rate. In short, while the proposition that the current population has an ethical responsibility for future generations remains unchallenged, more appropriate ways for addressing this ethical responsibility are being sought. That is, setting discount rates equal to the marginal productivity of the asset base may be desirable; however, practical application of this approach is more problematic.

For example, Perrings, Folke and Mäler (1992) argue that defining the marginal productivity of capital in circumstances where most of the ecological stock is not valued and production functions are neither smooth nor continuous is extremely difficult. Second, a social rate of discount that reflects the growth potential of the whole economy–environment system remains undetermined and is likely to remain so for some considerable time. Finally, both factors suggest that although we may believe that the real rates of social discount are currently too high, determining what the rates ought to be is not an easy task. As discussed in Chapter 3, a more important issue may be to determine the extent to which we need to increase other assets to compensate for any loss in 'natural' assets, namely, the conditions determining whether 'weak' or 'strong' sustainability rules should apply.

---

11 Mäler (1994); Pearce, Markandya and Barbier (1989); and Perrings, Folke and Mäler (1992) provide more discussion of the issues surrounding discounting.

Culture

> That land is a community is the basic concept of ecology, but that land is
> to be loved and respected is an extension of ethics. That land yields a cultural
> harvest is a fact long known, but latterly often forgotten. (Leopold 1970)

Culture can influence people's attitudes and preferences, and thus economic
activity. This, in turn, affects biodiversity loss. Culture shapes the way in which
society interacts with its environment, and defines and uses biodiversity (Berkes
and Folke 1992 and 1994). Cultural influences may occur at several levels of
society, such as local, national and global. What is interesting for biodiversity
loss is the conditions under which culture provides a stimulus for biodiversity
conserving or depleting activities.

A concept of 'ecosystem people' and 'biosphere people' may be used to discuss
the relationship between societies, cultures and their environment (Gadgil 1993;
Berkes, Folke and Gadgil 1993). 'Ecosystem people' can be depicted as subsisting
largely on resources produced or gathered from their immediate vicinity. They
frequently inhabit regions that are rich (or were once rich) in biodiversity and
have a personal stake in the environment. However, they often have little control
over the natural resource base of these regions.

'Ecosystem people' often develop a strong social culture that reflects their close
interaction and inter-dependence on the environment, both within and across
generations. Thus, society's culture can motivate individuals to utilize resources
more prudently than they would otherwise, and develop practices that are in tune
with ecological processes and functions. For example, 'ecosystem people' often
protect some biological communities or habitats, certain selected species and
critical stages of biological history to ensure a sustained use of resources (Berkes,
Folke and Gadgil 1994). The extent of cultural influence on individual behaviour
depends on a range of factors, for example the 'bonding' within the society. Box
4.6 provides an example from the Uttara Kannada District, India, where 'ecosystem people' display a strong cultural respect for the environment, which
encourages natural resource conservation.

'Biosphere people' can be characterized as enjoying access to resources from
all over the world, in the form of commodities such as food, drugs, fuel or
wilderness to which they can transport themselves. 'Biosphere people' frequently
transform natural resources with the aid of modern technologies, which increase
the rate and scale of environmental impact. They are part of an increasingly
integrated global society and may have control over major development decisions
affecting natural resource use. Because of their lack of integration and their
perceived independence from the environment, 'biosphere people' may fail to
develop strong cultural ethics for wise resource management. In addition, the
'biosphere society' is more transient, less community based and is thus less well
'bonded' with the environment. As a result, the biosphere culture may have less
influence on the behavioural patterns of 'biosphere people'.

This is not to say that all 'ecosystem people' develop a strong culture for
natural resource conservation. Nor should it be taken that all 'biosphere people'
have less connection to their culture or that the biosphere culture is necessarily

Box 4.6

The ecosystem people of Uttara Kannada, India

The people of Uttara Kannada District, located in the centre of a chain of hills making up the Western Ghats in India, fit the characteristics of 'ecosystem people'. Over time, they have developed a culture and traditions that reflect their inter-dependence on their environment. The culture and traditions support the sustainable use of biological resources and conservation of biodiversity.

For example, the 'ecosystem people' provide total protection to some sacred ponds and groves. The only surviving stand of *Dipterocarpus indicus* in Uttara Kannada occurs in a sacred grove to the goddess Karikanamma. Some 20 species of the genus *Ficus nervosa* – now recognized as a keystone resource – dot the countryside and are protected as sacred trees. The village forest of Kallabbe, managed by the local people, supports a larger standing biomass and a greater variety of trees than exist in nearby reserve forests.

Although the culture of the local population supports natural resource conservation, their efforts are being undermined by increasing demands through population growth and external pressures. For example, a number of sacred groves have been clearcut by the forest department and *Ficus nervosa* have been supplied to the plywood industry at a highly subsidized rate.

Source: Gadgil (1993)

less environmentally sensitive. What is important, however, is to acknowledge that culture does affect individuals' behaviour. Each individual is part of a culture, and is influenced by its social norms and sanctions. The cultural capital influences how societies relate to and use the natural environment (see Box 4.7).[12] As we move towards a more transient community – a less integrated and bonded society with fewer perceived connections to environment – local and natural cultural influence on individuals may decline, and cultural concern for natural resource use may be less sensitive to conservation.

At the same time, there is increasing recognition that society depends on a well-functioning environment. However, the question still remains as to whether or not humanity will be able to use the great creative activity of the current energy-rich world and the pervasive information network that has been developed, in order to find ways to reorganize and sustainably manage biodiversity, and the resilience of ecosystems, that form the basis of human welfare.[13]

12 Berkes and Folke (1992 and 1994) define cultural capital as the 'factors that provide human societies with the means and adaptations to deal with the natural environment and actively modify it'. Among these factors are people's views of the natural world and the universe, environmental philosophy, values and ethics, religious, local and personal knowledge of the environment, traditional ecological knowledge, the range of institutions that a society has at its disposal, cultural diversity and finally human capital – namely, the education, skills and know-how stored in human beings.
13 See the previous note for a definition of cultural capital.

Box 4.7

Natural, human-made and cultural capital

Natural capital is the basis, the pre-condition for cultural capital. Human-made capital is generated by an interaction between natural and cultural capital. Human-made capital, in turn, may cause an alteration of cultural capital. Technologies (tools, skills and know-how) which mask the society's dependence on natural capital encourage people to think they are above nature. The more extensive this change, the more similar types of technologies will be developed and the more impacts on natural capital there will be. Positive feedbacks between cultural capital and human-made capital are established which enhance this trend. There will be resource depletion and environmental degradation to feed an industrial society that requires ever-increasing amounts of raw materials and that generates ever-increasing amounts of waste. Therefore, cultural capital plays an important role in how we use natural capital to 'create' human-made capital. Thus, human-made capital is never value-neutral, but a product of evolving cultural values and norms.

Source: Berkes and Folke (1994)

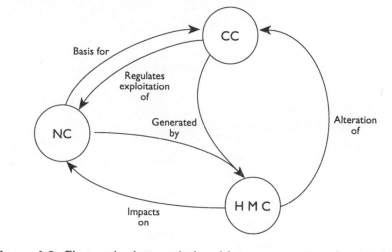

Figure 4.2: *First-order inter-relationships among natural capital (NC), human-made capital (HMC) and cultural capital (CC)*

Part II

ANALYSIS OF SELECTED SYSTEMS

5

Forests

We begin our examination of the problem of biodiversity loss in selected natural systems by looking at the world's forests. As noted in Chapter 1, forest conversion and degradation have been identified as critical factors in the global biodiversity problem because the vast majority of terrestrial species occur in forests. In particular, closed tropical forests are estimated to hold between 50–90 per cent of the world's species (Reid and Miller 1989; see also Chapter 1 of this book). Therefore, any attempt to address the problem of species loss is intrinsically related to the challenge of conserving forest ecosystems. However, in this chapter our concern is less with the problem of species extinction arising from deforestation than with the wider ecological and economic implications of global deforestation in terms of ecosystem functioning and resilience, and support of economic activity and human welfare.

Many of the papers prepared for the Beijer Biodiversity Programme address the issues surrounding deforestation, including its ecological and economic implications, the causes of forest conversion and degradation, and the management and policy responses to promote forest conservation. Most of the papers focus on tropical deforestation, although Holling et al (1994) make an important contribution to our understanding of ecosystem functions and the role of biodiversity in temperate forests.

IDENTIFICATION AND ANALYSIS

This section provides a review of the global status and trends in forest resources, discusses the ecological implications of biodiversity loss resulting from deforestation and reviews research on the causes of deforestation.

Global status and trends

In order to examine the problem of deforestation it is important to have a clear understanding of the status of forest resources and rates of forest conversion. In the past, estimates of deforestation have relied heavily upon data provided by government forest departments based on ground and aerial surveys. Not surprisingly, there has been much controversy over the reliability of such estimates, especially in tropical developing countries. In more recent years, developments have been made in remote sensing and satellite imagery which have greatly enhanced the quality of forest assessment.[1]

The Tropical Forest Resources Assessment (TFRA) collected statistical data to estimate tropical forest resources and rates of change using a deforestation model (FAO 1993). The total area of natural forests was estimated to be 1756 million hectares (mn ha) in 1990; approximately 36 per cent of the total land area in the tropics. Of this, tropical rainforests (718 mn ha) and moist deciduous forests (587 mn ha) together account for 74 per cent of all tropical forest area. On a regional basis, Latin America and the Caribbean contain the largest extent of tropical forest area (918 mn ha), followed by Africa (528 mn ha), then Asia and the Pacific (311 mn ha). Within the tropical zone, over half of the natural forest area is concentrated within three countries, namely Brazil, Zaire and Indonesia.

The extent of land area under plantations in the tropics is relatively small compared to that under natural forests. In 1990 total plantation area was 43.9 mn ha. The net area, after deducting for mortality and failures, is estimated to be 30.7 mn ha. This is less than 2 per cent of the total natural tropical forest area (FAO 1993).

Deforestation between 1981–90 was 15.4 mn ha each year (pa) on average, giving a compounded annual rate of deforestation of 0.8 per cent. Tropical deforestation was concentrated in Latin America and Caribbean (918 mn ha pa) and Africa (528 mn ha pa). Asia and Pacific experienced the lowest extent of deforestation, but due to its relatively small forest base exhibits the highest rate of deforestation at 1.2 per cent. Of the tropical forest countries, Brazil and Indonesia incur the highest extent of annual forest loss (3.7 and 1.2 mn ha pa respectively). However, the rates of deforestation are highest in those countries with relatively small forest resources, notably Philippines (3.3 per cent), Thailand (3.3 per cent), Costa Rica (2.9 per cent), Paraguay (2.7 per cent) and Malaysia (2.0 per cent).

Forests, of course, are not only destroyed but are regenerated naturally as secondary forests, regenerated by human intervention or renewed naturally by human management. Reafforestation refers to three separate processes:

- the restoration of previously existing forests (artificial regeneration);
- the artificial establishment of new forests on previously forested ground (reforestation); and
- the artificial establishment of forests in previously unforested areas (afforestation).

During 1981 to 1990 the reported forest plantations area increased annually on average by 2.6 mn ha and the net area (after deduction for mortality and failings)

---

1 The Food and Agriculture Organisation (FAO) of the United Nations is currently completing its 1990 Global Forest Resources Assessment (GFRA). This will form the most comprehensive database on the world's forest resources. The FAO studies are an amalgamation of various primary sources ranging from case studies and national statistics to satellite data. While a number of secondary sources, such as the World Resources Institute (WRI 1990), Sedjo and Lyon (1990) and Barbier (1993b), have pieced together regional or global reviews from more up-to-date primary sources, they often end up relying heavily on the older FAO figures. The GFRA encompasses three regional components: (i) tropical countries; (ii) industrialized countries; and (iii) non-tropical developing countries. The first two assessment components are now complete, and the assessment of non-tropical developing countries is due to be published in 1994.

by 1.8 mn ha pa. Thus, the net area planted each year represents only about 12 per cent of the total area deforested each year in the tropics. There is clearly a serious problem of tropical deforestation.

While net tropical deforestation appears to have increased over recent decades, in the temperate region forested area has remained broadly stable. The main reason for this has been that temperate deforestation has largely been replenished through reafforestation. For example, Sedjo and Lyon (1990) actually report a 2 per cent gain in temperate forest area since the Second World War. Of the global rate of reforestation (and afforestation) of roughly 15 mn ha per year in the 1980s, the bulk occurred in China (4.6 mn ha), the US (1.8 mn ha), Brazil (0.5 mn ha) and Europe (1.0 mn ha). An FAO estimate from the late 1970s placed the stock of plantation forest at 90 mn ha of which only some 12 mn ha were located in the tropics (WRI 1990).

According to Sedjo and Lyon (1990), 90 per cent of global softwoods (coniferous) stands are located in temperate regions. Yet, despite the growth of plantations and secondary forests, there are still substantial hardwood resources in many temperate regions, particularly in the former USSR, the US and Canada (466 mn ha). However, it is clear that for commercial forestry purposes, there is an important transformation of forest resources occurring in many temperate regions, from depletion of biologically diverse 'old growth' forests to plantations and secondary forests for timber production. Sedjo and Lyon (1990) report that 70 per cent of world demand for industrial uses of wood is based on softwoods, and that softwood supplies from temperate plantations and secondary growth forests are on the rise.

To summarize, concern over the loss of forest systems is increasingly focusing on the implications for global biodiversity. In the case of tropical forests, the large scale loss of forested areas is the main issue; in temperate regions, it is the replacement of more diverse 'old growth' forests by less rich plantations and secondary forests in many areas. In the remainder of this section, we examine further the ecological and economic implications of these changes to global forest systems as a way of determining whether current fears are justified.

Forest ecology and the role of biodiversity

Two important ecological impacts of forest loss are the effect on species composition and extinction, and, in turn, the implications of species and overall biodiversity loss for the ecological functioning and resilience of forest systems.

As noted above and discussed in Chapter 1, much popular concern over tropical deforestation has focused on the resulting loss in biodiversity, in particular as reflected in estimated rates of species extinction. However, Lugo, Parrotta and Brown (1993) offer a note of caution over many recent assessments of rates of species extinction and biodiversity loss associated with forest clearance. The basic models used to evaluate the relationship between extinction of species and deforestation rely on islands biogeography theory. Estimations are generally derived from an assumed species area relationship. As shown in equation (1), S is the number of species, A is the area and C is a parameter that depends on the type of species, its population density and the biogeographic region:

$$S = CA^Z \qquad (1)$$

The shape of the species area curve is determined by Z. Most regions of the world are characterized by Z factors between 0.16 and 0.39. Islands tend to have Z factors of about 0.35 while comparable continental areas have Z factors of about 0.20. Z factors tend to increase as the area under consideration becomes smaller. The predicted magnitude of species extinction in relation to forest area loss is a function of the Z factor. Unfortunately, our understanding of factors that affect the value of Z is still incomplete. Nevertheless, when values are low (< 0.20), the model predicts that more than 50 per cent of the land area can be deforested before the slope of the extinction curve rises rapidly with increasing deforestation. Conversely, at high values (> 0.60), extinction rates are almost proportional to deforestation rates (Figure 5.1).

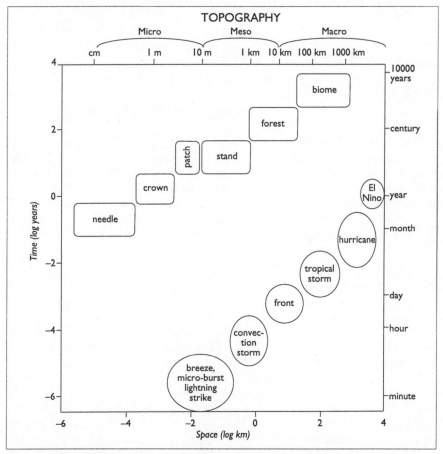

Source: Holling (1992)

Figure 5.1 *Relationship between deforestation and loss of species to extinction*

Limited bird and plant data for the island of Puerto Rico indicate that the model over-estimates extinction rates even when Z values are extremely low (0.15). Lugo, Parrotta and Brown (1993) propose that the model is constrained in its consideration of the full range of factors affecting species extinction. In particular, the model fails to take into account land use after deforestation and implicitly assumes that land is biotically sterile after forest clearance. Furthermore, habitat diversity is not accounted for in the species area model, except in the implicit assumption that larger areas have more habitats. Finally, the model is based on the analysis of a single species, while it may be more useful to look at assemblages of species in biodiversity loss.

For example, Lugo, Parrotta and Brown (1993) provide a case study from Puerto Rico where plantations have been established on degraded lands when agricultural activity is no longer possible due to poor soil productivity. Management practices that facilitate natural successional processes and the development of species rich understories have enabled greater levels of biological diversity to prevail, and may serve as refuges for threatened species, although efforts to re-establish forest land use activities are unable to offset the full, and often irreversible, losses of species diversity resulting from the original forest conversion. Box 5.1 presents several examples of management actions that increase the number of species on biologically impoverished or degraded sites.

Box 5.1

Management actions for species diversity

There are a range of management actions that could be undertaken to promote species diversity. Some of these are listed below.

- Diversification of habitats within agricultural landscapes through adoption of agroforestry systems, maintenance of vegetation in uncultivated corridors, or tree islands between fields, along roads and waterways, and around wetlands and other uncultivated sites.
- Recycling of sewage and other non-toxic organic wastes through degraded sites to increase soil organic matter, stimulate soil microbial activity and accelerate natural succession.
- Use of proven reclamation techniques in mining areas and/or derelict industrial and urban sites.
- Control of fire, unregulated livestock grazing and excessive fuelwood collection to allow natural recovery processes to enhance biological diversity.
- Multiple seeding of deforested, severely degraded sites.
- Use of tree plantations as foster ecosystems for native tree species.
- Improving soil fertility, particularly soil organic matter.

Source:Lugo, Parrotta and Brown, 1993

The work of Lugo, Parrotta and Brown (1993) implies that the existing species area model provides unreliable estimates of species loss resulting from tropical deforestation. Further research is required to develop the conversion/extinction model further to enable better estimation of species loss and changes in species composition associated with forest clearance, particularly where such clearance leads to secondary forest regeneration or the establishment of plantations. Such research will in turn enable more reliable assessment of overall biodiversity loss resulting from deforestation.

However, as we have argued in Part I, we need to know more than just how many species are being lost. We also need to know if we are losing key species and processes that may undermine the resilience of the ecosystem. Research in this area for forest systems is only just beginning.

Holling et al (1994) discuss the key ecological functions and properties of temperate forests. The authors emphasize that the choice of scale of observation and function is crucial in determining the perception of what diversity is, and how it is generated and operates. Boreal forests, located on the granite shield of eastern continental North America, provide an example of a hierarchical structure where each level of the hierarchy has its own scale ranges in both time and space, as shown in Figure 5.2. The functions and properties of boreal forests differ at the various levels, as discussed below.[2]

Forest patches can vary in scale, reflecting combinations of fire size and intensity, soil characteristics, stand age and meteorological conditions. They are typically about 30 m across and cover the range of competitive influences on a single mature tree. The key processes influencing diversity at the patch scale are biological processes of plant competition for nutrients, light and water. The foundations for biochemical cycling, energy accumulation and storage are controlled at the patch scale by photosynthesis, respiration, decomposition and nutrient dynamics, depending upon the tree species, understorey vegetation and microbial communities.

The patch properties of texture and variety allow some species, such as soil organisms, to live their whole lives within the patch. Other species, such as insects, live in the patch during their immature stage. Many other animals, such as birds and mammals, operate at a larger scale, where the relation between stands of trees is the primary determinant of their existence and functions.

For example, in the wet eastern boreal forests, birch, spruce and balsam fir prevail. A competitive ordering of sequence occurs based on capacity to compete for light, whereby birch flourishes early, followed by spruce and then fir. In the fire-induced, drier, mid-continental boreal, poplar, birch and jackpine predominate. The sequence of succession begins with birch and poplar appearing quickly after fire, because they resprout from the roots of fire-killed trees. Jackpine grow more slowly and often do not predominate until several years after a fire. However, jackpine generally die after 100–120 years, making way for cedar and white spruce. Given a typical fire sequence of 100 years, jackpine emerge as the main upland dominant species in boreal forests.

Beyond the scale of a patch is a stand of trees, which originates from a specific disturbance event. Boreal forest stands can cover over 500 ha, depending on

---

2   The following sub-section on forest ecology and biodiversity is drawn from Holling et al (1994).

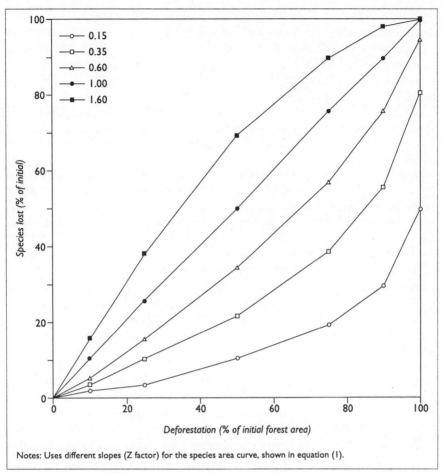

Notes: Uses different slopes (Z factor) for the species area curve, shown in equation (I).

Source: Holling et al (1994)

Figure 5.2 *Space and time hierarchy of the boreal forest and atmosphere*

disturbance processes such as fire or insect outbreak. These disturbance processes may be contagious or spread over space. Once they exceed a patch size, they become self-propagating and free from control by the originating trigger, for example, weather. The critical process-controlling boreal forest stand dynamics are abiotic and zootic disturbances, for example, storms, fires, insect outbreak, grazing by mammals and disease. These processes can transform the outcome of plant competition and growth at the patch scale, thereby maintaining diversity that would otherwise be constrained.

For example, although fir can frequently out-compete spruce, it is particularly vulnerable to periodic attacks by an insect defoliator, the spruce budworm. In unexploited forests, outbreaks occur in a quasi-cycle period, ranging from 40 to 100 years, and disturbed areas may reach 500 ha. Given that spruce is less vulnerable to budworm, and birch not at all vulnerable, insect disturbance shifts the balance of competition between the dominant species. Between outbreaks, the rapidly growing balsam tends to dominate spruce. During outbreaks, however, spruce is able to sustain itself until the surviving understorey of balsam catches up. The diversity of species at the stand level is determined by a combination of competition within the plant patch operating over tens of meters at yearly scales and budworm dynamics operating over hundreds of meters and decades.

The scale beyond the stand level is the contiguous forest. At this scale, abiotic and zootic factors are again important, but their influence is often determined by climatic conditions. For example, the properties of tree species, such as fir and spruce, are correlated with the intensity of budworm outbreaks, which depend on differences in regional climate. The full geographic area of budworm modified forest extends over a range of climatic regions. In western Ontario, the warm dry spring favours budworm survival and spruce is more abundant. In New Brunswick, warm dry springs are less frequent, and balsam fir and spruce are found in more equal proportions. Further east, in Newfoundland, the cool maritime climate enables the fir to dominate.

The geographic scale of the continental boreal forest biome covers groups of interactive ecosystems of coniferous and mixed forests, and of bogs, wetlands, rivers and lakes, across North America and Eurasia. The timescale applicable here is several lifetimes of trees. At this scale, disturbance events are periodic, and disturbances are endogenously determined and are an inherent part of ecosystem succession.

At the biome scale, a periodic disturbance may be a windstorm that 'clearcuts' many hundreds of hectares of trees as part of a normal process whereby extremes of weather intersect with increasing vulnerability of ageing trees. For different tree species in different forest regions, the natural disturbances may include insect outbreak, windstorm or drought, which create the preconditions for fire. Sustainability and diversity at the biome scale may maintain successional cycles of stand level boom and bust to produce a perpetuating mosaic of stands of trees of different ages, covering 100 to 1000 hectares over the boreal forested region.

The discussion so far has shown that at each of the hierarchical levels of boreal forests, a different cluster of processes control ecosystem function. Plant and local biogeochemical processes dominate at small scales. At intermediate scales, zootic and abiotic disturbance processes dominate. At larger scales, climatic, geophysical and global biochemical processes are more important. The interaction of all these processes across hierarchical levels, and temporal and spatial scales, determines diversity.

What does this tell us for the ecology of biodiversity loss? One universal feature of the processes that ecologists have identified at each scale is the cycle of birth, growth, death and renewal, although each with its own speed and geographical coverage. The capacity to renew after disturbances, such as insect outbreak or fire, is key to sustainability and diversity. Resilience and recovery are determined by the fast release and reorganizational sequence, as discussed in detail in Chapter 2.

Research to date indicates that only a small set of species and physical processes are critical in forming the structure and overall behaviour of terrestrial ecosystems (Holling et al 1994). On this basis, priority for investments in protecting and enhancing biological diversity should be placed on structuring variables. A key challenge for ecologists is identifying the critical set of species and physical processes in ecosystems. These determine the capacity of ecosystems to produce ecological resources and services.

However, a note of caution is required in that there are insufficient long term studies of whether the loss of rare species leads to slow shifts in ecosystem structure or function. In addition, current 'passenger' species may evolve to become the critical 'driver' species of the future. As discussed in Chapter 2, a better term for the former is life insurance species.

In sum, given the ecological implications of forest loss discussed above, focusing conservation efforts on saving global forests purely on the grounds of avoiding species extinction or changes in species composition may be inappropriate. Equally, priorities for conservation may be set on the basis of 'species richness' without any consideration of whether the species comprising a given area have an impact of ecosystem structure at specific scale ranges and on the key process that forms that structure. For example, Southgate and Clark (1993) note that current conservation efforts concentrate heavily on the Amazonian rainforests. While conservation of the species rich Amazonian forests is undoubtedly important, conservation efforts in other species rich and often more threatened forest are not receiving the same level of attention. Conservation efforts should prioritize key ecosystems, reflecting the need for a diverse range of ecosystems, and allocate resources and research accordingly to determine more fully the role of biodiversity in supporting ecosystem functioning and resilience.

Economic implications of forest degradation and loss

If current rates of biodiversity loss through forest degradation and conversion are 'excessive', it is because important economic values are disappearing as a consequence of this loss in biodiversity. This may be occurring because current policy and management decisions affecting forest resource use are not taking these values into account. To illustrate why this may be the case, we will briefly review the type of economic values lost as forests are cleared and degraded.

As noted above, forest degradation and conversion inevitably implies some loss of biological resources and diversity. As a result, there may be some loss of economic values. This may occur either because certain biological resources may have an actual or potential economic value in their own right, or because biodiversity loss results in disruptions to ecological functioning and resilience more generally.

The range of economic values associated with biodiversity loss have already been introduced in Chapter 2. The loss in use values as forests disappear or are degraded refers to the loss in biological resources that have potential economic value as commodities extracted from the forest, such as timber and non-timber forest products, as well as genetic material for the pharmaceutical industry, biotechnology or scientific research. Loss or degradation of forest resources can also affect various 'services' derived directly from the 'intact' or 'conserved' forest, such as recreation, tourism and education. The natural ecological functions of forest ecosystems can also be affected by biodiversity loss, and, of course, more directly through widespread deforestation and degradation. The result may be significant impacts on human welfare through the decline in ecological 'services', for example, protecting watersheds, regulating climate and storing carbon. Other, often less tangible, values may also be lost, including the foreclosing of future uses of the goods and services provided by a well-functioning forest system, and the loss in value from knowing that such a system no longer 'exists' or cannot be shared with one's children or future generations. Assessment of the values arising from biodiversity loss through deforestation and forest degradation therefore amounts to assessing these key values of the forest system.

Some of the values of forests, such as timber products, non-timber forest products, watershed protection, recreational values and so forth, may affect only populations in the country in which the forest is situated. Some of the 'regional' environmental functions of forests, such as the protection of major watersheds, may have transboundary spillover effects into more than one country. In addition, the world's forests, especially tropical forests, are also increasingly considered to provide important 'global' benefits, such as a major store of carbon and as a source of most of the world's biological diversity. Because of the complex linkages between the various ecological functions of forest systems that result in local, regional and global benefits, forest conversion and degradation must inevitably have repercussions for human welfare beyond the impacts in the immediate vicinity of forest areas. In particular, the continuing disruptions in ecological functioning and resilience of forest systems may reduce their ability over the long term to 'maintain' the earth's store of biodiversity. Any disturbance to this function is on such a large scale, and involves so many complexities and uncertainties, that the likely economic consequences are impossible to comprehend.

However, much of current forest conversion and degradation could be avoided if many of the more quantifiable economic values of forest systems described above were considered in forest management and development decisions. Unfortunately, they rarely are. One major problem is that many important values are not reflected automatically in market prices. As a consequence, such values need to be explicitly assessed, quantified and incorporated into decision making concerning forest use.[3] Although economists have for a number of years been developing methods to account for the full range of economic benefits accruing to society from forest ecosystems, current project and investment evaluation procedures and policy analyses that affect forest use rarely employ these methodologies. Even qualitative assessment of benefits is often avoided. In the absence of any relevant information on the full range of economic benefits arising from forest systems, decisions that affect these ecosystems are made without a complete understanding of the economic consequences of all available options. Better knowledge of the costs and benefits of alternative forest land use options would allow policy makers to make more appropriate land use planning decisions.

There have been numerous attempts to identify and assess forest values during the past decade. A recent literature review by the London Environmental Economics Centre (1992) of economic analyses of tropical forest land use options

---

3 For reviews of the approach and methodology as applied to temperate forest systems, see Johansson and Löfgren (1985) and, as applied to tropical forests, see Barbier et al (1992) and LEEC (1992).

noted that there has been an emphasis on the valuation of non-timber forest products, followed by timber, agriculture (crops and livestock) and wildlife. There have been far fewer studies of the value of tourism and 'environmental' uses (such as watershed protection, nutrient cycling and carbon sequestration) of tropical forests. Although these environmental attributes may be highly significant, they are often extremely difficult to value.

The failure to consider fully the range of values associated with forests and the biodiversity they contain has important implications as to whether we are currently exploiting these systems 'sustainably'. Forests can be considered as a form of 'natural' capital. That is, they have the potential to contribute to the long run economic productivity and welfare. Too often, decisions concerning forest depletion and conversion are taken without considering the full opportunity cost of these decisions. In short, we do not know whether it is worth 'holding on' to forests as an economic asset because we do not know or bother to take into account the potential economic benefits that the natural forest resource yields (Barbier 1992).

Each choice or land use option for the forest – to leave it standing in its natural state, or to exploit it selectively, for example, for timber or non-timber forest products, or to clearcut it entirely so the land can be converted to another use, such as agriculture – has implications in terms of values gained and lost. The decision as to what land use option to pursue for a given forest area, and ultimately whether current rates of deforestation are 'excessive', can only be made if these gains and losses are properly analysed and evaluated. This requires that all the values that are gained and lost with each land use option are carefully considered.

The decision over which forest land use option to pursue depends on the relative returns to the alternative uses. The following simplified example is used to illustrate the economics of land use decision making. Consider the choice between clearing the land for agricultural production and sustainably managing the forest for timber production. If the discounted net returns of sustainable timber production (NPV^T) exceed the net returns from converting the forest for agricultural production (NPV^A), then it will be in the direct economic interest of the individual, or society, to sustainably manage the land for timber production.

$$NPV^T \quad > \quad NPV^A \qquad (2)$$

That is, so long as sustainable forest management for timber production leads to economic rent greater than that derived from forest clearance for agricultural production, then there exists an incentive to conserve the forest for timber production.[4] Moreover, if timber production is done on a sustainable basis, then sustainable management of forests has the chance of being an economically attractive alternative to competing forest land uses over the medium to long term.

The above example is extremely simplified and does not reflect the full complexities of decision making in practice (such as a range of alternative land

---

4 As indicated in Chapter 4, economic rent is the net return to a unit of land. This value is the residual, or surplus, remaining after the costs of all other factors of production are netted out.

use options, other political objectives, conflicts between individual and society decisions, valuation of costs and benefits, and so on). However, it does illustrate an extremely important point – that in order for sustainable forest management to be a viable forest land use option, it must yield net returns that are greater than those derived from competing uses.[5] The following case study provides a specific example of the application of this principle to the establishment of a protected area with limited human use.

Munasinghe (1994) presents the preliminary results from a World Bank study that assesses the costs and benefits across different socio-economic groups resulting from the creation of Mantadia National Park in Madagascar.[6] Like many other tropical developing countries, Madagascar is one of the world's most ecologically rich countries, but is also one of the world's most economically poor countries. In response to the severe threat of forest degradation and biodiversity loss, Madagascar is considering creating additional parks and national reserves. To offset the opportunity costs imposed on local people by park creation and increase the likelihood of forest protection, nature tourism and buffer zone activities have been included in some park projects.

Two of the more important and more difficult to measure economic impacts of national park creation are the costs incurred by local villagers and the benefits received by foreign tourists. The opportunity cost approach, travel cost method and contingent valuation approach were used to assess these values in the new Mantadia National Park. The preliminary results are presented below and summarized in Table 5.1.

Table 5.1   *Valuation of Biophysical Reserves in Madagascar*

Items valued	Valuation technique	Aggregated net present value (20 years and 10 per cent DR)
1. Direct use benefits of forest by local villagers – agriculture, fuelwood, crayfish, crab, tenreck, frog.	Opportunity cost (production function approach)	US$566,070
2. Net benefit of forest for local villagers – including use and non-use costs and benefits.	Contingent valuation	US$673,078
3. Direct use benefits of tourists – tourism benefits only	Travel cost	US$796,870
4. Net benefit of park creation for tourists – may include tourism and other perceived benefits and costs of park creation, such as lemur conservation	Contingent valuation	US$2,160,000

Source: Based on Munasinghe 1993 and Kramer 1993.

5   For a recent review of methodology and valuation techniques as applied to such an assessment of tropical forest land use options, see Barbier et al (1992).
6   See Kramer et al (1992) and Kramer (1993) for more details about this study.

The opportunity costs of park creation incurred by local villagers includes the forgone benefits they previously derived from the forest, such as fuelwood, fish, animals, grasses and fertile land for shifting agriculture. A survey of 351 households in 17 villages within a 7.5 km radius of the park boundary was conducted. The survey indicated that most households engage in shifting cultivation and rely on forest clearance for their land. In addition, they obtain significant quantities of fuelwood, crayfish, crab, tenreck and frog from the forest. Using market prices in conjunction with estimates of the quantity of products extracted from the forest, the opportunity costs to villagers of losing access to Mantadia National Park were estimated to be US$91 per household each year on average, or US$556,010 in present value terms for all households. This was considered an upper estimate of the benefits derived by local villagers from the park, as it does not take into account access to alternative forest resources outside the park.

The contingent valuation method (CVM) uses survey techniques to establish the value of non-marketed goods and services derived from the forest. Demand for non-marketed goods is established first by describing a simulated market to the respondents and then asking them directly to reveal their preferences in terms of some common denominator.[7] The CVM approach was used in both the village and the tourist survey. A travel cost study was also administered to tourists visiting the nearby small Perinet Forest Reserve, adjacent to Mantadia National Park. The questions were phrased in terms of how much more the tourists would have been willing to pay for their trip if the new park had been created for their visit. The data from the tourist survey were then supplemented by information on the costs of travel and expenditures

The CVM survey of the villagers established that on average a compensation of 108 kg of rice would make the villagers as well off with the park as without the park. For all households covered by the survey, this implies a necessary one-time compensation of approximately US$673,078 for all use and non-use benefits that the villagers derive from the park. The CVM and travel cost studies of tourists yielded estimates of the net present value of tourism benefits associated with the park amounting to US$796,870 and US$2.16 million respectively.

Several important lessons for economic valuation of the costs and benefits of a forest land use option can be drawn from this study. First, valuation techniques need to be adapted to local situations – in this case rice was used as the basis for measuring the value of forest benefits forgone by villagers through the establishment of the protected area. Second, careful application of valuation techniques in relevant decision making situations can provide useful indications of which forest values are being affected by the choice of land use. However, it is important to keep in mind what is actually being measured by the valuation technique, for example, direct use benefits, net benefits including use and non-use benefits, and so forth and the reliability of data and the methodologies in assessing these different benefits. Even more important, although this study

---

7　Blamey and Common (1993) stress that problems of 'embedding' and 'citizen type responses' may undermine CVM in practice. Researchers applying CVM techniques need to be clear about the possible range of behavioural motivations involved in response making, and about what the purpose of seeking those responses is, in order to obtain meaningful and useful responses to CVM questions.

was concerned with the establishment of a protected area to conserve biological diversity, it did not assess the role of the biodiversity of the forest in maintaining ecosystem functioning and resilience. Consequently, it could not determine whether loss in biodiversity through direct exploitation of the forest by the villagers would have affected their ability to sustain these uses over time.

Providing estimates of the economic costs and benefits associated with park creation is often an important step in alerting policy makers and project designers to the need to take the opportunity costs of different socio-economic groups into account in forest land use decisions. Appropriate measures to compensate the 'losers' from park creation, in this case local villagers, may be required to ensure support for successful park creation. However, the potential benefits of park creation, such as providing local employment and demand for locally produced goods, also need to be considered. Estimates of the potential ecotourism benefits from park creation may be used to formulate policies to 'capture' some of this value, which can then be channelled back into park management and conservation. Chapter 10 looks at national and local conservation management issues in more detail.

MANAGEMENT AND POLICY

This section addresses the market and policy failures that encourage deforestation, briefly reviews current forest conservation efforts, and discusses the policy options for improved forest conservation and management.

Market and policy failures affecting forests

In Chapter 4 we described how market and policy failures can create incentives that lead to excessive exploitation of biological resources and conversion of habitats that result in biodiversity loss. Here we provide some examples of how market and policy failures contribute to the process of deforestation.

In the forest and related sectors of most tropical developing countries a range of market failures prevail, including incomplete information and markets, externalities, open access exploitation and public environmental goods, uncertainty and imperfect competition. These market failures lead to a distortion of economic incentives, such that the full value of forests is not taken into account in forest land use decisions. As a result, excessive deforestation occurs. Economic policies may create additional incentives for deforestation, further exacerbating the problem of unnecessary forest clearance and degradation. In general, sectoral policies have the most immediate and visible impacts on deforestation, but many broader fiscal, monetary and international policies can also have important effects (see Figure 5.3 and Box 5.2).

Panayotou and Ashton (1994) describe market and policy failures leading to perverse incentives for deforestation in Asia. Market failures are considered endemic to forestry because of the long gestation period of tree species (which are therefore subject to greater uncertainties and higher discount rates), insecure

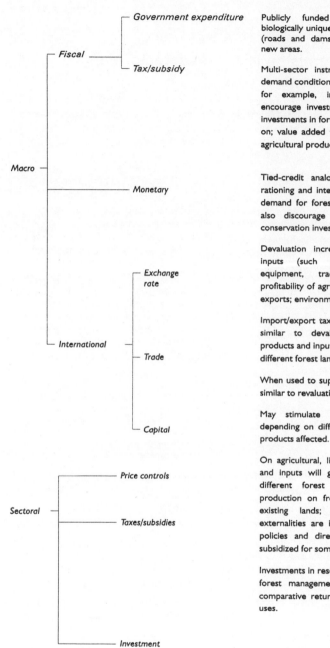

The following text accompanies the branches of the diagram:

Government expenditure

Publicly funded agencies can protect biologically unique areas; public infrastructure (roads and dams) may encourage opening new areas.

Tax/subsidy

Multi-sector instruments can alter general demand conditions and thus use of resources; for example, income tax breaks may encourage investments in land speculation, investments in forest industries, mining and so on; value added taxes can affect forest and agricultural products.

Monetary

Tied-credit analogous to subsidies; credit rationing and interest rate rises may reduce demand for forest land conversion, but can also discourage forest management and conservation investments.

Exchange rate

Devaluation increases prices of imported inputs (such as, petroleum, logging equipment, tractors), which increase profitability of agricultural and forest product exports; environmental effects uncertain.

Trade

Import/export taxes and quotas have effects similar to devaluation but on selected products and inputs only; may alter returns to different forest land uses.

When used to support over-valued currency, similar to revaluation of exchange rate.

Capital

May stimulate or reduce deforestation depending on different forest land uses and products affected.

Price controls / Taxes/subsidies

On agricultural, livestock, forestry products and inputs will generally affect returns to different forest land use options and production on frontier lands compared to existing lands; generally, environmental externalities are ignored in sectoral pricing policies and direct costs of deforestation subsidized for some activities.

Investment

Investments in research and extension, and in forest management can affect yields and comparative returns to different forest land uses.

Source: Barbier et al (1993b)

Figure 5.3 *Economic policies and deforestation*

Box 5.2
Economic policies and deforestation

In general, sectoral policies have the most immediate and visible impacts on deforestation, but many broader fiscal, monetary and international policies can also have important effects. Repetto (1990) suggests that a useful way of conceptualizing how the impacts of government economic and pricing policies affect deforestation is by visualizing a set of 'concentric circles' moving outward from the forest:

- at the hub are policies that directly affect timber and forest management, that is to say, forest revenue structures, tenurial institutions governing privatization of forest land and enforcement of traditional use rights, reforestation incentives and administration of timber harvesting concessions;
- in the next circle are policies directly influencing the demand for forest products, that is to say, trade and investment incentives to promote wood-using industries, and energy pricing towards fuelwood substitutes;
- in a third circle are policies directly affecting extensions of the agricultural frontier and the rate of conversion of forest land, that is to say, agricultural credit, tax and pricing incentives for frontier agriculture, including policies affecting the relative price of new forest land, the incentives for cultivation at the intensive as opposed to the extensive margin and the concentration of landholdings, as well as public investments that indirectly spur frontier expansion, such as road-building, and public services, such as agricultural research and extension;
- in the outer circle are macroeconomic policies that indirectly affect deforestation, that is to say, exchange rate policies affecting forest product exports, policies affecting capital markets that influence investors' time horizons, demographic policies, trade and investment policies affecting labour absorption and rural–urban migration.

property rights and significant externalities. Policy failures in the form of short term concession arrangements and low 'rent capture' through stumpage fees also occur. Furthermore, subsidies for logging and forest conversion to pastures and plantations, and linking land titling to land clearing have promoted forest land clearance. Finally, infrastructure investments, such as road building, have provided further incentives for deforestation.

Studies examining the factors contributing to deforestation include Binswanger (1989) and Mahar (1989), who highlight the role of subsidies and tax breaks, particularly for cattle ranching, in encouraging land clearing in the Brazilian Amazon. More recent analysis by Schneider et al (1990) and Reis and Marguilis (1991) emphasize the role of agricultural rents, population pressure and road building in encouraging small scale frontier settlement in this region. Schneider et al (1990) described the pressure on forests in frontier areas as 'nutrient mining', whereby the depletion of forest ecosystems usually begins with logging. Burning reduces pest incidence and also converts biomass to ash, which provides minerals, other than nitrogen which is lost during combustion, needed for crop production. Cattle ranching usually represents the last phase of nutrient mining, which may lead to long term land degradation.

Southgate and Clark (1993) note that the term 'mining' also reflects the lack of reinvestment of earnings derived from forest exploitation. Open access resource exploitation drives resource rents down to zero, so that land and forest product prices fail to reflect their full economic value. Instead, the price of resources gravitates to the opportunity cost of labour needed to extract them. The lack of resource rents constrains investment opportunities and locks the frontier population into a treadmill of dependence upon nutrient mining. Once the forest and soil nutrients in one area have been thoroughly depleted, colonists still find themselves impoverished and need to move to new forest areas to make a living.

There have been several statistical analyses of the causes of tropical deforestation in recent years. There are a number of important caveats that need to be borne in mind when looking at these studies.[8] First, all analyses suffer from problems of reliability and accuracy of data. Data limitations make it difficult to distinguish between production and conversion forests across the tropics. For example, if log production is mainly from conversion forests, then timber extracted is essentially a precursor or by-product of agricultural conversion, which is the principal factor in the resulting deforestation. In addition, due to the level of aggregation, the analyses are not sensitive to the different types of forests and different patterns of wood use.

However, statistical approaches can provide interesting insights to the existence and relative importance of relationships between deforestation and factors thought to contribute to forest conversion. Table 5.2 provides a review of studies conducted in South-East Asia (Panayotou and Ashton 1994). The most important factors found to contribute to deforestation are population, roads and crop prices. Other important factors have been log prices, poverty and lagged agricultural productivity.

Table 5.3 presents the results of a tropics wide analysis of the relationship between forest clearance and timber production, agricultural yield, population density, income growth and tropical forest stock (Burgess 1993 and 1994). The analysis was conducted for 53 countries, and supports the hypothesis that round-wood production and population density lead to greater forest clearance, while increases in income per capita and improvements in agricultural productivity can offset deforestation. The results also suggest that countries with smaller than average forest area are more likely to mine their remaining forest at a high rate.

Persson (1994) explored the role of macro-economic policies in deforestation in Costa Rica using a computable general equilibrium (CGE) model. The main reasons for deforestation are thought to include low land prices (which fail to reflect the total social opportunity value of the rainforest), undefined property rights (which make the private costs of deforestation lower than the social cost of deforestation), high interest rates (which imply that the value of future gains from the forest are lower than the current gains from deforestation), and macro-economic policies (such as taxes, which create incentives for excessive deforestation).

---

8   A comprehensive review of recent studies can be found in Burgess (1993 and 1994).

Table 5.2   *Statistical analysis of the causes of deforestation in South-east Asia*

	Thailand 1	Thailand 2	Philippines 1	Philippines 2	Peninsular Malaysia
Author	Panayotou & Sungsuwan	Tungpan & Panayotou	Kummer	Kummer	Vincent and Yusuf
Geographical unit	Province	Province	Province	Province	Country
Period	1973–82	1973–88	1970–80	1970	1904–88
Data	Panel	Panel	Cross-section	Panel	Time series
Method	OLS	OLS	OLS	OLS	OLS
Specification	Log-Log	Linear	First Dif	Log–Log	Linear
Dependent variable	Deforest	Deforest	Deforest	Deforest	Agric Area
Independent variable	Elasticity Estimates (t statistics in parentheses)[a]				
Population	1.51 (9.7)			0.54 (NA)	0.08 (2.4)
Roads	0.11 (1.4)	0.28 (2.12)	0.23 (2.4)	0.28 (NA)	
Agriculture (crop price)	0.32* (1.7)	1.60* (3.0)	0.41 (4.2)		
Logging (log price)	0.41* (4.1)		0.32 (3.2)		
Productivity	0.38 (1.9)				
Forest size		0.14 (5.6)			
Income per capita		0.98 (3.3)			
Lagged agricultural area					0.97 (38)
DF[b]	55	70	64	66	81
R^{2c}	0.80	0.75	0.49	0.58	0.99

*Assuming a supply price elasticity of 1.
[a]Significance test for each variable.
[b]Degrees of freedom.
[c]'Goodness of fit' for the regression.

Source: Panayotou and Ashton (1992).

Persson (1994) analysed changes in various policies using a static CGE model of an open economy, with a dynamic feature due to the inclusion of the discount rate and the future value of forested land. The model is a development from

Table 5.3 *Analysis of causes of deforestation in tropical countries*

Dependent variable: Five-year change in closed forest area (log forest area 1985–log forest area 1980)

Explanatory variable	Estimated coefficient (t statistic)
constant	−0.1009 (−4.188)
X1 (log of closed forest area as a percentage of total area 1980)	0.01253 (1.609)
X2 (population density 1980)	−0.0474 (−2.695)
X3 (roundwood production per capita 1980)	−0.0849 (−2.3029)
X4 (real GNP per capita 1980)	0.000195 (1.8098)
X5 (agricultural yield 1980)	0.02301 (1.1298)
X6 (dummy Latin America)	−0.06809 (−2.4086)

Estimated elasticities
X1 = 0.0125
X2 = −0.0285
X3 = −0.0186
X4 = 0.1870
X5 = 0.0339
X6 = 0.0216

R^2: 0.268
F statistic: 2.8089
Number of observations: 53

Source: Burgess (1993, 1994)

previous CGE modelling exercises in that it includes undefined property rights, and a functioning market for logs and cleared land. Deforestation is seen to arise from activities by squatters and directly from the forest sector.

The preliminary results of the model indicate that defining property rights leads to a fall in deforestation by squatters, especially when the discount rate is lower than the future value of the forest. Given a situation of well defined property rights, combined with a low discount rate, an increase in taxes on land decreases total deforestation. If the fall in taxes is registered on capital rather than land, then the user price of capital services is reduced. This leads to a relative gain in capital intensive sectors of production, such as agriculture and other industries. As output is seen to expand in the agricultural sector, more land is needed and a higher price paid for cleared land. This results in increased squatters' deforestation activities. Increased taxes on output in the agricultural sector are seen to reduce agriculture and related production, lessening deforestation by squatters. However, deforestation from the forest sector increases due to released resources from the agricultural sector.

Public policies also have an important influence on the pattern of forest-based industrialization and its implications for long term economic development and deforestation. Vincent and Binkley (1991) note that stumpage prices (the prices of harvested logs at the stand) have a crucial role to play in the interrelated dynamics of timber reserve depletion and processing expansion, particularly in facilitating the transition of the forest sector from dependence on old growth to secondary growth forests and in coordinating processing capacity with timber stocks. Unfortunately, in most developing countries, stumpage prices tend to be administratively determined rather than set by the forces of supply and demand, thus understating stumpage values and failing to reflect increasing scarcity as old growth forests are depleted. A number of economic and environmental distortions result:

- old-growth forests are depleted too rapidly;
- forest land is inappropriately cleared for agriculture or other uses;
- inadequate and inappropriate investment is made in second growth forests;
- inefficient processing facilities are installed;
- decisions on log and lumber trade policies are inefficient and encourage unsustainable management practices;
- elaborate and counter-productive capital export controls are needed to ensure that resource rents are not repatriated.

Vincent and Binkley (1991) explore three case studies of long term forestry policy and development: logging in Peninsular Malaysia which is mainly of old growth tropical forests; in Ghana which logged over most of its old growth tropical forest but has poorly developed its secondary forest; and in Chile which produces timber mainly from second growth (such as plantation) temperate forests. In Malaysia, wood prices – timber charges, log prices and sawnwood prices – have been kept artificially low at every stage of forestry development, from log exporter to exporter of primary products to embryonic exporter of downstream products. The result has been the development of processing capacity that exceeds the forests' sustained yield capacity. Like Malaysia, Ghana has shown little success in establishing plantations as an alternative source of timber to the natural forest. Artificially low royalty rates for natural forest timber mean that concessionaires' incentives to invest in plantations are limited and, at the same time, through their impact on delivered log prices, have helped encouraged the over-expansion of domestic processing capacity. In contrast, in Chile the crucial policy issue has been how to build up an efficient industry based on the nation's increasing supply of timber from privately owned plantations (mainly of *Pinus radiata*). Initial success seems to have come from providing private investors with secure, long term tenure for plantations and additional planting incentives. Another key policy has been to permit the export of logs, which forces domestic mills to pay world prices for sawlogs, pulpwood and woodchips, and to be more efficient.

Improper policies also have an impact on timber forest management and its environmental effects in industrialized countries. Logging fees or royalties for timber harvested from public lands are also based on administrative pricing. The standard calculation is to take the short-run derived demand lumber price at the mill minus harvest, extraction and (log to lumber) conversion costs in order to determine the royalty (Hyde, Newman and Sedjo 1991). Such pricing methods are not related to long-run 'user' costs or environmental values and, in many instances, do not even approximate market and economic scarcity values for timber.

For example, in Australia state forest agencies generally set timber harvesting royalties by administrative means, which are then negotiated with individual buyers as part of a package that includes processing commitments. The royalties are usually adjusted in the short term in line with changes in inflation and in the long term in line with changing market conditions. A recent study compared the resulting administrative royalty pricing in the 1980s with market-derived prices. The study indicated that processors were prepared to pay 49 to 74 per cent above royalty levels for low grade logs, 34 to 48 per cent extra for medium grade logs and 27 to 40 per cent extra for higher quality logs. Old growth forest hardwood sawlogs and softwood sawlogs were generally priced below market price; pulplog royalties were found to be both above and below market price (Resource Assessment Commission 1991).

As outlined by Wibe (1991), other problems also exist with regard to ensuring that private investors and concessionaires in OECD countries produce timber at a long-run privately efficient level. First, markets for forest land in these countries are far from perfect and free, preventing any investment in forestry from being fully capitalized through selling the standing timber or planted stand. For example, in the Nordic countries, and Germany and France, restrictive regulations exist on the market for forest lands. In addition, regulations on the buying and selling of forest land usually imply large transaction costs, especially when holdings are small, which is normally the case. The result is that private forest owners tend to invest too little in regeneration and/or reforestation. Second, concerning publicly owned forest lands in OECD countries, the major problem is in securing efficient contracts with private forestry activities. For example, in Canada, where 11 per cent of forest land is owned by the federal government and 80 per cent by the provinces, provincial governments sell licenses to private concessionaires for 20 to 50-year periods. They usually have the right to harvest the area once, with some restrictions on maximum annual cuts. Concessionaires can also obtain volume licenses that allow them the right to harvest a certain volume of timber in an area. However, such contracts often exclude any regulation of long term damage and degradation of the stand or of any environmental impacts. Nor are these values incorporated in the licence fee, which is usually set very low and, in some areas, is close to zero.

Subsidies in OECD countries, particularly for plantation establishment, are now recognized to have direct and indirect environmental impacts, as several case studies have revealed (Jones and Wibe 1992; Wibe 1991). For example, in Sweden subsidization of forest land drainage to increase timber production has led to the loss of over 30,000 ha of wetlands annually. In the UK in the 1980s, tax concessions on afforestation were increased but not for the purchase of land. Investors therefore had an incentive to minimize land purchases and increase their tax shelters by locating coniferous plantations on land of poor or negligible agricultural value, such as wetlands, heath and moorland, but which have high environmental value as natural wildlife habitat and for other amenities. The tax concessions were repealed in 1990, although they have been replaced by direct afforestation grants to farmers.

The long-run economic effects of subsidizing forest plantations may also have indirect environmental impacts (Jones and Wibe 1992; Wibe 1991). If such subsidies lead to more afforestation on agricultural or wild lands, then the expansion in supply could reduce prices and profitability. In Italy, this has caused skilled owners of established plantations to be replaced by less skilled 'new' (and subsidized) owners, with implications for productive efficiency and timber stand management over the long term. In the US and Germany, state intervention has facilitated below-cost sales by public forest companies, reduced profitability for the whole sector and discouraged private investment. The result is inefficient forest management and sub-optimal levels of exploitation. In Spain, the non-priced environmental benefits of traditional forestry systems of holm and cork oak woodlands in the Dehesa regions have led to under-investment in private holdings; however, public intervention has been to plant conifers, poplars and eucalyptus, which have altered the characteristics of plantations in these regions and actually increased local environmental degradation.

The qualitative and quantitative studies reviewed above indicate that in recent years significant steps have been taken in the research and analysis of forest clearance and degradation. Our understanding of the underlying and proximate causes of deforestation is improving all the time. However, we still have much to learn. Perhaps more importantly, we need to translate our understanding of the problems into relevant policy actions to improve the management and conservation of the world's forests. The following briefly introduces policy options for improved forest management and biodiversity conservation.

Policy options for forest management and biodiversity conservation

The previous discussion has shown that there is genuine cause for concern over the excessive exploitation and rapid depletion of the forests in many regions, but especially in tropical countries. Much of this results from the widespread prevalence of market and policy failures that have distorted the incentives for sustainable forest management. Failures in concession, tenure and pricing systems have produced counter-productive incentives that lead to the 'mining' of production forests, and tax breaks and subsidies have encouraged the conversion of forest land to agriculture and other uses. Therefore, a crucial first step in reducing deforestation is the correction of existing domestic market and policy failures, and ensuring 'proper' economic incentives for efficient and sustainable management of forests. This may be considered as a necessary precursor to any additional forest conservation and management policies and investments. Below we look at the role of project investments and international policies in forest conservation and management.

Past approaches to forest conservation at a project level have included habitat protection – demarcating land as state parks which are protected from use. These have often been unsuccessful due to conflicts over resource access between local populations who resent the loss of access to resources and park managers. In addition, habitat protection for biodiversity conservation has proved to be well beyond the reach of the developing world's park services, which are often understaffed and underfunded.

More recent approaches to biodiversity conservation have been through 'people-oriented' projects, or Integrated Conservation Development Projects (ICDPs). A review of ICDPs across all developing regions has indicated the promise of this approach. However, it also indicated a number of shortcomings (Wells 1992). We will discuss ICDPs in more detail in Chapter 10, particularly their potential role in reconciling biodiversity conservation and resource use by local communities.

The implications of prevailing economic incentives for 'nutrient mining' activities at forest frontiers are daunting for all forest conservation activities, including ICDPs (Southgate and Clark 1993). In order to overcome these powerful incentives for depletion, a new look at the linkages between agricultural development and habitat conservation is required. Thus, while the local situation remains important, it is also necessary to look at the broader economic influences on resource use and management at frontier areas.

For example, Southgate (1991) demonstrates in a statistical analysis that farmers and ranchers encroach very little on natural habitats in countries where crop and livestock yields have improved, through research and extension, irrigation investment and related measures. Conversely, where productivity trends have been flat, increasing demands for agricultural commodities, brought on by population or income growth or expanded exports, have led inevitably to land use conversion. Thus, in order to ensure the success of biodiversity conservation, appropriate economic incentives are required at the project level. Finally, to ensure the long term viability of conservation efforts in developing countries, it is essential to improve production, income and employment in other areas, including cities, towns and other places where agriculture is already established.

Such developments and improved incentives need to be complemented by better institutional frameworks for ensuring that appropriate incentives are encouraged at the forest level among local communities and individuals. Critical to this process is the elimination of open access conditions, such as those contributing to the 'nutrient mining' process discussed above. Coupled with this must be policies and approaches that balance local people's traditional rights to resources with increasing their responsibilities for improved resource management. In some cases this may call for legalizing informal rights and access arrangements; in others, establishing effective local management regimes and incentives is required (Gadgil, Berkes and Folke 1993).

As we will discuss in more detail in Chapter 10, sanctions and other interventions in the international timber trade have been proposed as an alternative means of coercing tropical timber producer countries into reducing forest exploitation, and the subsequent loss of biological diversity and other environmental values.

In addition, trade measures are increasingly being explored as part of multilateral negotiations and agreements to control excessive forest depletion, to encourage 'sustainable' timber management, and to raise compulsory financing for timber producing countries that lose substantial revenues and incur additional costs in changing their forest policy.

Using a theoretical model, Barbier and Rauscher (1994a and 1994b) analyse the impact of trade policies on deforestation. The main result of the analysis is that if importing nations want exporting countries to conserve more of their forests, trade interventions that seek to affect the terms of trade against the export of tropical timber products are in the long run a 'second best' policy option. Improving domestic incentives for forest conservation is much more important. Under certain conditions, trade interventions may even be counter-productive. In contrast, international transfers, which reduce the dependency of the producer country on the exploitation of forest for export earnings, are more effective in promoting conservation of the forest stock.

An additional finding of the Barbier and Rauscher (1994a and 1994b) analysis is that if the producer country values its tropical forests solely as a source of timber export earnings, then it will aim for a smaller stock of the forest in the long run than if it also considers other values provided by the forest. Understanding the full range of benefits accruing from their tropical forests, such as watershed protection, genetic diversity, tourism and micro-climatic functions, is important to determine the direct social value of forest conservation.

Recent empirical studies have supported these analytical results of our model (Barbier et al 1993b; Vincent and Binkley 1991; Hyde, Newman and Sedjo 1991). Generally, these studies have also concluded that trade intervention is a 'second best' option for controlling deforestation. Instead, the problem should be tackled at the source, which means improving forest sector policies, and removing market and policy failures that are encouraging excessive forest degradation and clearance at the stand level.

CHALLENGES TO BE ADDRESSED

This chapter has raised numerous key challenges to be addressed by ecologists and economists to ensure sustainable forest management and biodiversity conservation. The following are of particular note.

- Ecologists need to identify key species and processes in forest ecosystems to enable prioritizing of conservation efforts. Meanwhile, efforts to improve ecosystem conservation need to continue, but should become more fully integrated in forest management practices and development strategies.
- At the heart of sustainable forest management is the correction of existing domestic market and policy failures. Until these are corrected, other attempts to encourage sustainable forest management are likely to be undermined and may even be counter-productive.
- An important area for further research is the economic valuation of forest goods, services and environmental attributes, including their role as a store

and source of biodiversity. Ecologists and economists need to work together on this to develop and improve identification, assessment and valuation techniques.

■ Conservation projects need to be designed so that they are sensitive to prevailing socio-economic conditions and the incentives for conservation derived from these conditions, particularly the use and management of forest resources by local communities.

■ Finally, international policies to promote forest conservation need to be carefully analysed and designed to prevent countervailing responses by tropical forest countries. In particular, interventions that restrict the economic opportunities (such as trade bans and taxes) may produce perverse results. Enabling incentives, such as financial support for conservation programmes, may prove more effective in the long run.

The development of consistent and comprehensive approaches to begin tackling these challenges will go a long way towards reconciling forest management for human use and biodiversity conservation. Instituting such approaches across all forests of the world should form an integral part of any global strategy to control biodiversity loss.

6

Wetlands

This chapter explores ecological and economic issues concerning the loss of the world's wetlands. Several Beijer Biodiversity Programme papers have indicated that the main policy challenge is wetland valuation. However, the role of wetland biodiversity in supporting ecosystem functioning and resilience has not been treated explicitly, nor valued directly. The importance of this role can only be gleaned indirectly from the importance of well-functioning wetland systems for economic activity and human welfare.

Although wetland areas tend to be treated as 'wastelands' that would be more valuable converted to other uses, these natural systems often perform essential ecological 'services' that support and protect economic activity and livelihoods. Unfortunately, these 'natural' values are often ignored in decisions to convert or exploit wetlands. Thus proper valuation of the ecological services and resources that wetlands provide is necessary for their proper management and conservation. This issue is the main focus of the following chapter.

IDENTIFICATION AND ANALYSIS

The use of the term wetlands covers a wide variety of inland, coastal and marine habitats. The enormous range of wetland types can be sub-divided into 30 categories of natural wetlands and nine human-made ones (Dugan 1990). Included in these categories are mangroves, which are basically coastal forest systems, floodplains, which are areas that may be only periodically flooded but otherwise dry, and gravel pits, which have since accumulated water. Essentially, any habitat that is significantly 'wet' for sufficiently long periods of time can be classified as a 'wetland'. Thus the international treaty on wetland conservation, the Ramsar Convention, officially defines wetlands as:

> areas of marsh, fen, peatland or water whether natural or artificial, permanent or temporary, with water that is static or flowing, fresh, brackish, or salt, including areas of marine water the depth of which at low tide does not exceed six metres.[1]

Global status and trends

The difficulty of determining what habitats are 'wetlands' with any precision, and the extensive and diverse variety of wetland areas, have hindered accurate

---

1 The full title of the Ramsar Convention is the Convention on Wetlands of International Importance, Especially as Waterfowl Habitat. It functions as an international treaty and serves as the principal inter-governmental forum to promote international cooperation of wetland conservation. There are more than 60 contracting parties currently, with others considering signature. For further details see Dugan (1990).

estimation of the global status of these ecosystems. However, it is generally believed that approximately 6 per cent of the world's land area is covered by wetlands, whereas in 1900 global wetland area may have been twice as much (Turner et al 1994). More recent scientific estimates suggest that there are approximately 5.3 to 5.7 million km^2 of freshwater wetlands in the world. Canada is thought to contain the most wetland area – around one-quarter of the global total (WCMC 1992).

More difficult still is determining the rate of wetland loss. The most accurate estimates appear to be for the US and other advanced industrialized countries. The original wetland area of the continental US may have been around 890,000 km^2 of which only 47 per cent is left. Although in Europe there has been extensive creation of artificial wetlands such as reservoirs, fishponds and gravel pits, by the end of the 1970s France may have lost 10 per cent of its wetland area, whereas The Netherlands and the UK may have lost around 60 per cent (WCMC 1992). In New Zealand, it is estimated that over 90 per cent of natural wetlands have been destroyed since European settlement (Dugan 1990). Although the rate of wetland conversion in advanced industrialized countries may have been slowing down since the mid-1970s due to better conservation and management policies, the rate of loss in many countries may still be high (Turner and Jones 1991).

Estimating wetland loss in developing countries has been even more problematic. Although difficult to determine, best guesses would suggest that the rate of loss in many areas is equivalent to that experienced by the US during this century (Barbier 1993c and 1994b). However, the extent of wetland loss varies greatly from region to region. For example, many of the wetlands of South America are still in pristine condition, whereas the wetlands of the Caribbean have been intensively exploited, and those of Central America and Mexico are in a more 'mixed' condition (WCMC 1992). Many wetland areas in Africa, the Middle East, Asia, Australasia and Oceania are also under threat. In general, the most sustained pressure on tropical wetlands appears to be on coastal mangrove areas and river floodplains (Dugan 1990).

Although there are natural causes of wetland loss, the major threats are clearly from human activity that results in conversion or modification of wetland areas or in pollution (Table 6.1). As indicated in Table 6.2 in developing regions over-exploitation of resources and over-use for recreation are also important threats. Thus the factors determining wetland loss epitomize the proximate and underlying driving forces for global biodiversity loss that we discussed in Chapter 4. In the rest of this chapter we will discuss this problem by focusing on the particular aspects emphasized by the Beijer Biodiversity Programme papers that address wetland loss: wetland valuation and incentives for improved management.

Table 6.1   *Causes of wetland loss*

	Estuaries	Open coasts	Floodplains	Freshwater marshes	Lakes	Peatlands	Swamp forest
Human actions							
Drainage for agriculture, forestry and mosquito control	•	•	•	•	o	•	•
Dredging and stream channelization for navigation and flood protection	•			o			
Filling for solid waste disposal, roads, commercial and residential	•	•	•	•	o		
Conversion for aquaculture/mariculture	•	o	o	o	o		
Construction of dykes, dams, levees, and seawalls for flood control	•	•	•	•	o		
Discharges of pesticides, herbicides, nutrients from domestic sewage	•	•	•	•	•		
Mining of wetlands for peat, coal, gravel, phosphate and other materials	o	o	o		•	•	•
Groundwater abstraction			o	•			
Sediment diversion by dams, deep channels and other structures	•	•	•	•			
Hydrological alterations by canals, roads and other structures	•	•	•	•	•		
Subsidence due to extraction of groundwater, oil, gas, and other minerals	•	o	•	•			
Natural causes							
Subsidence	o	o			o	o	o
Sea-level rise	•	•					•
Drought	•	•	•	•	o	o	o
Hurricane and other storms	•	•				o	o
Erosion	•	•	o			o	
Biotic effects				•	•	•	

Notes: • Common and important cause of wetland degradation and loss.
   o Present but not a major cause of loss.
Source: Dugan (1990)

Wetland values

Natural wetlands perform many important ecological services for humankind – prevention of storm damage, flood and water flow control, support of fisheries, nutrient and waste absorption, and so forth. Wetlands can also be used for recreation and water transport, and their diverse resources can be directly exploited for fishing, agriculture, wildlife products, wood products and water supply. When properly measured, the total economic benefits to human welfare of a wetland's ecological functions, its services and its resources may exceed the economic gains of converting the area to an alternative use. Some economic

Table 6.2   *Major threats to wetlands: Asia, Latin America and the Caribbean*

Threat	Incidence (per cent of sites)
A Latin America and the Caribbean	
Pollution	31.0
Hunting and associated disturbance	30.5
Drainage for agriculture and ranching	19.0
Disturbance from recreation	11.5
Reclamation for urban and industrial development	10.5
Forestry activities	10.0
Fishing and associated disturbance	10.0
B Asia	
Hunting and associated disturbance	32.0
Human settlement/accroachment	27.0
Drainage for agriculture	23.0
Pollution	20.0
Fishing and associated disturbance	19.0
Commercial logging/forestry	17.0
Wood cutting for domestic use	16.0
Watershed degradation/soil erosion/siltation	15.0
Conversion to aquaculture ponds or salt pans	11.0
Diversion of water supply	9.0
Over-grazing by domestic stock	9.0

Source: WCMC (1992)

studies have valued the benefits of temperate wetlands.[2] But to date, little analysis of tropical wetland benefits has been undertaken. Yet recent studies across the developing regions of the world have suggested that tropical wetland systems – whether inland freshwater systems or coastal, mangrove systems – may have a crucial role to play in economic development.[3]

Although the value of wetlands in terms of providing essential ecological 'services' and resources are significant, efforts to determine these values and incorporate them in development decisions have been too few. As the Beijer Biodiversity Programme Papers make clear, this is one area where economists and ecologists should be working together to make a significant contribution through improved analysis.

'Valuing' a wetland essentially means valuing the characteristics of a system. Any system, whether natural or humanmade, can be characterized by three concepts:

■ stocks;
■ flows; and
■ the organization of these stocks and flows.

---

2   For reviews, see Gren et al (1994); Farber and Costanza (1987); Turner (1991); Turner and Jones (1991); and Turner et al (1994).
3   For reviews, see Barbier (1993c, 1994b and 1994c) and Dixon (1989).

These three system characteristics have parallel concepts in both ecology – structural components, environmental functions and diversity – and economics – assets, services and attributes. Table 6.3 summarizes the linkages between these basic system characteristics, and their ecological and economic counterparts.

Table 6.3 *Ecological and economic system characteristics*

General system characteristics	Ecological system characteristics	Economic system characteristics
Stocks	Structural components	Assets
Flows	Environmental functions	Services
Organization	Biological and cultural diversity	Attributes

Source: Adapted from Aylward and Barbier (1991)

In ecology, a distinction is usually made between the regulatory environmental functions of an ecosystem (such as, nutrient cycles, micro-climatic functions, energy flows and so on) and its structural components (such as, biomass, abiotic matter, species of flora and fauna, and so on). This distinction is useful from an economic perspective, as it corresponds to the standard categories of resource stocks or assets (namely, the structural components) versus environmental flows or services (namely, the ecological functions). In addition, ecosystems as a whole often have certain attributes (biological diversity, cultural uniqueness/heritage) that have economic value either because they induce certain economic uses or because they are valued in themselves.

Figure 6.1 indicates some of the standard techniques available for measuring the various economic values of wetlands.[4] However, it is important to acknowledge that, even if fully quantified and aggregated, the sum total of all conceivable economic values of a wetland – its total economic value (TEV) – may fail to reflect the total primary value (TPV) of the ecosystem (Gren et al 1994). The TPV reflects the total 'life support service' of an ecosystem as an integral whole, which is essentially the existence, functional operation and maintenance of the

---

4 Further discussion of these economic techniques as applied to wetlands can be found in the references listed throughout this chapter. For good introductions to environmental valuation techniques in general, see Dixon et al (1989), and Dixon and Hufschmidt (1986). Chapters 2 and 3 discussed generally the economic approach to valuation, and the basic concepts of use and non-use value as employed by economists. However, some of the categories of economic value indicated in Figure 6.1 need further explaining here.

A special category of value is option value, which arises because an individual may be uncertain about their future demand for a resouce and/or its availability in the future. There is a general consensus in the economics literature that option values are not a separate form of value but represent a difference between ex ante and ex post valuation (Smith 1983; Freeman 1984). If an individual is uncertain about the future value of a wetland but believes it may be high or that current exploitation and conversion may be irreversible, then there may be quasi-option value derived from delaying the development activities. Quasi-option value is simply the expected value of the information derived from delaying exploitation and conversion of the wetland today. Again, there is a consensus that quasi-option value is not a separate component of benefit but involves the analyst properly accounting for the implications of gaining additional information (Fisher and Hanemann 1987). In contrast, however, there are individuals who do not currently make use of tropical wetlands but nevertheless wish to see them preserved 'in their own right'. Such an 'intrinsic' value is often referred to as existence value. It is a form of non-use value that is extremely difficult to measure, as existence values involve subjective valuations by individuals unrelated to either their own or others' use, whether current or future. An important sub-set of non-use or preservation values is bequest value, which results from individuals placing a high value on the conservation of tropical wetlands for future generations to use. Bequest values may be particularly high among the local populations currently using a wetland, in that they would like to see the wetland, and their way of life that has evolved in conjunction with it, passed on to their heirs and future generations in general.

entire ecosystem that is behind the ecological services and resources of value to human beings. In other words, the wetland and its functional relationships in their entirety are the source of TPV, which is over and above the combined economic value of the various wetland 'characteristics'. Thus TEV is in some sense a total 'secondary' value which is always less than TPV. On the other hand, going beyond TEV to measure the extra 'glue value' that comprises TPV is extremely difficult.

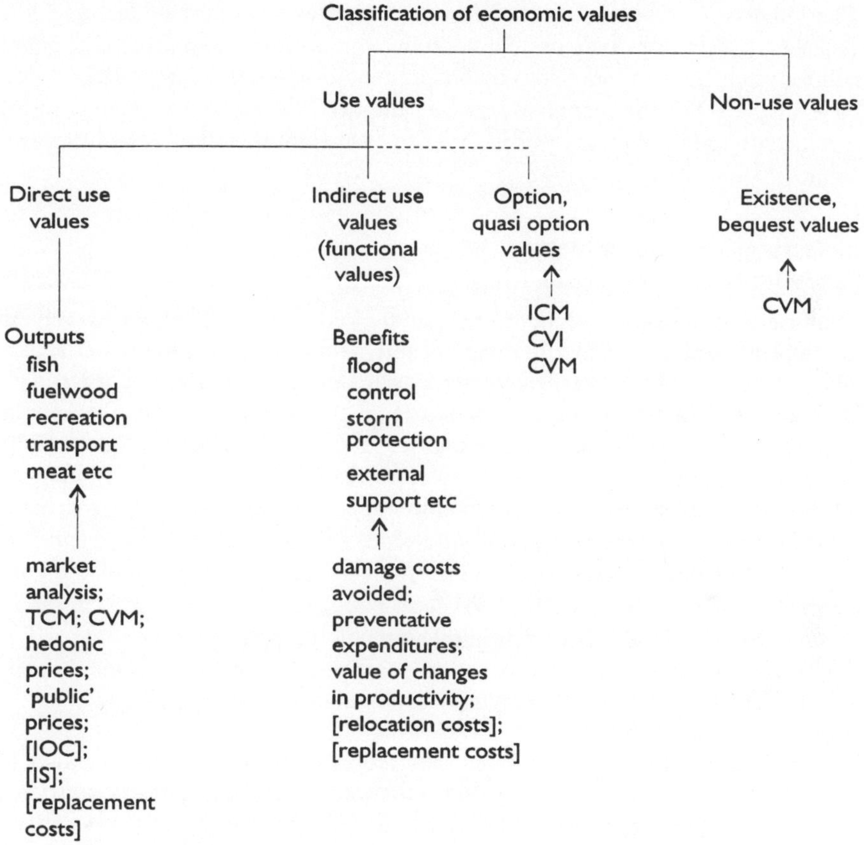

Classification of economic values

Use values		**Non-use values**

Direct use values	Indirect use values (functional values)	Option, quasi option values ↑ ICM CVI CVM	Existence, bequest values ↑ CVM
Outputs fish fuelwood recreation transport meat etc ↑	Benefits flood control storm protection external support etc ↑		
market analysis; TCM; CVM; hedonic prices; 'public' prices; [IOC]; [IS]; [replacement costs]	damage costs avoided; preventative expenditures; value of changes in productivity; [relocation costs]; [replacement costs]		

Notes: ICM = individual choice models.
        CVI = conditional value of information.
        CVM = contingent valuation method.
        TCM = travel cost method.
        IOC = indirect opportunity cost approach.
        IS   = indirect substitute approach.
        [ ] = valuation methodology to be used with care.

Source: Barbier (1994b); adapted originally from Barbier (1989)

Figure 6.1 *Valuing wetland benefits*

Assessing the economic use and non-use values of wetlands and other ecosystems is therefore essential, but nevertheless falls short of putting an aggregate value on wetlands. As will be argued in the next section, however, it is very rare that an assessment of the full TEV of ecosystems – let alone its full aggregate value, or TPV – is necessary in most wetland management decisions.

MANAGEMENT AND POLICY

The important economic benefits derived from wetlands must be factored into decisions concerning their use. In addition, the presence of market and policy failures often leads to more conversion and modification of wetlands than necessary. In the following section we discuss the need for assessing wetland values and incentives in policy analysis in order to ensure appropriate wetland management.

Assessing wetland values

The use and non-use values of temperate wetlands – which are largely in developed countries – may differ significantly from those of tropical wetlands – which occur mainly in the developing world. For example, many tropical wetlands are being directly exploited, often through non-market, 'informal' economic activity, to support human livelihoods, for example through fishing, hunting, fuelwood extraction and so on, whereas recreation/tourist use may often be limited. In contrast, direct exploitation to support livelihoods – except perhaps commercial fishing or forestry in some areas – may be small for most temperate wetlands, but their recreational value is often significant. Valuation of the non-commercial direct use of wetlands by local populations can be critical in determining the economic value of tropical wetlands to developing countries. The failure to take this value into account is often a major factor behind policy decisions that lead to the current over-exploitation or excessive degradation of tropical wetland systems.

Direct uses of the wetlands would therefore include both consumptive uses of its resources (such as, livestock grazing, fuelwood collection, forestry activities, agriculture, water use, hunting and fishing) and non-consumptive uses of wetland 'services' (such as, recreation, tourism, in situ research and education, and navigation along water courses). Direct uses of wetlands could involve both commercial and non-commercial activities, with some of the latter activities often being important for the subsistence needs of local populations. Commercial uses may be important for both domestic and international markets. In general, the value of marketed products (and services) of wetlands is easier to measure than the value of non-commercial and subsistence direct uses (see Figure 6.1). As noted above, this is one reason why policy makers often fail to consider subsistence and informal uses of tropical wetlands in many development decisions.

Various regulatory ecological functions of tropical wetlands may also have important indirect use values. Their values derive from supporting or protecting economic activities that have directly measurable values. For example, the groundwater recharge function of floodplain wetlands may have indirect use value through its replenishment of aquifer systems that supply water for domestic use and agriculture. The storm prevention function of mangrove swamps may also have indirect use value through the protection afforded coastal property and economic activity. The biological diversity of a wetland ecosystem may also have an important role in maintaining regulatory functions, for example, changes in species diversity may affect how well support and protective services function and, in some cases, even their availability. The indirect use value of an environmental function is related to the change in the value of production or consumption of the activity or property that it is protecting or supporting.

However, as this contribution is non-marketed, goes financially unrewarded and is only indirectly connected to economic activities, the indirect use values of regulatory environmental functions may be difficult to value (Aylward and Barbier 1992). Increasing evidence from studies of temperate wetland systems suggests that the values of these functions may be substantial.[5] Although few valuation studies of key environmental functions in tropical wetlands have been conducted, the available evidence suggests that the economic value of regulatory environmental functions may be highly significant.[6]

A major problem in valuing regulatory environmental functions is the lack of scientific data on ecological relationships and functions, especially in developing countries. This is particularly the case for techniques that attempt to estimate potential environmental damages that may result from having these functions impaired or disrupted (see Figure 6.1). However, recent advances in the methodology for valuing non-marketed environmental goods and services suggest that in many instances the data requirements for valuing wetland functions may not be too overwhelming. The production function approach may be especially promising. It is used to value changes in productivity by incorporating a wetland as an 'input' to the production process of economic activities it is supporting or protecting (Barbier 1994b and 1994c; and Mäler, Gren and Folke 1994).[7]

Evaluation of the various option and non-use values of wetlands requires the use of even more sophisticated techniques (see Figure 6.1). In general, these approaches have so far been used sparingly for temperate wetlands and not at all for tropical wetlands. One such approach used is contingent valuation methods (CVM), which attempt to elicit through direct survey methods the 'willingness to pay' by individuals for various ecosystem valuables. CVM can be employed for both use and non-use values.

For example, CVM was recently used to assess through an 'on-site' survey of users the value to these individuals of protecting the recreation and environmental quality benefits of the Norfolk Broads in England from increased flood-

---

5 See the references and case studies cited in Gren et al (1994); Turner et al (1994); and Turner and Jones (1991).

6 See the references cited in Barbier (1994b and 1994c), in particular Adams and Hollis (1988); Lal and Dixon (1990); Ruitenbeek (1992); Twilley (1991); and Yañez-Arancibia and Day (1988).

7 As Mäler, Gren and Folke (1994) make clear, the production function can also be applied to determine the economic values of economic activities within wetland areas, in particular direct uses of resources such as fuelwood, hunting and foraging for subsistence uses that are non-marketed and difficult to value otherwise. In addition, Smith (1983) suggests that the approach can be used for other important non-marketed environmental benefits, such as recreation. Ellis and Fisher (1987) and Freeman (1991) provide examples of the use of the production function approach to value the contribution of mangroves in the Gulf of Mexico to blue crab fisheries. See also the Gotland case study by Gren (1992) and cited in Gren et al (1994), and Turner et al (1994), which is also discussed briefly below.

ing. The on-site research produced value estimates of £77–244 per household per annum, or a total annual user value of £6–25 million based on forecast visitations. The study also attempted an estimate of non-use or 'existence-type' values through a parallel off-site mail survey across Great Britain. Households living near the Broads had a higher non-use value (£12.45 per household, yielding an aggregate annual value of £32.5 million) than those in the rest of Great Britain (£4.08 per household, yielding an aggregate value of £7.3 million). However, these latter results did not adequately distinguish between past users of the Broads and pure non-users, and cannot therefore be classified as pure non-use values.[8]

Assessing development and conservation options

To make consistent choices between wetland conservation, preservation and development options, or between a decision to halt, modify or continue with an activity that is inflicting damage on a wetland, requires the application of a consistent appraisal methodology for evaluating the alternative options. At the heart of the appraisal methodology is the determination of the various costs and benefits associated with each option. Critical to this assessment of costs and benefits is the choice of appropriate valuation techniques, as indicated in Figure 6.1 and discussed above.

Barbier (1994b and 1994c) suggests essentially three broad categories of assessment, with each category corresponding to each major type of policy decision concerning wetland use that generally needs evaluating:[9]

- *impact analysis* – an assessment of the damages inflicted on the wetland from a specific environmental impact (such as oil spills);
- *partial valuation* – an assessment of alternative resource allocations or project options involving wetland systems or resources (for example, whether to divert water from the wetlands for other uses or to convert/develop part of the wetlands at the expense of other uses); and
- *total valuation* – an assessment of the total economic value of the wetland system (for example, for national income accounting or to determine its worth as a protected area).

Under the first approach, assessing a specific environmental impact involves valuing the changes in the wetland resulting from that impact. For example, assume that discharges of oil are regularly polluting an estuarine wetland, affecting both fish production and water quality in the wetlands. The costs of this activity are the losses in wetland values arising from damage to the ecosystem and its resources. These damages would amount to the losses in net production benefits (namely, the economic benefits of production less the costs) from the impacts of the oil spills on the fishery plus the losses in net environmental benefits in terms of poorer quality water supplies for wetland and neighbouring

---

8 This case study is summarized in Gren et al (1994) and Turner et al (1994). The original reference is Bateman et al (1992). However, the CVM approach must be used with caution; for a critical evaluation see Blamey and Common (1993).

9 In what follows, it is assumed that all costs and benefits are discounted at some positive rate into present value terms.

settlements, as well as for general ecosystem functioning. Thus, by assessing and valuing these losses we would arrive at an estimate of the net production and environmental benefits of the wetlands, NB^W, that are affected by the oil spills. The total cost of this impact, C^I, in terms of damage to the wetland are these forgone net benefits:

$$C^I = NB^W \qquad (1)$$

Dixon and Hufschmidt (1986) and Dixon et al (1989) provide case studies of applying this particular approach in the overall context of economic appraisal of environmental impacts. For example, in the analysis of the cost-effectiveness of various options for disposing of waste water from a geothermal power plant on the island of Leyte in the Philippines, it was necessary to decide which means of waste water disposal from the plant would protect the environment in the most cost-effective manner. For some of the options, the costs of the environmental impacts in terms of lost marine fishery and rice production were quantified. Other environmental costs, such as energy loss, lost riverine fishery production, human health effects and amenity impacts, were not possible to quantify. For example, the analysis showed that the quantifiable environmental costs of releasing untreated waste disposal into the Bao River or into the Mahiao River were quite high, accounting for 41 per cent and 35 per cent of total measurable costs of these options respectively. Both options may also seriously contaminate the marine ecosystem with unknown and unquantifiable effects.

Another variation of the impact analysis approach is to evaluate the loss of wetland benefits by comparing them to the costs of providing humanmade alternatives where feasible. Under certain conditions, this replacement cost approach can provide a minimum estimation of the forgone wetland benefits, but the strict equality of equation (1) no longer holds.[10] Gren et al (1994) and Turner et al (1994) discuss a case study conducted by Folke (1991) of the Swedish wetland system – the Martebo mire – on the island of Gotland in the Baltic Sea. The analysis used replacement cost analysis to compare alternative human-made technologies to wetland produced goods and services. The results are indicated in Table 6.4. They show that it takes a considerable amount of (undiscounted) investment and industrial energy to replace various goods and services provided by the wetland system.

The second assessment approach, that is, partial valuation of wetland benefits, may be required when one or more development options may lead to alteration or conversion of wetland systems. That means choices involving diversion,

---

10 However, as argued by Aylward and Barbier (1992) and indicated in Figure 5.1, this replacement cost approach is not ideal and should be used with extreme care. The implicit assumption of replacement costing is that the replacement is worthwhile, and this implies that the benefits of the human-made replacement exceed the costs of providing such benefits. At the same time, the benefits of the human-made option should be the same as those of the ecological services that it is replacing. Unfortunately, the value of these ecological services is now equated with the costs of the option replacing it. These two conditions are therefore mutually exclusive: the benefit–cost ratio cannot be both greater than and equal to one at the same time. In fact, often the costs of replacements are extremely high and may exceed the benefits of the ecological services that are being originally replaced. Thus an important assumption underlying the application of the replacement cost approach is that the demand for services would be the same regardless of the method and costs of providing it (either human-made or 'ecological') and that the costs of the replacement are less than the value of the ecological services that it is replacing. In practice, it is very difficult to determine whether such an assumption is valid and it is not verified in the case study by Folke (1991) discussed here.

Table 6.4   *Replacement monetary and energy costs for Martebo mire, Gotland Island, Sweden*

Replacement technologies	Monetary costs 1/	Energy costs 2/
Redraining and clearing of ditches and streams (g)	50–56	0.200–0.330
Dams for irrigation	57–205	0.200–1.167
Pumping water to dams	11–36	0.025–0.225
Irrigation pipes and machines (h)	58–184	0.230–1.045
Artificial fertilizers (g)	935–1345	8.130–19.095
Regulating wire	10–18	0.060–0.200
Pumping water to stream (h)	7–11	0.015–0.070
Well drilling	33–53	0.080–0.300
Water quality controls	12–40	0.020–0.180
Water purification plant	32	0.180–0.230
Nitrogen and saltwater filtering (h)	0–460	0–3.290
Water transport (h)		
– humans	0–500	0–4.050
– domestic animals	0–335	0–2.175
Pipeline to distant shore (h)	0–990	0–5.570
Mechanical sewage treatment and storing (g)	625–750	1.360–4.265
Silos for manure from domestic animals (g)	370–950	1.160–5.405
Sewage transport	63–126	0.165–1.020
Sewage treatment plant	3–200	0.005–1.170
Nitrogen reduction in sewage treatment plant (g)	40–45	0.085–0.255
Hatcheries		
– farmed salmon (b)	210–250	0.720–1.670
Endangered species (b)	68–314	0.120–1.965
TOTAL	**2585–6900**	**17,950–46,865**

Notes: 1/ Undiscounted monetary costs valued in 1000 SKr 1989 (6 SKr = US$1).
   2/ Energy costs in fossil fuel equivalents TJ (10^{12} J).
   (g) Technologies replacing loss in the performance of the wetland's biogeochemical process.
   (h) Technologies replacing loss in the performance of the wetland's hydrological cycle.
   (b) Technologies replacing loss in the biological part of the wetland.
Source: Gren et al (1994) and Turner et al (1994); original source Folke (1991).

allocation or conversion of wetland resources should compare the opportunity costs of the proposed options in terms of the subsequent loss in wetland benefits. For example, assume that there is an upstream irrigation project on a river that is providing water for agriculture. If this project diverts water from a wetland downstream, then any resulting loss in wetland benefits must be included as part of the overall costs of the project. Given direct benefits (such as irrigation water for farming), B^D, and direct costs (such as, costs of constructing the dam, irrigation channels and so on), C^D, then the direct net benefits of the project are:

$$NB^D = B^D - C^D \tag{2}$$

However, by diverting water that would otherwise flow into the downstream wetlands, the development project may result in losses to floodplain agriculture and other primary production activities, less groundwater recharge and other external impacts. Given these reductions in the net production and environmental benefits, NB^W, of the wetlands, then the true net benefits of the development project (NB^P) are $NB^D - NB^W$. The development project can therefore only be acceptable if:

$$NB^P = NB^D - NB^W > 0 \tag{3}$$

If the forgone wetland benefits are significant then the failure to assess the loss of wetland benefits will clearly lead to an over-estimation of NB^P. This is tantamount to assuming that there is no opportunity cost of diverting floodwater from the wetlands, which is rarely the case. Moreover, it may not be necessary to measure all affected wetland benefits; for example, if one or two impacts prove to be sufficiently large to render the development project uneconomic. In any case, it is not necessary to measure all wetland benefits but only those benefits which are affected by the development project – which is why this approach is called a 'partial valuation'.

A partial valuation was conducted to assess the economic importance of the Nigerian Hadejia-Jama'are wetlands, and thus the opportunity cost to Nigeria of its loss, by estimating some of the key direct use values the floodplain provides to local populations through crop production, fuelwood and fishing (Barbier, Adams and Kimmage 1991).[11] The economic analysis indicates that these benefits are substantial on both a per hectare basis and a water input basis – namely, the minimum and maximum amount of floodwater required to sustain them. This proves to be the case even when the agricultural benefits were adjusted to take into account the unsustainability of much pump-irrigated wheat production within the wetlands. As indicated in Table 6.5, the present value of the aggregate stream of agricultural, fishing and fuelwood benefits was estimated to be around N850 to N1280 per ha, or around N240 to N370 per 10^3m^3 (with 'maximum' flood inputs).[12]

The economic importance of the wetlands suggests that the benefits it provides cannot be excluded as an opportunity cost of any scheme that diverts water away from the floodplain system. When compared to the net economic benefits of the Kano River Project, the economic returns to the floodplain appear much more favourable (see Table 6.5). This is particularly the case when the relative returns to the project in terms of water input use are compared to that of the floodplain system. The result should cause some concern, given that the existing and

11 See Barbier, Adams and Kimmage (1991) for further details on the analytical approach of the study, including the difficulties encountered, and Barbier (1993c) for a retrospective review. Both papers also discuss possible alternative approaches to valuing the groundwater recharge function of the floodplain.
12 At 1989/90 prices, 7.5 Nigerian Naira (N) = US$1.

Table 6.5 *Comparison of net present value of economic benefits*

Kano River Project Phase I and Hadejia-Jama'are Floodplain, Nigeria
(N7.5 = US$1, 1989/90)

Per hectare a/	(8%, 50 yrs)	(8%, 30 yrs)	(12%, 50 yrs)	(12%, 30 yrs)
HJF (N/ha)	1276	1176	872	846
KRP (N/ha)	233	214	158	153
Per water use b/				
HJF (N/10^3m^3)	366	337	250	242
KRP (N/10^3m^3)	0.3	0.3	0.2	0.2

Notes: a/ Based on a total production area of 730,000 ha for Hadejia-Jama'are floodplain (HJF)
and a total crop cultivated area of 19,107 ha in 1985/6 for the Kano River Project Phase I
(KRP).
b/ Assumes an average river flow into Hadejia-Jama'are floodplain (HJF) of 2549 Mm^3
and an annual water use of 15,000 m^3 per ha for the Kano River Project Phase I (KRP)

Source: Barbier (1993c) and (1994b); original source Barbier, Adams and Kimmage (1991)

planned water developments along the Hadejia-Jama'are River system, such as the Kano River Project, will continue diverting water from the floodplain.

A case study of alternative nitrogen abatement measures in Gotland, Sweden also illustrates the partial valuation approach. The different nitrogen abatement strategies include restoration of a degraded wetlands, expansion in the capacity of sewage treatment plants and a reduction in farmers' use of nitrogen. In comparison with the other strategies, restoration of the wetlands not only improves water quality but also provides numerous ancillary environmental benefits – essentially the result of reviving an entire ecological life support system.

The results of the analysis are displayed in Table 6.6. In measuring water quality benefits, a production function approach employing a hydrological model of Gotland was used. This was linked to a monetary measure obtained from a contingent valuation estimation of the willingness to pay for nitrate reduction in drinking water in Sweden. An estimate of 200 kg/ha per year for the nitrogen purification capacity of wetlands was obtained from Swedish field research. As indicated in Table 6.6, the water quality benefits of wetland restoration alone outweigh the returns to the alternative nitrogen reduction strategies. In order to measure the ancillary environmental benefits of wetland restoration, the replacement cost measures for nitrogen abatement, water buffering, supply of energy and provision from the Martebo mire study on Gotland were used (see Table 6.4). These were adjusted to account for the difference between an unexploited and restored wetlands. Nevertheless, the ancillary environmental benefits accounted for nearly two-thirds of the total marginal value of restoring wetlands (see Table 6.6). The results of the study suggest that a dollar invested in water restoration would yield over eight times the return of a dollar invested in the next best nitrogen reduction strategy.

As the name implies, the final assessment approach involving total valuation of a wetland system requires an appraisal of all the net benefits of a wetland. If the objective of the total valuation is to measure, say, the economic contribution

Table 6.6 *Marginal values of nitrogen abatement, Gotland Island, Sweden*

(SKr per kg N-reduction)

Abatement strategies	Water quality	Ancillary environmental benefits	Total
Restoration of wetlands	259	600	859
Sewage treatment plants	104		104
Agriculture	5		5

Source: Gren et al (1994) and Turner et al (1994); original source Gren (1992)

of the wetlands to the welfare of society as part of a resource accounting exercise, then the objective should be to value as many of the net production and environmental benefits, NB^W, of the wetlands as possible. Another objective requiring total valuation would be the need to determine whether or not the wetlands should become a protected area with restricted or controlled use. The total net wetland benefits would therefore have to exceed the direct costs, C^P, of setting up the protected area (including any costs of relocating or compensating existing users) plus the net benefits forgone, NB^A, of alternative uses of the wetlands:

$$NB^W > C^P + NB^A \qquad (4)$$

Ruitenbeek (1992) uses this approach in evaluating the trade-offs between different forestry options in a mangrove system in Bintuni Bay, Irian Jaya, Indonesia – although in this example the comparison is between the total economic value of a wetlands preserved through a cutting ban and the total economic value generated by various forestry development options, ranging from partial selective cutting to clearcutting.

An important feature of the analysis is that it explicitly incorporates the linkages between mangrove conversion, offshore fishery productivity, traditional uses, and the imputed benefits of erosion control and biodiversity maintenance functions. To the extent that these linkages exist, then some of these direct and indirect uses become mutually exclusive with more intensive mangrove exploitation through forestry options. The 'optimal' forest management option will therefore depend on the strength of the environmental linkages. The results indicate that the clearcut option is optimal only if no environmental linkages exist – a highly unrealistic assumption. At the other extreme, a cutting ban is only optimal if the linkages are very strong, that is to say that mangrove alteration and conversion would lead to immediate and linear impacts throughout the ecosystem. Even if weak interactions exist, an 80 per cent selective cutting policy with replanting is preferable to clearcutting. However, given the considerable uncertainty over the dynamics of the mangrove ecosystem, and that alteration and conversion may be irreversible and exhibit high economic costs, the analysis concludes that there is little economic advantage to cutting significant amounts (for example, more than 25 per cent) of the mangrove area.

An interesting attempt to indicate the total primary value (TPV) of a wetland was conducted in the study of the Martebo mire in Gotland, Sweden, discussed above. TPV was estimated by using gross primary production (GPP) – the amount of energy captured via photosynthesis in the wetland system. In ecology, GPP is used as a common measure of an ecosystem's potential to generate all goods and services, or its life support function, and thus serves as an approximate indicator of TPV. Folke (1991) estimated the annual loss in the life support function of the Martebo mire from exploitation to be about 730 tetrajoules (TJ or 10^{12} joules) of GPP in terms of solar energy capture. This is equivalent to a loss of 55–75 TJ in fossil fuel equivalents. The energy costs of replacing the wetland goods and services indicated in Table 6.4 are nearly as high (18–47 TJ in fossil fuel equivalents). However, these technical replacements were only a partial substitution for elements of the overall ecosystem life support function and fell short of restoring the original ambient environmental quality.

Assessing market and policy failures

The above examples illustrate the fact that the values of wetland resources and functions are significant, and should not be ignored in development decisions that affect wetland systems. However, too often decisions to convert or degrade wetlands are taken without considering their 'natural' benefits. In particular, the failure of markets to reflect fully the values of many environmental functions provided by wetlands means that individuals rarely take into account these values in their private land use decisions. In many regions, the direct costs of wetland conversion are often subsidized, either directly or indirectly, by governments. Public investments themselves, such as in dams, irrigation, urban development, agricultural projects and other infrastructure, routinely fail to consider the environmental impacts on wetlands.

The result is that excessive wetland conversion and degradation can be traced to the prevalence of market and policy failures that adversely affect the incentives for wetland management and conservation. The general role of these failures as an underlying cause of global biodiversity loss was discussed in Chapter 4. Turner et al (1994) and Turner and Jones (1991) list and discuss briefly the wide range of information, market and intervention failures that lie behind the rapid pace of wetland conversion and degradation the world is currently experiencing.

By not addressing these market and policy failures, we will continue to lose many important wetland systems that provide essential ecological services and resources. As Tables 6.1 and 6.2 make clear, the land, water and other resources contained within wetland systems are being converted and over-exploited for economic activities that are easily recognized as yielding immediate development benefits to both individuals and governments. As Gren et al (1994) maintain, the crux of the market and policy failure problem is information failure – a general lack of appreciation of the full economic value of conserved wetlands, particularly their regulatory environmental functions. Thus related to the lack of appropriate economic incentives for wetland conservation are the valuation issues discussed throughout this chapter.

CHALLENGES TO BE ADDRESSED

Loss of the world's wetlands is an increasing economic problem because important values are lost, some perhaps irreversibly, when natural wetlands are converted or degraded. The role of biodiversity in supporting wetland system functioning and resilience is not well known; however, the values provided by many well-functioning wetland systems to human welfare would suggest that this role is extremely important. Although difficult to estimate, the total life support function of wetlands may be particularly significant, as 'wetlands' comprise a diverse range of marine, coastal, estuarine and freshwater habitats.

The choice of whether or not to convert or exploit wetlands can only be made if the gains and losses associated with each wetland use option are properly analysed and evaluated. This requires that all wetland values – whether marketed or non-marketed – should be considered where appropriate.

As this chapter has made clear, the valuation issue is the most important policy challenge to be addressed by ecology and economics, and is particularly suited to the ecological–economics approach advocated in this book. Improvements need to be made in estimating the benefits of environmental regulatory functions, which are behind many of the important ecological services that benefit human welfare. In addition, we need to further our understanding of how biodiversity supports the ecological functioning and resilience of wetland systems. Finally, as our knowledge of wetland values improves, we need to use this information to create the appropriate incentives for determining choice of various wetland uses. There will be many situations in which wetland conversion, modification and exploitation will be economically and ecologically justified. However, management of the world's wetlands is bound to improve as we begin systematically to correct prevailing market and policy failures that contribute to excessive conversion and exploitation.

7

Estuarine and Marine Ecosystems

This chapter looks at the ecology, economics and sustainable management of estuarine and marine resources and ecosystems. The frequent mismatch between the characteristics and functions of the ecological systems, and human institutions and policies developed to use them, has led to ecosystem degradation and biodiversity loss. Due to the increasing scale and impact of human activity on estuarine and marine biodiversity and environments, the management of species and populations needs to be designed in the context of their ecological structure in relationship with the ecosystem of which they are part. A better understanding of these resources and ecosystems is required to enable improved management and sustainable resource use. Based on studies performed within the Beijer Institute's biodiversity programme, this chapter provides case studies that address the relationships between the ecology, the resources, and the management regimes in estuarine and marine ecosystems.

IDENTIFICATION AND ANALYSIS

In this section we:

- present an ecological characterization of estuarine and marine ecosystems, and discuss the ecological implications of biodiversity loss in these habitats;
- review the direct and indirect impacts of economic activities on estuarine and marine ecosystems; and
- identify ecological and economic analyses that have been undertaken on estuarine and marine degradation and management.

Ecological characteristics of estuarine and marine ecosystems[1]

Coastal and estuarine ecosystems form the interface between continental lands, and oceanic islands and their surrounding seas. Estuaries are coastal indentations with restricted connection to the ocean which remains open at least intermittently. They vary in form and size, from large areas, such as the Chesapeake Bay in the US and the Baltic Sea, to shallow coastal lagoons behind barrier islands, peninsulas and spits. Estuaries are among some of the most productive ecosystems of the world. The biological diversity of estuaries and coastal waters is strongly coupled to their surrounding environment. Many marine species require

---

1 This sub-section draws on the contribution of Costanza, Kemp and Boynton (1993); Hammer, Jansson and Jansson (1993); and Holling et al (1994) to the Beijer Biodiversity Programme.

Box 7.1

The herring (clupea harengus) in its life support environment

Offshore areas are to a great extent influenced by physical forces like wind, waves and currents, whereas in coastal areas biological production and interactions are more pronounced. The open sea is a pulsed system of energy fixation during the light season with a dormant period during winter. The Baltic pelagic (offshore) system starts the year with a big explosion of phytoplankton in March–April, half of which settles to the sea bottom serving as food for bottom-living animals, including fish larvae. The next plankton bloom is in July and is also a major food source for fish larvae and other species in the food web, that lasts through the autumn. Fish migration and reproduction are triggered by the pulsing behaviour of its life support environment, as a consequence of the seasonal variations in light, temperature and water quality.

The annual rythm and dependence of both offshore and coastal areas for life support is illustrated by the spring spawning herring in the Baltic Sea. In the summer the adult herring mainly feed in the offshore (pelagic zone) system utilizing the maximum occurrence of zooplankton in July. When the plankton are getting scarce in late autumn the herring switch to microscopic shrimps congregations near the sea bottom (soft bottom). By the end of the year they pause in their feeding and form large schools in the coastal archipelago (phytal zone) where they remain and spawn in May. The spawning results in a wide geographical spread of roe in the archipelago. The coastal system provides optimal hatching conditions and sufficient food for the young larvae, before it migrates out from the coast.

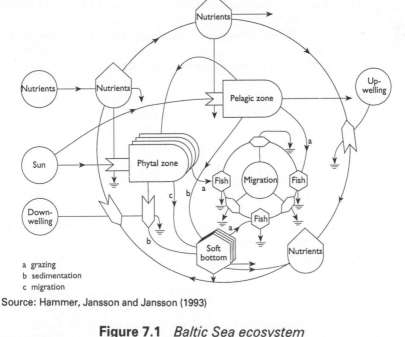

a grazing
b sedimentation
c migration

Source: Hammer, Jansson and Jansson (1993)

Figure 7.1   *Baltic Sea ecosystem*

estuaries for a portion of their life cycle, for example numerous fish species migrate between systems and a variety of organisms have pelagic larval stages, such as barnacles. Box 7.1 provides an example of the onshore and offshore dependence, and the migratory pattern of the spring-spawning herring in the Baltic Sea.

As an aquatic interface, coastal and estuarine ecosystems contain a mixture of freshwater and oceanic species, but fewer species than similar communities in lakes and oceans. This is because estuaries generally experience widely varying conditions of temperature, salinity, concentrations of a wide variety of chemicals, and plant and animal densities, much of which are mediated by water movement often over short time scales. The large and unpredictable variations in salinity and water movement tend to limit the number of animal and plant species capable of adapting to these rigorous physical conditions.

Many estuarine species occupy broader 'ecological niches' than in their original fresh or marine water environments, because the organisms need to adapt continually to a rapidly changing environment. The selective advantages of specialization are less pronounced and most organisms are characterized as generalists. For example, the American oyster (*Crassostrea virginica*) can grow well across an extreme salinity range, feed successfully on a broad range of algal species and detritus, stop feeding during cold periods of the year when food is limited and can survive extended periods of low oxygen conditions.

The buoyancy of water and the rapid water transport associated with tides, winds and pressure gradients provide a means for rapid dispersion and easy mobility for resident organisms, such as mussels and barnacles. As a consequence, many organisms have high fecundity and depend on water transport for larval dispersal. Isolated populations in estuaries tend to be rare and functional replacements for estuarine species are usually possible. For example, over a whole estuary – such as the Chesapeake Bay – reproduction of the American oyster favours one location in some years and other locations at other times. The larval stage of the oyster is pelagic, which ensures wide dispersal and colonization of available habitats, and replenishment of areas that have become depopulated.

Since there are few endemic species in estuaries, this has implications for maintenance of species assemblages and functional diversity. They are open to active migrations, passive entry via river and tidal flows, and accidental introductions by humans. This ensures a continual supply of normally occurring and also new species. However, while local extinctions of species are relatively rare and generally of short duration in estuaries, local population extinctions may occur. Estuaries also tend to be characterized by high resilience to unpredictable events. For example, in the Chesapeake Bay plankton communities, benthic populations and fish populations recover rapidly after major storms. The buffering capacity displayed by many estuarine ecosystems rests on three primary factors:

- the relatively small standing ecological structure;
- the high degree of organism mobility; and
- the prevalence of generalist species.

However, in estuarine ecosystems functions depend on a much lower species diversity (albeit a larger abundance per species). For example, compared to the marine North Sea the brackish estuary of the Baltic Sea has less than one-tenth of the macro-animal species to help perform necessary ecosystem functions. This implies that if a single major group of species is wiped out (for example, by disease) the ecological structure and even the resilience of the system may be challenged. Semi-enclosed seas, where species entrance to the system is constrained, are particularly prone to such threats.

There are several important differences between estuarine/marine ecosystems and terrestrial ecosystems. The first is the virtual absence of physical structures that can be used for habitat creation in the former ecosystems. For example, plant canopies are common in terrestrial environments but rarely exist in most estuarine and marine ecosystems. However, there are some exceptions, such as shallow coastal systems with sea grasses, kelp systems, near-shore ecosystems with abundant recruitment and coral reefs.

For example, coral reefs in stable, tropical marine environments are able to develop unparalleled species diversity. Such systems create complex structures which lead to multiple ecological niches and high species diversity. However, coral reef systems cannot survive highly variable environments because their organisms are not adapted to widely varying physical conditions. Similarly, in the patchy coastal system of the Baltic Sea, numerous functional niches exist. These functional niches harbour dense food webs with several species acting as 'insurance capital' for the ecological functions.

A second important difference between terrestrial and marine/estuarine ecosystems is the extent to which species actively shape their environment. The pattern of ecosystem evolution described in Chapter 2 is generally appropriate for terrestrial systems and aquatic environments that display physical attributes, and substrates that enable the development and evolution of a complex biological community. Such terrestrial and aquatic ecosystems demonstrate a capacity to absorb and modify specific ranges of variability without changing into a different state. This control of variability over some, but not all scales, gives them an inherent resilience. Under these conditions species actively shape their environment.

This is not the case in open ocean systems, partly due to the difference in the physical properties of air and water. Pelagic organisms of the ocean exist in an environment of water without any fixed substrate, and therefore need to adapt to the existing environment and its variability. These species are not capable of shaping their environment nor controlling its variability. In addition, recent research has shown that many organisms in coastal ecosystems go through a pelagic oceanic phase where the controlling ecological processes are physical rather than biological. The phase of physically controlled variability is often of great significance in determining inshore patterns of diversity, as shown in Box 7.2 with a case study of barnacles on the Californian coast.

A third important difference between terrestrial and marine/estuarine ecosystems is the spatial and temporal scales of physical variability. Steele (1991) stresses that it is inappropriate routinely to apply rules from land management to the management of estuarine, coastal and marine ecosystems. Although some

---

Box 7.2

Intertidal and pelagic ecosystem interactions: the case of the barnacle

Previous generalizations of rocky intertidal ecological systems were based on studies of biological interactions. System diversity was explained through competition, predation and intermediate disturbance at the site of the adult animals in the coastal area. However, recent research at the 'full ecosystem' level has revealed the importance of the physical processes in pelagic environments affecting the larvae recruitment to intertidal rocky shores.

For example, on the Californian coast, adult barnacles that are attached to the rocks steadily release larvae into the sea during the spring and early summer. The larvae are carried offshore to fronts separating the upwelled water from the warmer and fresher water of the California Current. There the larvae feed on the abundant plankton algae of the nutrient rich upwelled water. As the upwelling season wanes, the fronts move to shore returning the larvae to the adult habitat where they settle and metamorphose into small adults.

However, the return of mature larvae to the rocky shores occurs in episodic pulses that bring about large fluctuations in barnacle abundance. These fluctuations are determined by interactions of physical forces of the winds, the upwelling and the California Current. If wind relaxation occurs for extended periods, the front can collide with the coast and deposit its accumulated larvae, thereby producing a recruitment event. The major cause of population fluctuations lies in the ocean phase of the life cycle, rather than the coast, where the adults compete for space and incur predation and disturbance, as previously assumed.

Source: Holling et al (1994).

---

ecological generalizations between land and sea may exist, we first need to recognize the substantial differences in scale between physical and biological responses in marine, terrestrial, and freshwater systems and sectors. From a landscape view perspective, Jackson (1991) claims that in coral reefs the predictability of coral distribution, abundance and diversity increases with spatial scale. When scale is increased it is possible to observe successional states that result from differences in coral life histories and vulnerability to disturbance, such as effects of storms on recruitment, differences in resource use and recovery of biotic relationships. Indeed, scale is of great relevance for predictability and sustainable management of dynamic and self-organizing systems (Costanza et al 1993).

Direct and indirect impacts of economic activities on biodiversity

Marine and estuarine biodiversity have been adversely affected through:

- direct use of marine and estuarine resources; and
- the indirect impact of land based activities on these ecosystems.

Poor estuarine and marine management has directly led to the misuse and overuse of resources, for example through excessive harvesting of fish stocks. A pattern of 'sequential exploitation' of fish resources has occurred, whereby fish stocks are gradually depleted from accessible to less accessible areas and from valuable to less valuable species (Berkes 1985; Grima and Berkes 1989). Extraction of the less abundant and remote resources has been made possible through the increased use and development of energy intensive technologies, such as improved and larger sea vessels.

The development of the New Bedford fisheries in the US clearly illustrates the situation where increasing resources and energy intensive technologies are required to exploit fish stocks of rising scarcity. In this fishery, the total harvest in 1988 was 30 per cent less than it was in 1968, but 300 per cent more direct fuel was used to catch it (Cleveland 1991). A similar trend is seen in the fisheries around the Island of Gotland, Sweden, where there was a 50 per cent increase in total catch between 1920 and 1973, but a 400 per cent increase in the direct fuel that was used to catch the fish (Zucchetto and Jansson 1985).

Fisheries in Sweden have an extensive history of specialization following the pattern of sequential exploitation, otherwise known as 'boom and bust' (Hammer 1994). The offshore and growth oriented fisheries which developed after the Second World War became so widespread by the late 1960s that they caused a threat to the reproduction of major fish stocks. Due to high levels of natural variability, initial cases of species over-exploitation were not detectable until the problem became severe. The pattern of 'boom and bust' has also characterized the North Sea herring fisheries and the Baltic cod fisheries, with ensuing declines in both stocks (Hammer, Jansson and Jansson 1993).

Similarly, harvesting salmon has followed an exploitative development sequence, starting with accessible salmon in coastal areas, to offshore salmon fisheries and recently to farming salmon in cages. The shift in technology from nets and small boats, to larger and larger vessels, and finally to cages, has increased the demand for non-renewable resources and fossil energies, as well as the impact on coastal and marine environments.

The over-exploitation of fish stocks and the failure to take into account the structure, function and resilience of the ecosystem upon which the fish stocks depend have led to the impoverishment of marine and estuarine ecosystems. In many cases, inappropriate management and over-exploitation have resulted in a fall in the quality and the quantity of fish harvested, and a decline in the fish industry. In regions and communities that are highly dependent on fish and fish related industries there have been severe adverse socio-economic effects (Regier and Baskerville 1986).

Land use activities, such as urbanization, infrastructure development, industrialization, forestry and agriculture, may also indirectly incur detrimental environmental impacts on marine and estuarine ecosystems, and their biological diversity. For example, point source pollution, runoff from rivers and drainage basins, and atmospheric downfalls can degrade marine and estuarine ecosystems.

Nutrient runoff has caused severe local eutrophication of coastal waters and has contributed to a long term eutrophication of many estuarine and marine systems. For example, the annual input of nitrogen into the Baltic Sea has increased four times since the beginning of the century, with the most drastic increase taking place in the last four decades. Sixty per cent of the nitrogen stems from river inputs, 30 per cent from atmospheric deposition and about 7 per cent from municipal sources (Larsson, Elmgren and Wulff 1985).

The introduction of pipe draining for crop-land runoff has reduced the potential for natural fresh water systems, such as wetlands, to 'filter' the polluted water. While this large scale technical approach to the problem of crop-land drainage has boosted agricultural productivity, it has also increased the nutrient loadings of coastal and estuarine waters, and caused significant changes in their biological diversity (Folke, Hammer and Jansson 1991). The increased nutrient load has led to extensive algal blooms, decreasing water transparency and depth distribution of benthic vegetation of great importance as nursery areas for many aquatic species, including commercially valuable fish. It has also caused a shift towards more pelagic fish species and less of others, such as cod (Hammer, Jansson and Jansson 1993).

Toxic substances including DDT, PCB, dioxin, toxaphen and other chlorinated organic compounds, and heavy metals such as mercury, lead, cadmium and zinc tend to accumulate and become concentrated in the upper trophic levels of estuarine and marine food chains, often in important commercial fish and shellfish. The bio-accumulation of hazardous substances in fish has caused decreased reproduction of fish-eating birds and sea mammals, such as sea eagles, otters and seals in many areas of the world.

Research has shown that the toxification and eutrophication of the Baltic Sea and the Chesapeake Bay has altered energy, carbon and nutrient flows with subsequent changes in species composition and biological communities (Costanza, Kemp and Boynton 1994; Hammer 1994). Ecological systems that are stressed in this way often exhibit larger and more irregular fluctuations, and are often even more difficult to predict and manage than undisturbed natural environments. An important concern is that long enduring perturbations into coastal and marine environments, such as the continuous input of various wastes, may be a more severe threat to the ability of these systems to generate ecological services than occasional unpredictable events like storms, pest-outbreaks, algal blooms or oil spills. Continuous perturbations may undermine the capacity of an ecosystem to absorb unpredictable events and lead to loss of ecological life support.

Ecological and economic analyses of estuarine and marine degradation and management

Based on the Beijer Biodiversity Programme papers, we have analysed the ecological structure and relationships in estuarine and marine ecosystems, emphasizing the value of conserving biodiversity for the maintenance of diverse, resilient and functioning life support systems. We have also discussed the various impacts of economic activity on these ecosystems, in terms of direct effects from human uses and indirect effects from land based activities. The rest of the chapter reports on case studies within the Biodiversity Programme that analyse:

■   the policy failure of not taking into account the functions of estuarine, coastal and marine ecosystems in fisheries management; and
■   the economics of alternative management regimes for marine parks, fish farming and the value of biodiversity on island ecosystems.

We highlight efforts by ecologists and economists to analyse together the issue of a sustainable use of aquatic biodiversity.

MANAGEMENT AND POLICY

Fisheries management is often depicted as a renewable resource management problem, as discussed in Box 7.3. There are several specific issues that arise in the conventional approach to fisheries management. The first is the problem of open access resource use – whereby open access to fisheries may encourage excessive harvesting of fish stocks. The second is the impact of rapid technical changes in fishing vessels, which has enabled both the scope and scale of fishing activities to increase. As described in Box 7.3, both these characteristics can lead to the over-harvesting of fish stocks.

More recently, research has shown that management regimes are often developed with a poor understanding of fish ecology and rarely takes into account how the fish resources inter-relate with the marine or estuarine ecosystem as a whole. The concept of maximum sustainable yield has been in focus in fisheries management. But, as stressed by Ludwig, Hilborn and Walters (1993), due to the complexity, variability and uncertainty of how most estuaries and marine systems behave, the concept is hard to apply successfully.

In addition, some methods of fishing – in particular the creation of intensive fish farms – have adverse environmental impacts ('environmental externalities') that are not reflected in management decisions. Furthermore, government subsidies to the fish industry may have further distorted incentives for fish harvesting and promoted the development of an over-capitalized industry. Finally, fisheries management regimes often fail to look at 'external effects' on marine and estuarine ecosystems, for example, through polluted agricultural runoff, even though this may affect the ability of the marine/estuarine ecosystem to produce fish resources. This section looks at these management problems in more detail and provides case studies where possible.

Hammer (1994) describes offshore fishing communities in terms of 'biosphere people' as discussed in Chapter 4. Offshore fishing communities have become linked into global markets, and now use more sophisticated and effective fishing techniques and technology. The predominating fisheries management strategies have aimed at smoothing out and dampening natural fish stock fluctuations in order to achieve stable yields. To some extent this has been made possible by subsidies and advantageous loans for the construction and running of larger sea vessels. However, the rapid over-capitalization of the offshore fisheries has locked the system into a rigid structure, whose operations are detached and unable to respond to the ecological systems upon which they depend. Costanza, Kemp and Boynton (1993) also support the notion that financial incentive structures that

Box 7.3

Fisheries management as a renewable resource problem

The basic fisheries management problem is essentially a renewable resource problem and can be illustrated by Figure 7.2 below. The upside-down, U-shaped curve represents the natural growth rate of the resource $G(Q)$ which is a function of the size of the resource stock (a fishery). If the resource stock is either too low, Q_L, or too high, Q_M, the growth rate is zero. In contrast, population level Q^* leads to a maximum sustainable growth yield growth rate, as this is the maximum harvest level (that is, $q = G(Q^*)$) that can be sustained indefinitely without depleting the population.

In Figure 7.2 harvesting of the resource is represented by the upward sloping curve q, which is assumed to be a properly regulated, common property fishery. Note that at stock level Q_p, where the harvesting rate just equals the growth rate of the resource $(q = G(Q_p))$, the population is at a stationary state level. Given the relationship between the harvesting rate and the resource stock as shown, this stationary state must be stable in the long run. For example, if the initial resource stock is less than the stationary state level ($Q_O < Q_P$), the natural growth rate will exceed the harvesting rate. This means that the population will grow until it reaches the stationary state level, Q_P, where growth is just offset by harvesting. On the other hand, if $Q_O > Q_P$ harvesting will exceed natural growth. The population will therefore decline until, once again, the stationary state level Q_P is attained. So, no matter what the initial resource stocks are, given the rate of harvesting represented by curve q, the population will eventually settle down to the long run equilibrium represented by Q_P.

A frequent problem that occurs in fisheries is the breakdown of common property rules, thus creating a situation of open access resource use. When this occurs, users of the resource tend to harvest more for a given stock level as they will now ignore any user and externality cost. Thus curve q_c now represents the new

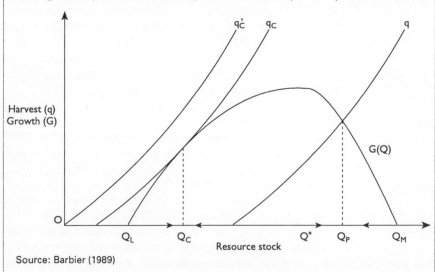

Source: Barbier (1989)

Figure 7.2   *The optimal depletion of a renewable resource*

harvesting rate. The new stationary state level should now be Q_c but this is not always sustainable in the long run. As the diagram shows, if the resource is initially greater than this level ($Q_0 > Q_c$) then harvesting exceeds natural growth and the stock will decline to Q_c as a long run equilibrium. If the initial stock is much lower, ($Q_0 < Q_c$), then harvesting will still exceed natural growth. As a result, the resource will not increase to Q_c in the long run but will instead decline towards zero. Hence, an open access resource may be exhausted to extinction if the initial stocks of that resource are too low.

A second problem that occurs in fisheries management is when the value of the harvested resource increases or technological change lowers the per unit harvesting costs. Under these conditions, users will be able to harvest even more for a given stock level. In Figure 7.2 this is represented by curve q_c, which has shifted even further to the left. As a consequence, harvesting always exceeds the natural growth rate, irrespective of the initial stock level, and the resource will eventually be exhausted.

have been developed for offshore fishing often lead to fishing activities that undermine the health and resilience of estuarine and marine ecosystems.

Faced by declining, poorer quality and more remote fish stocks, the fish industry has recently been developing intensive aquaculture management schemes through various forms of 'fish farms'. For example, intensive shrimp farming now occurs in ponds in coastal mangrove forests in South America and South-East Asia (for example, Bailey 1988; Primavera 1993). However, similar problems to offshore extensive fishing are occurring due to the sectorial focus in management on increased production at the rearing site. The capacity of the ecosystem and its species to support the expanding industry with resources and by processing its waste is hardly ever accounted for, and may undermine the objective of production maximization.

Aquaculture is often considered to be an economically efficient and environmentally benign alternative to marine and estuarine fisheries. However, in some cases, such as cage farming of Atlantic salmon, aquaculture is a more resource demanding system than the alternative system, in this case offshore salmon fisheries. At the same time the support from marine and coastal ecosystems, and the demand for ecological services, has not decreased. Aquaculture production still relies upon the maintenance of a healthy coastal and marine ecosystem for the provision of environmental functions, such as a large flow of water to flush waste products and to maintain adequate oxygen levels around the farm. The marine water surface area required to produce the food given to the salmon in the cages is about 1 km^2 per tonne of salmon that is produced. This area is similar independently of whether a salmon is cage farmed or caught in fisheries.

Salmon farming in cages highlights a further problem associated with intensive aquaculture. That is, as a throughput system it generates environmental impacts associated with the use of chemicals, medicines and antibiotics, as well as eutrophication derived from the use of artificial feed. Box 7.4 shows that when the external cost of eutrophication is included, the cost of production is estimated to be SKr 30/kg of salmon produced at the firm level. Given that the price of cage cultured salmon was approximately SKr 30/kg when profitability was at its peak, it suggests that the external costs of salmon production are high and may even outweigh the benefits of salmon production. Additional risks associated with salmon production include the potential outbreaks of diseases and parasites in the farms that may affect the surrounding natural flora and fauna, including other commercial fish and shellfish species. Farmed salmonids escaping from the cages are a substantial problem, since they migrate to rivers with natural populations, and may infect this stock and change the natural, and often highly specialized, genetic characteristics. The loss of marine and estuarine biodiversity may adversely affect the provision of ecological services, thus constraining the capacity for further fish farming. If the degradation goes too far there may be an irreversible decline in the system structure and its biota (Folke and Kautsky 1989 and 1992). In fact, conversions of natural marine and estuarine ecosystems to expand salmon farming have made it necessary to restore these ecosystems in order to maintain the farming systems (Regier and Baskerville 1986).

Box 7.5 shows how fish farming could be developed to be more organic and in tune with its coastal ecosystem through a combined culturing of seaweed, mussels and salmons. Integrated marine/estuarine and land use systems have already been developed in some areas. For example, the Pacific Basin is especially rich in customary marine tenure systems which provide ecologically sustainable yields that are resilient to external pressures (Ruddle, Hviding and Johannes 1992). East Asia and Oceania also had, and to some extent still have, a wealth of these integrated systems. In ancient Hawaii, both freshwater and seawater fish ponds were integrated with agriculture, and whole river valleys were managed as integrated systems, from the upland forest (left uncut by taboo) all the way to the reef, as shown in Figure 7.4. Both freshwater and seawater fish ponds were managed in synergy with agriculture, as a total food production system. Waste from one system was used as a resource in the other system. In this case, some 10 to 20 species were cultivated in four different kinds of fish ponds. Although the number of cultivated species was lower than in the natural environment, both agriculture and aquaculture production systems were relatively diverse, and 'in tune' with natural ecosystem processes and biodiversity (Gadgil, Berkes and Folke 1993). These institutions evolved with their resource base and were able to balance resource use rights against responsibilities (Berkes, Folke and Gadgil 1994).

Nelson and Serafin (1992) argue that thinking in terms of sustainability means assessing the biodiversity of an area in relation to changes in land use, and with regard to equity or access to opportunity for all involved groups and persons. This requires availability to information, and the involvement of those affected and those knowledgeable about the local situation. For this purpose a land and resource use survey called the abiotic, biotic and cultural or ABC resource survey has been developed. The survey provides for systematically mapping geology, soils, forests, coastal areas, wildlife habitat, land use, land tenure, social and any other relevant information in an area in relation to conservation and development. The ABC method has, over the years, been increasingly used to assess land use changes in terms of the inter-relationships between nature and culture, for example, in park management, and river and coastal planning. Such a pluralistic

Box 7.4

Internalizing external costs of salmon farming

Salmon farming in cages requires lots of resources collected by fishing vessels operating over vast marine ecosystems. Salmon farming also releases substantial amounts of waste and pollutants into coastal and estuarine environments. In the Rio Declaration the international community argued that a major cause of environmental degradation is due to the fact that polluters do not pay for the pollution they cause. Therefore, national authorities should strive to promote the internalization of environmental costs. The internalization is an attempt to narrow the differences between the private and social value.

Large amounts of money are spent on reducing outlets of nutrients from point sources to coastal waters. In Sweden, a major measure to reduce municipal sewage effluents has been to build sewage treatment plants. The costs for reducing outlets of nutrients from sewage treatment plants can be interpreted as Swedish society's willingness to pay at the margin for nutrient reductions. The cost of eutrophication to Swedish society from a fish farm producing 100 tons of salmon would then be at least SKr 425,000–725,000, or around 4–4.55 SKr per kg nutrients released from the farm. This estimate covers only parts of the external environmental costs generated by the fish farming industry.

What would the production cost look like for the salmon farming industry if fish farmers would have to pay the external costs to society of the nutrient releases they cause? That is, if the cost of eutrophication caused by the salmon farming were to be internalized. During the 1980s, when the fish farming industry boomed, the highest price paid to the farmer for cage cultured salmon in Sweden was about SKr 30 per kg. Due to the enormous expansion of farmed salmon production, not only in Scandinavia but worldwide, there has been a considerable drop in prices. Internalizing the cost of eutrophication at the level of the firm would increase the production cost to more than SKr 30 for each kg of salmon that is produced. With the costs of eutrophication internalized, the production cost actually exceeds the highest price paid for farmed salmonids in the 1980s, the decade when profitability of salmon farming in cages peaked.

Hence, internalizing only one of several non-priced social costs can in some cases be sufficient to reveal whether an industry behaves in a sustainable fashion or not. Ideally, not only the external costs of eutrophication but all external costs (some of which would be very difficult to estimate) should be included in the cost of production. This would, of course, further eliminate the profitability of farming salmon in cages in coastal waters.

Source:Folke, Kautsky and Troell (1994)

approach is applied in a literature review of biodiversity and coastal management, and planning for areas in the US, Canada and Poland (Serafin and Nelson 1992).

Costanza, Kemp and Boynton (1993) suggest that the '4P' approach should be tested in the management of coastal and estuarine ecosystems. This is a flexible environmental assurance bonding system, a variant of a deposit refund system combining the polluter pays and the precautionary principles (namely, the '4Ps'). Strong economic incentives are provided by the bonding system to reduce

Box 7.5

A combined aquaculture system in coastal waters

Figure 7.3 is a sketch of a combined aquaculture system of seaweed, mussels and salmon in coastal waters. Waste from the salmon cage is used as a food resource for the mussels and seaweeds, and parts of the mussels are fed to the salmon. This would not only reduce resource use, waste problems and other environmental impacts, but, if effectively dimensioned, it will also transform excess nutrients from domestic sources into biomass and marketable products, that is, seaweed, mussels and salmon. The integrated system is taken to be an improvement in comparison to the unsustainable cage farming of salmon in monocultures. The economic and ecological feasibility of such systems is being tested in the coastal waters of southern Chile.

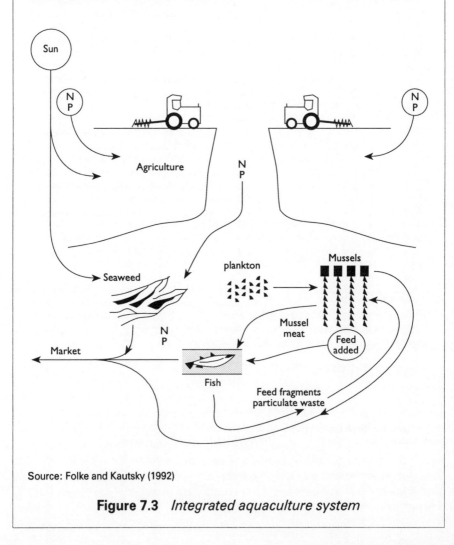

Source: Folke and Kautsky (1992)

Figure 7.3   *Integrated aquaculture system*

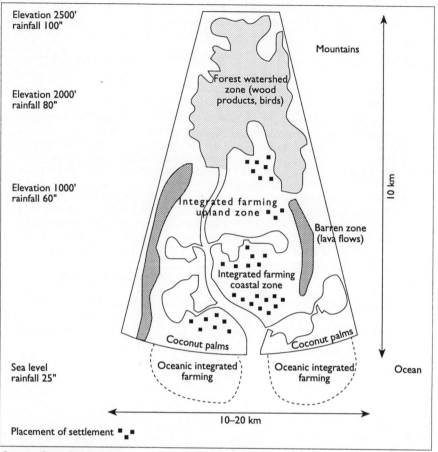

Source: Costa-Pierce (1987)

Figure 7.4   *Integrated ecosystem management in ancient Hawaii*

pollution, to research the true costs of activities that impact on biodiversity and ecological resilience, and to develop new innovative and cost-effective pollution control technologies. Further discussion of the use of such instruments in controlling biodiversity loss generally can be found in Chapter 9.

Dixon, Scura and van't Hof (1993) analyse how private incentives can be made consistent with the protection of marine parks in the Caribbean. They investigate the trade-offs between prevention of biodiversity loss in the Bonaire Marine Park and the use of the area to generate income, usually from tourism and sport diving. They found that with the right institutions and incentives marine parks can be effective means of protecting marine biodiversity and ecological resilience while still allowing direct use of the marine ecosystem. Dixon, Scura and van't Hof also stress the importance of ensuring that a larger share of the economic benefits of tourism are retained in the local economy. Their combined ecological and economic study is briefly summarized in Box 7.6.

In another study from the Carribean Islands, Narain and Fisher (1994) value the ecological service of lizards for the exports of sugar cane, bananas and cocoa,

Box 7.6

Meeting ecological and economic goals in marine parks

A study on the Bonaire Marine Park, in the Caribbean, combined an ecological analysis of carrying capacity with an economic analysis of the recreational value of the park, in terms of scuba diving. The private sector revenues were estimated at US$23 million per year and the governmental at just below US$9 million per year. The costs of establishment, subsequent rehabilitation, initial operation annual costs were calculated at about US$0.6 million. The direct and indirect income from the diving activities are, however, dependent on the quality of the marine park. Too many divers and impacts from other human activities, such as yachting and improper disposal of waste, degrade the marine park. Hence, increased dive tourism may begin to result in measurable degradation of the marine environment. Thereby, the social carrying capacity becomes limited by ecological carrying capacity. But, as stressed earlier in this book, social carrying capacity is to a large extent dependent on the behaviour of humans toward their environment. Hence, if the behaviour of divers and the management of the park are improved there is an opportunity to increase dive tourism. But the expansion is completely dependent on the premiss that this proper and sustainable behaviour is strictly followed. Otherwise the Bonaire Marine Park and the revenues it generates will collapse.

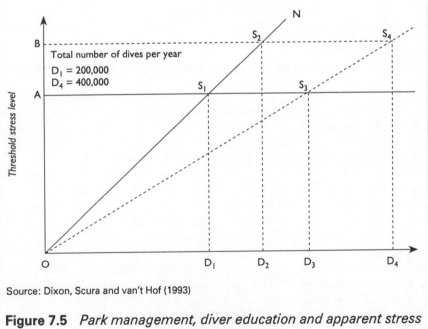

Source: Dixon, Scura and van't Hof (1993)

Figure 7.5 *Park management, diver education and apparent stress threshold*

through the application of a production function approach. Lizards prey on the pests that reduce the yield of these primary commodities. Without the lizards the cost of cultivation rises through an increase in the demand for pesticides. Their study on the economic valuation of the ecological service provided by lizards is summarized in Box 7.7.

Box 7.7

Modelling the value of island biodiversity using a production function approach

The Greater and Lesser Antilles in the Carribean rely heavily on the export of sugar cane, bananas, and cocoa. These exports form the basis for the economic well-being of the human population on these islands. The Anolis lizard feeds on insects that otherwise would reduce the production of the primary commodities for export. A reduction in the lizard population implies a need for an increase in the use of pesticides to combat the pests. Hence, the lizard can decrease the cost of cultivation by reducing the demand for pesticides. A production function approach was used to estimate the value of the lizard in the food production. First estimates and preliminary results indicate that the value of lost output due to a 1 per cent reduction in the population of Anolis lizard would correspond to about US$670,000. The maximum possible value of lost annual production would be US$455 million. This is the case if there were to be a catastrophic decline in the lizard population, perhaps to the point of extinction.

Source:Narain and Fisher (1994).

Hammer, Jansson and Jansson (1993) note that fisheries management often fails to take into account the 'external driving forces' that reduce fish quantity and quality. These 'external driving forces' may include land use activities, such as urbanization, infrastructure development, industrialization, forestry and agriculture, which have environmental impacts on coastal and estuarine ecosystems, and their biological diversity. It has been argued that a successful management of large estuaries requires that the economic activities and the external driving forces in their drainage basins are addressed (Folke, Hammer and Jansson 1991; Norton and Ulanowicz 1992). Such an approach has been extensively applied to the management of the Great Lakes drainage basins (for example, Friend 1993). Integrated ecological and economic studies with the purpose of improving the environmental condition of the Baltic Sea, are presently under way for the whole Baltic Sea drainage basin, in another major research programme of the Beijer Institute.

CHALLENGES TO BE ADDRESSED

There are several critical challenges to be addressed by ecologists and economists working together for biodiversity conservation in estuarine and marine ecosystems.

■ First, it is important to monitor and improve our understanding of the dynamics of estuarine and marine ecosystems, including their resilience and thresholds. This will assist in the development of management regimes that are sensitive to the species and its ecosystem, and that respond to environmental changes. Making management adaptive to the pulses and fluctuations in estuarine and marine ecosystems is a particular area that needs further research. Management practices that are more in tune with ecological processes and functions could, in the long run, provide a more sustainable, and potentially more efficient, use of coastal and marine biodiversity.

■ Second, more resource saving uses of marine and estuarine biodiversity need to be developed to offset the detrimental environmental impacts of fishing and other exploitative activities on the natural resource base. Further economic assessment and valuation of alternative uses of biodiversity, reflecting the full costs and benefits of any environmental impacts where possible, including the insurance value of aquatic biodiversity, also need to be undertaken to enable informed decisions over the allocation of demands for marine and estuarine resources.

■ Third, fisheries, aquaculture and other uses of estuarine, coastal and marine ecosystems need to be treated as integrated, rather than isolated, sectors. In particular, the external effects of land use activities (such as polluted water runoff) on fisheries need to be recognized, analysed and taken into account in fisheries management.

■ Finally, existing distortionary policies (such as subsidies for fisheries) that create incentives for misuse and overuse of estuarine and marine biodiversity need to be addressed. In addition, the pervasive problem of open access conditions to estuarine and marine resources, not only for resource users but also polluters, needs to be avoided.

8

Rangelands

The loss of biological diversity in rangelands is often not perceived as a key issue in the global biodiversity problem, especially when compared to the rapid rates of species extinction in the moist tropical forests. However, as this book has emphasized, the problem of biodiversity loss is not constrained to the direct costs of species extinction. Indeed, for rangeland ecosystems it is the impact of a change in the mix of species that is important. For example, a shift in the mix of vegetation biomass from palatable grasses to unpalatable grasses and woody plants reduces the ecological support function, namely, provision of fodder, required for livestock management. A decrease in the capacity of rangelands for livestock production has serious implications for current and future generations. In particular, some low income groups, such as nomadic pastoralists, are highly dependent upon rangeland production. In addition, the long term significance of biodiversity change in semi-arid regions makes the problem of biodiversity loss particularly acute.

In this chapter we look at the ecological and economic issues surrounding the problem of rangeland degradation. The research papers prepared for the Beijer Biodiversity Programme focus on two specific, but related, aspects of this problem:

- first, the need to revise our understanding about rangeland ecology and look at its implications for livestock management; and
- second, the need to address the prevailing problem of open access rangeland use, and appraise common property management regimes and social structures that have emerged to deal with this situation.

IDENTIFICATION AND ANALYSIS

Defining what constitutes a rangeland and measuring the rate of rangeland degradation is no easy task. Although much research effort has been put into exploring the status and changes in rangelands, we are still far from establishing a reliable rangeland database and monitoring system. However, it is clear that rangeland degradation is occurring at a substantial rate and that the socio-economic effects of this are significant. The following section looks at the current status and trends in rangeland degradation, and the recent insights into rangeland ecology.

Global status and trends

Rangelands are generally located in arid and semi-arid regions of the world. In their natural state, they consist of a vegetation mix of grasses and woody plants in various proportions. The extremes of pure grassland (such as prairies) and pure shrubland can be included in a definition of rangelands, but semi-arid savannah land is the more typical form of rangeland.

The primary determinants of rangeland vegetation are minimum temperature, plant available moisture and soil fertility. Rainfall, soil type, herbivores and fire are the major determinants of rangeland structure, and all four are strongly interactive as shown in Figure 8.1. Heavier textured soils with adequate water produce more palatable and nutritious fodder, and are relatively productive, but they are easily changed through management practices and may display substantial diversity of states in terms of woody to grass ratios, from open grassland with a few trees to dense thicket. These soils are highly sensitive to drought conditions, heavy grazing and fire. In contrast, the high woody biomass found on sandy soils is less productive, more resilient to such pressures and displays less interannual variation in fodder supply.

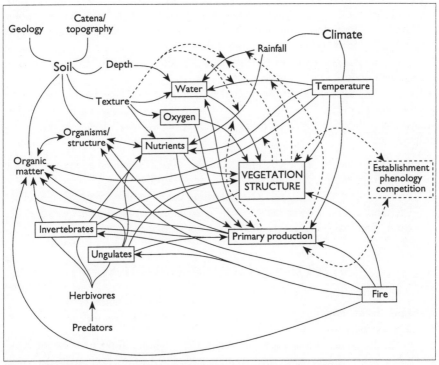

Notes: Solid lines are direct effects, broken lines represent secondary effects.
Source: Walker (1993)

Figure 8.1 *Generalized model of detriments of savannah structure*

Rangelands are mainly used for livestock production. Systems of rangeland management vary considerably, from nomadic pastoralism through mixed subsistence farming (relying mainly on livestock) to commercial ranching. The ecological structure of much rangeland was radically altered through human use many, many years ago. However, most rangelands are currently displaying signs of over-use resulting from current management regimes and technological developments (namely, water development, disease control, improved breeds and so on), which lead to greater pressure on the natural resource base (Walker 1993).

Change in grazing pressure is the most important cause of changes in the biodiversity mix in semi-arid savannahs. If economic pressure on a rangeland ecosystem causes it to 'crash', then economic activities dependent upon the rangeland will also be disrupted. A key underlying cause of such 'crashes' is the alteration in species diversity and its effect on rangeland resilience. The ecological and ensuing economic problems raised by biodiversity loss in rangelands provide a major driving force for improved analysis of rangeland degradation.

A selection of biological and physical indicators of range degradation have been proposed, and these are summarized in Table 8.1 (Behnke and Scoones 1993). These factors provide a broad indication of changes in the status of rangelands. However, the extent to which changes in factors such as soil, vegetation and livestock production constitute 'rangeland degradation' ultimately depends upon the definition of degradation being employed.

Table 8.1   *Biophysical indicators of rangeland degradation*

Soil changes	Decreased fertility Decreased water holding capacity Decreased infiltration Soil loss significantly in excess of soil formation
Vegetation changes	Changes in vegetation productivity over time, unrelated to rainfall patterns Changes in vegetation cover Changes of plant species composition of use to animals Shifts between vegetation transition states that result in decreased fodder
Livestock production changes	Changes in condition scoring of animals Changes in calving rates and death rates Changes in milk yields

Source: Behnke and Scoones (1993)

Rangeland degradation is often described in terms of its capacity to support livestock production. Using this approach, rangeland degradation can be defined as an irreversible decline in its potential for livestock production. Traditionally, changes in vegetation (such as vegetation productivity, vegetation cover, plant species, and vegetation states) have been used as the primary indicators of degradation.

Vegetation changes, however, may be an unreliable indication of changes in the functioning and resilience of rangelands for livestock production. In particular, large fluctuations in species composition, plant biomass and cover are characteristic of arid and semi-arid rangelands, due to the erratic rainfall patterns. Rangeland vegetation has adapted to, and is often capable of recovering from, natural disturbances, such as periods of drought. Therefore, while the productivity and composition of rangelands may appear disturbed in the short run, they may be resilient over a longer period and able to recover their productive capacity.

Under these conditions, degradation may be considered to occur only after the vegetation has passed, or is at the risk of passing, a critical threshold from which it irreversibly enters a lower productive state. One obvious problem for ecologists is to determine when vegetation is temporarily disturbed or has entered a permanently degraded state. Other factors, such as soil changes or livestock production, may prove more reliable indicators, or at least provide support to existing indicators, of range degradation.

Table 8.2 provides information on the global status of rangeland degradation, as part of a larger information base on desertification (Toulmin 1993; UNEP 1991). The statistics are based on data from the Global Assessment of Soil Degradation (GLASOD) programme carried out at the University of Wageningen in The Netherlands for the FAO, and data from the International Center for Arid and Semi-arid Land Studies (ICASALS) at the Texas Technical University, USA.

Table 8.2   *Status of desertification worldwide*

Land classification	Million hectares	% of total drylands
1 Degraded irrigated lands	43	0.8
2 Degraded rainfed crop lands	216	4.1
3 Degraded rangelands (soil and vegetation degradation)	757	14.6
4 Drylands with human-induced soil degradation (1 + 2 + 3)	1016	19.5
5 Degraded rangelands (vegetation degradation without soil degradation)	2576	50.0
6 Total degraded drylands (4 + 5)	3592	69.5
7 Non-degraded drylands	1580	30.5
8 Total area of drylands excluding hyper-arid deserts	5172	100.0

Source: Toulmin (1993); original source UNEP (1991).

Not surprisingly, different methods of estimating degradation produce substantially different results. In particular, estimates of degraded rangelands based on vegetation degradation alone produce far higher estimates of rangeland degradation (2576 mn ha) than that based on both vegetation and soil degradation (757 mn ha). As noted earlier, vegetation degradation may just be a temporary phenomenon resulting from a shift in rainfall patterns and thus a rather misleading indication of rangeland degradation. Toulmin (1993) stresses that the accuracy of information on rangeland degradation is extremely poor and can only provide a broad indication of the problem for policy makers. The usefulness of rangeland degradation data for planning and range management purposes is extremely limited.

Rangeland ecology revisited

In recent years, the conceptual framework providing the basis for rangeland ecology and the economics of rangeland management has been challenged. Like many other natural resource utilization problems, the traditional dynamic rangeland model ignores the major evolutionary properties of the natural system.

The basic model of rangelands dynamics is derived from Clementsian theory of ecological economics (Clements 1916). This is based on the theory of succession, whereby one association or community of plant species is assumed to replace another in an orderly and directional process. In the successional model, range condition is expected to change along a single, linear, or at least monotonic, gradient in response to rainfall and grazing pressure, as shown in Figure 8.2.

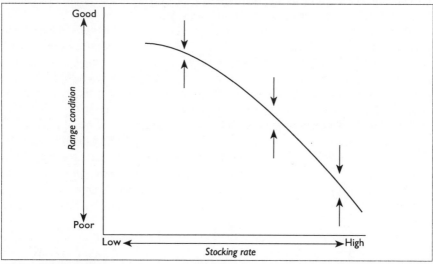

Source: Walker (1993).

Figure 8.2 *Assumed relationship between stocking rate and range condition*

Any particular rangeland site is depicted as having a single, persistent and characteristic vegetative state, called the climax, which represents the end stage of the succession. If this climax is disturbed, the vegetation would none the less return through a successional sequence to the climax, assuming no further disturbances. Inter-annual variation in rainfall causes vegetation to move up and down the successional gradient, and drought is assumed to exert pressure away from the successional tendency. Abnormal grazing conditions may also exert pressure in the opposite direction to the successional tendency, thus resulting in a dis-climax state. Fire may arrest the successional tendency, resulting in a sub-climax state (Walker 1993).

The management implications of the Clementsian theory involve selecting a stocking rate that balances the successional tendency, grazing pressure and pressures such as rainfall variation, so that a desired condition of rangeland is achieved. Management may aim to maintain the rangeland with little or no erosion and palatable perennial grasses in order to yield a sustainable and economically viable livestock offtake. In an equilibrium climax state, herd density has a dominant effect on herd dynamics.

Over the past decade there have been several criticisms of the Clementsian model and its ability adequately to characterize rangeland ecology. In some cases these criticisms have been based on a misunderstanding and misapplication of the model for rangeland management. The most common misperception of the Clementsian model is the notion of fixing the carrying capacity such that a constant herd density is maintained, regardless of the combined anti-successional tendencies of drought and grazing pressure. In addition, the multiple uses of livestock by pastoralists (for example, for meat, milk, draught, transport, manure, store of wealth and social obligations) may not be taken into consideration in the application of this model. Box 8.1 explores in more detail differences between various ecological and economic carrying capacities.

Other criticisms of the Clementsian model focus on its capacity to cope with a highly complex rangeland ecology. Although Clementsian successional processes are undoubtedly at work, the realities confronting rangelands are not adequately explored in this model. In particular, rangeland characteristics such as spatial variation and dynamics, event driven change, lag effects, thresholds, multiple trajectories of change and irreversibility need to be incorporated into the rangeland model (Solbrig 1993). This is discussed in more detail in Box 8.2.

Behnke and Scoones (1993) challenge the notion that any particular equilibrium climax state exists for some rangelands. They propose that some types of rangeland are in a state of dis-equilibrium or non-equilibrium. In systems that are 'away from equilibrium', density independent factors, such as rainfall, are seen to be the dominant factors explaining herd dynamics, rather than herd density.

Although we have learnt important lessons about rangeland ecology and the limits of the existing model, rangeland management still tends to rely heavily on the Clementsian linear succession model. This is partly because economists and rangeland managers are fixed into existing analytical frameworks and management strategies, but also because up until recently there has not been an alternative, easily understood and conceptually appealing model. As Walker (1993) eloquently describes the situation:

> Confronted with this array of complicating factors, the likely response of an applied economist, looking for a rangelands model, would be to throw up her hands in horror and turn back to Clements. It therefore behoves ecologists to provide a workable, alternative model.

One attempt to respond to the need for an improved rangeland model is

Box 8.1

Ecological and economic carrying capacity

Scoones (1993) distinguishes between economic and ecological carrying capacity of rangeland:

- ecological carrying capacity refers to the maximum number of animals the land can hold without being subject to density dependent mortality and permanent environmental degradation – this is determined by environmental factors;
- economic carrying capacity is the stocking rate that offers maximum economic returns and is determined by the economic objectives of the producers, namely, by their definition of productivity.

Livestock productivity can be measured in several ways, such as production per animal or production per unit area. Productivity may encompass beef production only (such as weight of beef produced per cow per year) or meat and beef production (such as measures of the productive energy of the pastoral system or protein output). When there are multiple economic uses of cattle (such as meat, beef, draught, transport, manure, store of wealth, social obligations and so on) finding a single unit of assessment is complex. Replacement cost, that is the value of marketed substitutes, can be used as an indication of the monetary value of the livestock. However, this may not adequately reflect all the use values, especially the non-marketed use values. In addition, the economic carrying capacity may need to take into account any trade-offs between competing uses, such as draught versus meat and milk.

Figure 8.3 indicates that different economic carrying capacities exist under different production objectives. While low stocking rates may be appropriate for beef production alone, under multiple use much higher stocking rates may be appropriate. The assumption that traditional pastoralists maintain uneconomically high stocking rates is often based on a misunderstanding of herders' objectives.

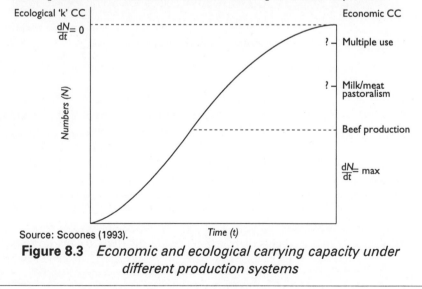

Source: Scoones (1993).

Figure 8.3 *Economic and ecological carrying capacity under different production systems*

Box 8.2
Rangeland models and dynamics

Rangeland models need to reflect the complex dynamics of rangeland structures and conditions.

- *Spatial variation and dynamics* – the basic Clementsian model assumes homogenous rangeland condition. However, site differences induced by the interaction of topography and rainfall, historical effects or community processes result in spatially and dynamically heterogeneous rangeland. For example, soil erosion, transportation and deposition in rangelands can operate at a number of scales simultaneously, resulting in a redistribution of water nutrients. This creates a mosaic of nutrious fodder patches offering high production potential, within a larger background area of poor quality vegetation with low production potential.

- *The significance of rare and extreme events* – the theory of plant succession is based on the assumption that continuous or very small incremental change in species composition is brought about through biotic reaction, namely, modification by plants and animals of the abiotic environment. While these changes do occur in rangelands, abrupt and discontinuous changes are also highly significant. Changes in rangeland species composition are often episodic, namely, occur in response to extreme or rare events, or a particular sequence of events, such as a very dry year following a very wet year, or two successive years of drought.

- *Lag effects, thresholds, multiple trajectories of change and irreversibility* – the succession model assumes linear, reversible changes in response to grazing pressure and fluctuations in rainfall towards a single stable state. However, in practice, rangelands are often characterized by a combination of lag effects, thresholds, irreversibilities and multiple trajectories of change towards a range of 'meta-stable' states. For example, soil degradation is essentially irreversibile, unless new deposition enabling soil development occurs, and often has a lagged, negative feedback effect on the ecological system. In addition, shifts in species composition within the grass layer may exhibit threshold effects, and different stable states may emerge from grazing pressure combined with changes in soil conditions.

Source: Walker (1993)

Westoby's 'state and transition model' (Westoby, Walker and Noy-Meir 1985). As described in Box 8.3, the state and transition model assumes that a potential array of rangeland states exists. Their existence, and movement between the different states, depends upon a combination of natural and humanmade events. States can be differentiated by their differences in species composition and the ability to move to a different state. A key insight of the state and transition model is that evolution occurs via discontinuous and often irreversible shifts from one 'persistent' locally stable equilibrium to another.

For example, grasslands of semi-arid east and southern Africa maintain a natural dynamic balance between two functionally different groups of grasses. One group is tolerant to grazing and drought, with the capacity to hold soil and water. The other is more productive in terms of plant biomass but is less drought

Box 8.3

The state and transition model of rangelands

The 'state and transition' model provides a conceptual model explicitly to examine rangeland dynamics. The basis of the model is as follows.

- There exist a number of possible rangeland states. States can differ in terms of their vegetation type (such as palatable and unpalatable grasses). They may also differ in their potential influence on future states (such as similar vegetative rangelands, but one contains seeds of woody plants and one does not).
- There are various transitional paths through which a range may move from one state to another. An ongoing stream of events dictates the movement along a transitionary path (for example, natural characteristics such as water and fire, or management actions such as stocking rates and burning).

Very simply, the state and transition model assumes that there exists a range of possible states and a catalogue of possible transitions between these states. Application of the model requires identification of the interacting 'landscape units' within the rangeland area and sub-division of the rangeland into these internally homogeneous units. Landscape units include the source, transfer and sink areas. A change in state may therefore reflect a change in composition and performance of the units, and/or a change in the proportions of the units. Practical application of the model obviously requires detailed knowledge of the specific rangeland, including rangeland changes and their causes.

The state and transition model implies various possible management opportunities and hazards. An opportunity consists of circumstances under which a state may change to a more preferable state, for example, to a more productive state. A hazard is the opposite, that is conditions under which a state has the potential to change to an inferior state. The objectives for management under the state and transition model are basically to seize the opportunities and to avoid the hazards, namely, opportunistic management.

Source: Walker (1993); and Perrings and Walker (1994).

resistant. Under the natural cycle of grazing by large herbivores, a diversity of species is supported that serves ecological functions of productivity on the one hand and drought protection on the other. However, stocking the range with ranched cattle at a 'sustained' moderate level of grazing can upset this balance. The modest and persistent grazing favours the productive over the drought resistent species. Thus diversity narrows to one type of function, drought protection is reduced, and the grassland may 'flip' and become dominated and controlled by woody shrubs of low value for grazing (Perrings and Walker 1994; Walker 1993).

The state and transition model provides a basis for taking the individual characteristics of rangeland ecosystems, such as rainfall, topography, soil type and biological composition, into consideration in rangeland management. In practice, the usefulness of the model crucially depends upon the manager's knowledge and understanding of the rangeland, ability to incorporate this information into the analytical framework provided by the state and transition model, and the manager's capacity to respond to the predictions of the model.

MANAGEMENT AND POLICY

Poor rangeland management practices, compounded by problems of open access and distortionary government policies, have contributed to rangeland degradation. In this section we address these management and policy issues in more detail.

Implications of rangeland ecology for management

In the previous section we introduced the management implications of the Clementsian theory, that is, selecting a stocking rate that balances the successional tendency, grazing pressure and pressures such as rainfall variation, so that a desired condition of rangeland (such as no erosion or palatable grasses) is achieved. It was also noted that misguided application of the traditional rangeland model can lead to inappropriate stocking levels and rangeland degradation. However, even 'proper' implementation of the Clementsian model can lead to adverse implications for rangeland ecosystems – simply because the dynamic evolution of the ecosystem is seldom accounted for. The problem of 'over-grazing' is addressed in Box 8.4.

Box 8.4
Ecological and economic over-grazing

Ecological over-grazing may be either 'fundamental' or 'current'. Fundamental over-grazing occurs when the equilibrium level of grazing pressure exceeds the level of grazing pressure corresponding to the maximum sustainable yield of the range. Current over-grazing occurs when the current level of grazing pressure exceeds that corresponding to the maximum sustainable yield of the range.

Economic over-grazing exists if the actual level of grazing pressure exceeds the economically optimal level of grazing pressure. The optimal level of grazing pressure is not necessarily the same as the level of grazing pressure corresponding to the maximum sustainable yield of the range. Whether optimal grazing pressure is greater or less than the maximum sustainable grazing pressure depends on the economic parameters of the system, namely, the relative prices facing resource users.

If relative prices are such that it is optimal to 'mine' the range, the optimal grazing pressure will exceed the maximum sustainable grazing pressure. This implies that fundamental ecological over-grazing will occur. If relative prices are consistent with the sustainable use of the resource, the optimal grazing pressure will be less than or equal to the maximum sustainable grazing pressure.

Source: Perrings (1993).

Walker (1993) discusses how spatially variable and dynamic rangelands require management regimes that are sensitive to local ecosystem changes over space and time. The effect of heterogeneous rangeland conditions on production depends upon several factors, including the mean annual rainfall, the degree of redistribution, the composition of species, and the shape of the vegetation growth response curve to changes in soil moisture and nutrients. For example, high production potential areas often develop within low production, poor vegetation regions. These areas are extremely sensitive to grazing pressure, and excessive grazing results in larger and larger patches, and a shift towards more extreme states of erosion and deposition. The failure of management regimes to take rangeland heterogeneity into consideration leads to zones of rangeland degradation with negative feedback effects on future livestock production.

Episodic effects on rangelands (that is to say, rare and extreme events, or a particular sequence of events, that drive rangeland structure) also need to be reflected in rangeland management decisions. What is more, episodic events combined with spatial variation can lead to a polarization of effects. For example, in source areas, the potential for change gets progressively less, and requires bigger and bigger events. In sink areas, episodic changes can occur in response to more frequent and smaller events. The failure of the management system to recognize and respond to significant events, and their potential impact across the rangeland, can again lead to excessive environmental degradation and a reduction in the potential for livestock production, especially in sensitive zones.

The state and transition model attempts to take the complex dynamics of rangeland ecology into account. In particular, it recognizes that fodder production may be variable in time and space, changes in vegetation and productive potential may be irreversible, and shifts in vegetation composition may occur episodically in response to events, such as a specific climate sequence and grazing pressure. As noted in Box 8.3, the objective of managers using the state and transition model is to understand the rangeland states and the potential transitory paths that are determined by a complex web of events. Managers need to be able to respond appropriately to opportunities and hazards that may present themselves, in other words, take an opportunistic management approach.

Underlying uncertainty about the various states that prevail, the potential for moving along transitory paths and specific rangeland responses to particular events, make the state and transition approach extremely difficult to manage. Management strategies are therefore necessarily risk based and attitudes towards risk generally depend upon how well managers can survive a severe loss. Management approaches therefore ultimately depend upon how well managers can predict range response and how risk averse they are. Predictions will improve and risks will be reduced the better the managers understand the dynamics and functions of the rangeland – including the role of biodiversity.

One particular requirement of the state and transition model is the need to respond quickly to opportunities and hazards. Attempts to maintain constant stock rates are frequently inappropriate. Instead, the ability to vary herd structure is required. In a commercial enterprise, this generally calls for variable herd stocking rates and browsing ranges. Flexible herd management has implications for herd composition, for example, a high proportion of readily saleable animals and low proportion of breeding females. The failure of management to respond at the right time and in the right way to specific events can have negative feedbacks into the rangeland ecosystem. This in turn has further implications for the productive potential of the rangeland and future management decisions.

Perrings and Walker (1994) use the insights provided by the state and transition model to consider the implications for decision making in the livestock sector. The main lesson drawn from the model is that 'evolution of the mix of vegetation species in semi-arid rangelands occurs via discontinuous and often irreversible shifts from one "persistent" locally stable equilibrium to another'. A locally stable equilibrium (or persistent state) implies that in the absence of grazing pressure and extreme natural 'events', the carrying capacity of the range will converge to some positive equilibrium value. Discontinuous change occurs when one state makes a transition to another state. The transition occurs when the locally stable equilibrium state is perturbed beyond the bounds of its stability. There are two potential and generally inter-related causes of this transition.

- An exogenous environmental shock (such as a severe or prolonged drought, fire or storms), which may cause the system to move beyond its limits and enter another state. However, management actions at the locally stable equilibrium state, such as a change in the stocking rate, the depletion of some existing species or the introduction of a new species, may create preconditions for the evolution of the locally stable system by altering its resilience to exogenous shocks.
- An endogenous force (such as an increase in livestock numbers, changes in vegetation or grazing patterns), which may drive the unstable system from one state to another. The limits of local stability of any given equilibrium (in the absence of further management intervention) define the threshold values for livestock, vegetation, water flows and so on. If these threshold values are exceeded, the system may undergo an irreversible change.

Two classes of decision problems are identified – those associated with the locally stable equilibrium rangeland states and those associated with transition between states; hence, the term state and transition model (see Boxes 8.3 and 8.5). If rangeland management is to be truly 'opportunistic' it must balance as well as exploit the conditions that make the system vulnerable to the combined effects of exogenous environmental shocks and endogenous forces. Management of key variables in the system, such as stocking rates as well as the overall mix of species, is important for determining the appropriate responses to external shocks and ensuring key threshold values are not exceeded by endogenous forces. The challenge is to let changes occur in the system that will lead to desired economic gain – such as improved productive value of the rangeland – while at the same time not allowing such changes to disrupt the overall resilience of the system and the economic activities dependent on it. Maintaining the biological diversity contained in a rangeland is obviously important to the overall resilience and functioning of the system, but as is the case with all crucial management decisions and responses, the exact amount of biodiversity conserved will depend critically on whether the system as a whole is at an equilbrium state or in transition.

Box 8.5
The state and transition decision tree

The state and transition decision tree provides a comprehensive framework for comparing rangeland management options, which may imply transition from one state to another. For example, two possible stocking strategies may exist for each state of the rangeland. Each strategy is assumed to involve a different optimal level of grazing pressure. The transition possibilities for each state are a function of the stocking strategy applied, plus some random event or set of events. Under any given stocking strategy the rangeland state may either persist or transmute into some other state. A comparison of the option can be made using the following decision tree.

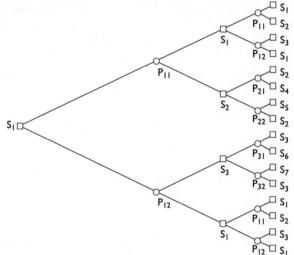

Figure 8.4 *The state and transition decision tree*

In Figure 8.4, the rangeland states, S_i, form decision nodes, to which correspond stocking strategies P_{ij}. Given an estimate for the probability of the events or shocks that drive the system, and given the sensitivity of any state to such events under each stocking strategy, the probability that a state will persist or transmute under a given stocking strategy will be known. The expected value of all stocking strategies and hence the optimal policy will be identified.

Source: Perrings and Walker (1994).

Perrings and Walker (1994) show that, if the optimal level of grazing pressure implies maintenance of rangeland resilience to natural shocks over time, then the solution derived from the state and transition model is the same as that derived from the range succession or Clementsian model. However, under the conditions assumed above, there is nothing to prevent the optimal level of offtake from being ecologically unsustainable. Optimal grazing may have negative feedback effects on the rangeland ecosystem and drive the system beyond the bounds of local stability. For example, the system may lose resilience to climatic shocks due to the stress resulting from continual exploitation by an economic activity (such as grazing).

Perrings and Walker (1994) extend the above analysis to address the problem of optimal resource allocation under discontinuous evolution of rangelands. This involves taking into consideration the prevailing and future possible states, as well as the transition between states. For example, stocking decisions at the prevailing state may cause the system to lose resilience. The opportunity cost of the loss of control that occurs around the unstable equilibria needs to be taken into account. If stocking densities threaten the stability of the prevailing state, then the full opportunity costs and benefits of all states reachable from the current state need to be taken into account.

The choice of appropriate stocking strategy can be made using the state and transition decision tree, which is introduced in Box 8.5. By assessing the full costs and benefits of alternative states, and the probabilities of reaching those states, the expected value of all stocking strategies can be determined and thus the optimal policy identified. Unfortunately, given the data constraints and our limited understanding of system functions, changes to the self-organization of ecosystems that lose resilience or local stability are not *a priori* predictable. High levels of uncertainty may undermine full implementation of this approach in practice. Even if this is the case, this approach provides a clearer framework for exploring the range of alternative rangeland management options and comparing these options.

To summarize, the traditional model of rangeland ecology has been revisited and revised to reflect more fully the dynamics of rangeland systems. This has implications for management strategies. Whereas in the past environmental economists have tended to argue that stocking densities are the key criteria for range management, range ecologists are claiming that 'opportunistic' range management strategies may be more efficient and potentially less environmentally damaging. The maintenance of biological diversity may be an important component of such opportunistic strategies; however, this and all management decisions must be sensitive to all the factors determining the overall resilience of the system, as well as to whether the rangeland is in an ecological equilibrium or a state of transition.

Ownership regimes, institutional structures and government policies

Having discussed models of rangeland management and their implications for rangeland degradation, we now turn to the role of other factors – in particular land tenure regimes, institutional structures and government policies.

A range of livestock management regimes exist, including nomadic pastoralists, mixed subsistence livestock farming and commercial ranching. These systems operate under a variety of land tenure systems, from open access resource use, to common property management, to private property resource rights. Open access and common property management regimes have frequently been blamed for the over-grazing and degradation of rangelands.

The origins of the view that common property and open access land use systems encourage over-use of the natural resource base are found in Hardin's 'tragedy of the commons'. Hardin (1968) asserts that private ownership of livestock on land without ownership inevitably leads to over-grazing, because there is little incentive for an individual using the commons jointly with others to limit their own use of the resource. This is based on the assumption that while an individual herder benefits fully from placing an additional animal on the commons, the costs of rangeland degradation resulting from this extra animal are shared proportionately by all users. Under these conditions, individual herders do not take the full user cost (namely, the loss of future use value of the rangeland) into account in their decision over herd size. As the commons is finite, sooner or later the total number of animals will exceed the carrying capacity of the land.

Hardin (1988) revisits his original article and provides more detail on the conditions under which the above pattern of resource degradation may occur. In his later work, he specifies the assumptions of open access to the commons and the self-interest motivation of the individual herder. Thus, earlier generalizations about the 'tragedy of the commons' and of 'common property management regimes', largely presumed in science and policy, were inappropriate (Feeny et al 1990). It is clear that the problem of tragedy of the commons is more a problem of open access resource use and can be more appropriately described as a 'tragedy of the unmanaged commons'.

In fact, all natural resources – including common property (or common pool) resources – may be well managed, depending on the effectiveness of the controls exercised by the society owning the resource. Three property rights regimes are possible in asserting effective control:

■ private property;
■ state property; and
■ communal resource property.

Each of these, and combinations thereof, can encourage sustainable resource use (Young and Solbrig 1993). Their relative effectiveness depends on the capacity to control access and regulate use of the resource – i.e., to eliminate open access conditions, balance resource use rights against responsibilities and legalize rights (Gadgil, Berkes and Folke 1993).

Systems of common property management may be well suited to the ecological characteristics of the rangeland, enabling flexible herd size and grazing patterns. They may also be well suited to the economic needs of the local society, in particular by providing a risk-pooling system for risk-averse individuals in a highly unpredictable and fragile environment. In addition, they may have evolved to deal with the range of production objectives of the livestock holders, including meat, milk, draught, store of wealth, social obligations and so on.

The literature provides many examples of efficient and sustainable resource use occurring under communal property management regimes.[1] However, while these regimes tend to be able to withstand internal pressures, they often break down under external impacts, such as government appropriation of land, distortionary taxes and subsidies. It is usually external factors that lead to deterioration of common land, rather than an inherent flaw in the communal property system itself.

The lack of resilience of communal property management regimes to external stresses and shocks frequently leads to proposals to revise the structure of resource management. Recommendations generally focus on the introduction of private property rights for scare resources. While this may be applicable in some situations, in many cases such policy recommendations fail to deal with the full range of needs that the existing institutional structures have evolved to serve. In these cases, a more suitable response may be to remove the external distortion, and then readjust communal property management regime accordingly (Young and Solbrig 1993). Several case studies that explore the problems of land tenure regimes, institutional structures and government policies are presented below.

Lane (1991) examines in detail the traditional land tenure arrangements of the Barabaig pastoralists in Tanzania. He shows that the original common property system of grazing rotation was an effective and sustainable form of pasture use. In recent times, due to external pressures from farmer encroachment and government appropriation of land, a new grazing pattern of rangeland use by the Barabaig has emerged. This latter pattern of rangeland use is relatively inefficient and leads directly to over-use of the range.

Government policies to establish commercial livestock activities through destocking pastoral herds, settlement and privatization of common land have exacerbated, rather than alleviated, the problem of inefficient and unsustainable rangeland use. In addition, the Barabaig have been alienated from their land and their traditional systems of land management have been undermined. Lane (1991) asserts that the failure to design policies in respect of existing, and potentially advantageous, common property management systems, has perpetuated the problem of inefficient and unsustainable rangeland use in Tanzania

Githinji and Perrings (1993) look at how institutional initiatives need to address the needs satisfied by the structures they replace, if they are not to provoke a conflicting evolutionary response on the part of those existing institutions. Case studies from Kenya and Botswana are used to explore this. The Kenyan case study has already been described in Box 4.5 on the role of institutional failure as a cause of biodiversity loss. Box 8.6 discusses policies for rangeland management in Botswana. Traditional rights and patterns of resource use have not been static, but have evolved in response to changing institutional, economic and environmental conditions. Property rights for scarce resources have tended to evolve in the general direction of private property. In many cases, the introduction of private property rights has not led to an improvement in productivity gains or

---

1 See for example, Berkes (1989); Bromley (1992); Feeny et al (1990; Gadgil, Berkes and Folke (1993); McCay and Acheson (1987); and Young and Solbrig (1993).

the social resilience of the community. In addition, an increase in environmental degradation often results.

Box 8.6

Patterns of rangeland use in Botswana

In Botswana, traditional livestock production involved pastoral nomads operating under individual herd ownership, with access to the range determined by the local community. The process of commercialization and participation in arable farming is much more advanced in Botswana than in other pastoral societies in sub-Saharan Africa. In particular, management of the two most vital resources for livestock production, pasture and water, became more exclusive under private ownership. Meanwhile, the traditonal regulatory authority of the chiefs declined and mechanisms for regulating grazing degenerated. For example, the badisa responsible for the care of rangeland disappeared, and range management decisions became more individualistic and less coordinated.

In 1975 the Tribal Grazing Lands Policy turned over the right of managing and planning land use from chiefs and their appointees, and vested this power in the Lands Board. This transition of power was based on the assumption that there was no incentive for individual households to decrease the amount of their stock, when such a reduction would only lead to an improvement in the range for others. However, the Lands Board failed to ensure that land and water allocation rights led to private stocking decisions that would be consistent with the sustainable use of the rangelands. This resulted in communal areas becoming open access resources with uncontrolled grazing. The next step was an extensive review of the agricultural sector, which has led to the fencing of remaining communal lands to ensure sustainable range management. This process has been affected by a range of institutional factors.

- The 'dual grazing rights problem' – where the Tribal Grazing Lands Policy ranch leaseholds retained rights of access to the communal land.
- Controlling access on the basis of ownership is complicated by the extensive use of mafisa (associate ownership), which allows transfer of livestock between households without changing ownership.
- The borehole syndicate was originally formed to exclude non-members from the use of the water. However, grazing around boreholes is intensive, due to the rights of access by syndicate owners, non-syndicate herdsmen with mafisa cattle from syndicate herdsmen, livestock owners who pay for the water, and those who have traditional right of access to the water even though they do not pay for the resource.
- Cattle are not only considered to be a production good that can be bought and sold, but also a store of wealth and the currency of a range of social obligations. For example, a significant incentive for cattle accumulation is for bridewealth. The breakdown of social institutions that supported young men in the provision of bridewealth has meant that young sons start their herds at an earlier age and hold greater cattle stocks to ensure sufficient bridewealth to meet their social obligations.

Source: Githinji and Perrings (1993).

Unemo (1994) looks at the environmental impacts of government policies and external shocks in Botswana. Most previous studies have used a partial analytical approach, which tends to constrain analysis to examination of the direct impact of government policies on one sector of the economy. By developing a computable general equilibrium (CGE) model for Botswana, the author is able to explore the effects of various macro-economic policies on the livestock sector. The framework of analysis provided by the CGE model enables examination of the 'knock-on' effects of these policies throughout the economy and analysis of several different policies simultaneously.

The level of government intervention in the livestock sector of Botswana is extensive and a number of distortionary incentives emerge from these interventions. For example, a range of subsidies to livestock production prevailed during the 1970s and early 1980s, including input subsidies, provision of slaughterhouse facilities, and extension and research services. Fiscal incentives also prevailed through the deductibility of investment in livestock and the ability to write off losses against income from other activities. Favourable trade agreements for beef exports through preferential access to the EC market also provided support to Botswana's livestock sector. Policies in other sectors, such as low grain prices and labour opportunities abroad, provided further stimulus for livestock expansion.

Unemo (1994) uses the CGE model to test the impact of several different policies on a range of indicators. Stocking rates (number of hectares of grazing land to head of cattle) provide an indication of the carrying capacity of the range, whereby a decrease in stocking rates is taken to reflect an increase in land pressure. The most surprising result comes from a 5 per cent fall in the price of diamonds – another major export commodity of Botswana. This results in a considerable increase in land pressure. In fact, according to the model, the stocking rate decreases by 12 per cent, implying an increased pressure on land resources. The elimination of the import tariff on crops and the imposition of an export subsidy in the meat processing sector worsens the land pressure slightly. Labour opportunities abroad for unskilled workers ease the land pressure, while a sudden increase in foreign exchange to the economy puts heavier pressure on the land. Box 8.7 presents the results of the analysis in more detail.

CHALLENGES TO BE ADDRESSED

In this chapter we have raised several key challenges to be addressed by rangeland ecologists and economists in the near future. In particular, the following points were noted.

- The need to improve our information on the extent and state of rangelands, and how they are changing over time.
- The need for ecologists to refine existing models of rangeland ecology and to work with economists to design appropriate management systems for livestock production in complex, dynamic and fragile ecosystems. Economists need to take into account the wide range of productive uses of cattle,

---

Box 8.7

The impact of government policies on rangeland degradation in Botswana

Using a computable general equilibrium (CGE) model, Unemo (1994) analyses the impact of governmental policies and external shocks on a range of indicators, including gross domestic product (GDP), stocking rate (number of hectares of grazing land per head of cattle) and water use in Botswana. Some of the main results of the analysis are summarized as follows.

- A fall in the price of diamonds by 5 per cent is seen to increase land pressure considerably, resulting in a decrease in stocking rates of as much as 12 per cent. This occurs through a decrease in income from mining which leads to a decrease in the demand for manufactured goods. This in turn makes investment in the livestock sector comparatively more attractive, thus leading to an expansion in land under livestock.

- Elimination of the 14 per cent import tariff on crops is seen to have no significant effects, although a decrease in the agricultural sector and a slight expansion of the livestock sector occurs. Stocking rates decrease by 0.07 per cent.

- The imposition of a 1 per cent export subsidy in the meat processing industry is seen to encourage an expansion in meat processing and livestock production. This translates into a decrease in stocking rates of 3 per cent.

- A reduction in the force of unskilled labour of 10 per cent was seen to lead to make all sectors, with the exception of mining, contract – especially the labour intensive, crop producing sector. GDP declined by 2.8 per cent but land pressure was reduced – stocking rates increased by 1.5 per cent.

- A sudden influx of foreign earnings by US$100 mn (16 per cent of total savings) boosted the manufacturing sector but led to a contraction in meat processing. However, livestock holding actually increased due to a factor movement into the less traded sectors. This results in an increasing land pressure shown by a fall in stocking rates of more than 2 per cent.

Source: Unemo (1994).

---

and the production objectives of herders, when determining appropriate management regimes.

- The need to examine appropriate responses to the breakdown of communal property management regimes due to external stresses. Improving the efficiency and sustainability of the prevailing system of resource use rights and responsibilities, rather than imposing an alternative property rights regime, may be more effective in managing the complex web of needs that the existing system had evolved to cope with problems such as uncertainty and risk aversion, flexible livestock herds and grazing patterns, and multiple uses of livestock. The need to appraise fully the effect of policy interventions on land use decisions, including any knock-on effects of policies in other, related sectors in the economy.

Part III

LESSONS FOR MANAGEMENT AND POLICY

9

Instruments and Tools for Biodiversity Conservation

In this chapter we are primarily concerned with whether the implications of biodiversity loss discussed throughout this book require the development of new conservation and environmental management strategies and 'tools'. We begin first with the policy implications of the need to respect system boundaries – in particular ecological limits and thresholds – to control the economic-environmental interactions that characterize the biodiversity problem (see Figure 1.1). As managing this problem essentially means policy prescriptions for influencing economic activity and incentives, we discuss in subsequent sections the extent to which traditional market based and regulatory instruments can be employed as opposed to the need for new instruments. Crucial to this discussion are the conditions under which the precautionary principle and safe minimum standards should be invoked – if at all. Our inquiry, therefore, starts with an exploration of the potential role of these two policy instruments in biodiversity conservation.

SYSTEM BOUNDARIES AND LIMITS: WHEN DO THEY MATTER?

In Part I we discussed how our lack of knowledge of ecological functioning and uncertainty for the future has raised concern over whether there are ecological limits to economic activity, and, in turn, whether consideration of the potentially irreversible and negative impacts on human welfare should lead us to respect such limits. As we noted before, such considerations have led to greater acceptance of the arguments for 'rules' that would ensure that humans should make some, but not unlimited, sacrifices for biodiversity. For example, one approach might be to accept the principle of a safe minimum standard – a sufficient area of habitat should be preserved to ensure the survival of species, sub-species or ecosystems, unless the costs of doing so are intolerably high. Similarly, arguments have been advanced in favour of a precautionary principle – in its broadest sense this implies that the opportunity set for future generations can only be assured if the level of biodiversity they inherit is no less than that available to present generations.

In this section we will address the issue of ecological limits by looking at the arguments for the precautionary principle and safe minimum standards as safeguards against the consequences of biodiversity loss. In the subsequent section, we examine the conditions under which these safeguards might apply and the inherent difficulties of translating them into practical policies.

The precautionary principle

The precautionary principle is increasingly being invoked as a public policy guideline for environmental issues. Recent international conferences in which this principle has been put forward include the Conference on Sustainable Development, Science and Policy in Bergen in May 1990, the Second World Climate Conference in Geneva in November 1990, the International Conference on an Agenda of Science for Environment and Development into the Twenty-first Century in Vienna in November 1991, and the United Nations Conference on Environment and Development – the 'Earth Summit' – in Rio de Janeiro in June 1992.

As noted by Myers (1993), the precautionary principle in essence asserts that there is a 'premium' on a cautious and conservative approach to human interventions in the natural environment where:

- our understanding of the likely consequences of the intervention is limited; and
- there are threats of serious or irreversible damage to natural systems and processes.

In such a circumstance, the 'burden of scientific proof' should therefore lie on 'would-be environmental disrupters' to demonstrate that their actions will not result in unacceptable ecological damage.

More formally, Perrings (1991) relates the precautionary principle to the notion of reserved rationality, whereby it may be rational for policy makers to proceed cautiously with an intervention in the natural environment to safeguard against the possibility of unexpectedly severe future costs – including the advent of sudden 'surprises' or 'catastrophes' (such as rapid climatic change or natural disasters). The need to proceed cautiously is reinforced by the lack of past 'experience' or 'history' with the type of environmental damages that may occur. This in turn may prevent decision makers from gauging accurately either the likelihood (or probability) of a catastrophic outcome or the scale (or magnitude) of the impacts on human welfare.

Consequently, the precautionary principle requires that an 'allowance' or a 'margin of error' be made for those uses of the environment that may result in unexpected and uncertain – though potentially large – future losses. This 'margin of error' can be translated into a 'safeguard allowance' or the sum total of 'preventive expenditures' that may be committed to mitigate any future damages associated with use of environmental resources today.[1]

However, it is conceivable that the future consequences of any environmental damage may be irrevocable, in the sense that uses of the environment today may cause profound and irreversible environmental damage which permanently re-

---

1 Perrings (1991) shows formally how the 'upped bound' on such preventive expenditures is equivalent to the difference between the expected, or reference, costs associated with a use of environmental resources and the decision maker's allowance for error in these expected costs as resulting from unknown future environmental damages. Costanza and Perrings (1990) demonstrate how such a principle may be applied through an environmental assurance bonding system, whereby environmental users would post a bond adequate to cover potential future environmental damages. This rather innovative application of the precautionary principal is discussed in more detail below.

duces the welfare of future generations. Many commentators on the current patterns of biodiversity loss note that this may be a characteristic feature of the future damages that are associated with species extinction, habitat destruction and, above all, loss of valuable ecological functions and ecosystem 'resilience' (see Ehrlich and Ehrlich 1992; Myers 1993 and the discussion in Part I of this book). If this is the case, then 'preventive expenditures' or 'safeguard allowances' alone may not be sufficient to avoid irreversible environmental costs being imposed on future generations.

This is basically the strong sustainability argument introduced in Part I. As natural environments disappear, the essential ecological services and resources they provide will increase in value relative to the ordinary goods and services in the economy produced by humanmade capital. Moreover, if this increasing ecological scarcity involves the loss of essential ecological life support functions, and the disruption to the overall resilience of natural and managed ecosystems, then there are limits to the substitution between natural and humanmade capital. Consequently, invoking the precautionary principle in terms of specific payments or expenditures to future generations cannot 'compensate' them adequately for the environmental consequences stemming from the loss of biodiversity. Proponents of strong sustainability would argue that such funds could only be invested in humanmade assets that are imperfect substitutes for essential environmental functions, or only partially rehabilitate degraded natural systems and services, including ecological resilience. The only way of maintaining the economic opportunities available to future generations – that is to say, ensuring that development is truly 'sustainable' – is to prevent irrevocable disruptions to ecosystem functions and resilience through biodiversity loss.

Safe minimum standards

If the welfare of future generations can only be assured if the level of biodiversity they inherit is no less than that available to present generations, then the precautionary principle begins to approximate more closely the policy of invoking safe minimum standards. Box 9.1 describes the latter policy in more detail. It clearly has a long history associated with the concept of avoiding species extinction. For example, more than 40 years ago, Ciriacy-Wantrup (1952) argued that as a result of irreversible extinction of a species, future societies may discover that they have forgone significant benefits. If there were close substitutes for the goods and services of the threatened species, and if there was a technological bias favouring those substitute goods, then the costs of preserving a minimum viable population of the species and its required supporting habitat would be small.

As explained in Part I, the current global biodiversity crisis cannot be reduced simply to a problem of species extinction. Rather, biodiversity loss results in a more fundamental problem of irrevocable loss of essential ecological functions and processes. Nevertheless, proponents of the safe minimum standard approach would argue that this principle should be extended to provide the necessary safeguards for ensuring that future generations inherit at least the same level of biodiversity as available to current generations.

Box 9.1
The safe minimum standard and biodiversity conservation

The concept of a safe minimum standard (SMS) as a policy for conservation has a fairly long history in resource economics that can be traced to Ciriacy-Wantrup (1952). SMS has generally been thought of in the context of species extinction. Adopting the SMS as a policy objective would essentially mean strict avoidance of extinction in day-to-day resource management decisions. Exceptions would occur only when it is determined explicitly that the costs of avoiding extinction are intolerably large or that other social objectives must take precedence.

As outlined by Bishop (1993) the basic arguments in favour of a SMS strategy for biodiversity conservation are as follows.

- The SMS rule is generally considered a 'pragmatic step' towards the attainment of an efficient and sustainable economy built on appropriate inter-generational natural resource endowments and an optimal path of capital accumulation over time.
- However, because such an economy does not exist today, and because of ignorance of the future and market (as well as policy) failures, there is great risk in the present practice of 'trading off' biodiversity through market transactions – in the sense that giving up two species for ten hospital beds would constitute a net gain for society. The result is excessive levels of biodiversity loss.
- The criterion of 'intolerable costs' none the less implies that there are limits on how much society should 'pay' for biodiversity conservation. However, the burden of proof lies on those seeking a relaxation of the SMS to determine costs that are 'intolerable' from those that are 'merely substantial'.
- A SMS strategy is therefore a practical safeguard for biodiversity conservation until economies have moved on to a development path that is both efficient and sustainable, including the elimination of pervasive market and policy failures that are biased against biodiversity conservation. Once such an ideal is attained, then biodiversity conservation can be assured through market mechanisms and public policy, and the SMS rule need no longer apply.

However, the SMS strategy carries its own risks.

- The current generation's ignorance over the future value of biodiversity and/or what constitutes 'intolerable costs' also limits the effectiveness of the SMS strategy in conserving the 'optimal' level of biodiversity. Some biodiversity that may be of great value to future generations may be lost. Alternatively, some biodiversity that has little value may be saved.
- In addition, a SMS strategy is likely to yield outcomes that trade-off biodiversity conservation and overall economic efficiency. Under the SMS rule, economic development opportunities that would have yielded positive net benefits to both present and future generations but would also have contributed to biodiversity loss, may be abandoned.
- The costs associated with SMS may not be borne equally across all members of society or all countries. Thus for the sake of intra-generational fairness and, indeed, even to induce some countries to cooperate in a global SMS strategy, it may be necessary to incorporate mechanisms for compensating income groups and countries that are disproportionately affected.

- It may be difficult to manage the transition from the 'second best' economy governed by safe minimum standards for biodiversity conservation to the 'ideal' economy, whereby appropriate market mechanisms and public policies ensure efficient and sustainable management of biodiversity. A critical issue is the timing of the transition, including the speed of adjustment and the degree to which the SMS should be 'relaxed' over time.
- It is possible that the elimination of many market and policy failures concerning resource use and environmental degradation may by themselves be sufficient for conserving biodiversity. The need for SMS can therefore be overly exaggerated in many cases.
- SMS rules for the avoidance of species extinction are less problematic than extending such rules to preserve critical ecosystems and ecological functions. In particular, the margin of error in terms of assessing their future value or the associated costs of their conservation is much greater. Consequently, determining the 'optimal' level of conservation and the appropriate trade-off with economic efficiency objectives is that much more difficult.

For example, Perrings, Folke and Mäler (1992) suggest that safe minimum standards are likely to be an essential part of a global biodiversity conservation strategy, given the considerable uncertainty associated with the future environmental impacts of current economic activities, the non-market and public goods nature of environmental assets, and the irreversibility of species extinction and loss of ecological functions. In particular, if the existence of ecological thresholds means that unknown irreversible environmental effects may be catastrophic, then the rate of environmental exploitation should not just be slowed down but ultimately restricted.

Bishop (1993) takes this argument a step further by maintaining that, in the absence of an efficient and sustainable economy protecting the interests of future generations, the adoption of a safe minimum standards strategy is the best policy for ensuring this objective (see also Box 9.1). Albeit somewhat crude, safe minimum standards seek to increase the welfare of future generations by conserving biological resources and diversity, that may prove useful and valuable in the future, and that would otherwise have been lost. Given our ignorance of the future, the strategy would increase the options available to future generations, thus increasing the likelihood that the economy is on a sustainable path. Safe minimum standards by themselves will not guarantee that the economy will ever reach such a sustainable path. However, they will ensure that future generations are better 'compensated' by receiving a larger resource endowment than in the absence of such standards. Just how much larger that endowment will be depends on the willingness of the current generation to tolerate the costs of biodiversity conservation through more, as opposed to less, stringent enforcement of safe minimum standard rules.

However, as in the case of the precautionary principle, the conditions under which safe minimum standards for biodiversity conservation should be applied are difficult to determine. To some extent they already underline the physical limits involved in more conventional environmental policies such as tradable permits for pollution, and legislation ensuring preservation of species and habitats, for example, the current US Endangered Species Act. Taken as a whole, however, existing environmental policies clearly do not guarantee that future generations will inherit a level of biodiversity that is no less than that available to present generations.

SAFEGUARDS FOR THE FUTURE: WHEN DO THEY APPLY?

The precautionary principle and safe minimum standards approach to biodiversity conservation present a fundamental challenge to develop more innovative policies for respecting ecosystem limits and thresholds. This is one important area for future research in ecological economics. However, there remain some fundamental questions concerning our present capability and willingness to evolve the precautionary principle and safe minimum standards into concrete policies.

First, it is clear from the discussion of strong sustainability that application of such approaches to environmental problems requires decision makers today to be ethically more concerned about inter-generational equity than they appear to be at present. As discussed in Part I, current attitudes to inter-generational equity as revealed through policy decisions would suggest that modern societies emphasize the enhancement of welfare today with little consideration of the implications for future generations. The underlying assumption is generally that future generations will enjoy the same or even higher levels of welfare than we do currently. Consequently, the potential threat that biodiversity loss poses to the economic opportunities available to future generations receives little weight in economic decisions made today.

In contrast, invoking safe minimum standards and policies based on the precautionary principle to control biodiversity loss would represent a profound shift in attitudes by the present generation in favour of inter-generational equity. Employing safe minimum standards would essentially mean placing 'limits' on economic activities to ensure that they do not impose irreversible environmental costs on future generations. Only slightly weaker, the precautionary principle can be interpreted as saying that if it is known that an action may cause profound and irreversible environmental damage which permanently reduces the welfare of future generations, but the probability of such damage is not known, then it is inequitable to act if the probability is known (Perrings 1991). Either policy would signal a significant shift in current attitudes to inter-generational equity. It is not clear that we are prepared – if ever – to countenance such a change in our ethics.

Second, there are important intra-generational aspects that need addressing. As noted in Part I, the world's resource endowment, and particularly its biodiversity, is not distributed equally. On a global level, the costs of implementing policies based on safe minimum standards or the precautionary principle are likely to appear more 'tolerable' to one country compared to another. Thus, those countries that are more directly dependent on resource exploitation and conversion to achieve a higher level of economic development may not accept any global conservation strategies that disproportionately affect them unless they are adequately compensated by other countries.[2] As will be discussed in Chapter 10, this issue of international compensation for biodiversity conservation is a crucial feature – and stumbling block – in current negotiations over international environmental agreements.

Even within individual countries, the costs of implementing the precautionary principle or safe minimum standards will not be distributed equally. The effect of such policies will essentially be to allocate a country's resources – for example, its capital, labour and natural resources – away from economic activities that threaten ecological thresholds. Such structural economic changes are not costless, and the costs should be expected to rise with the speed of implementation of precautionary principle and safe minimum standards. Moreover, in the short or medium term it may be difficult to allocate human and humanmade capital from one economic activity or sector to others. Some degree of structural unemployment and loss of capacity will result. On the other hand, economic sectors and activities that do not threaten ecological limits will most likely gain by the imposition of limits and penalties on environmental exploitation, as the additional costs to them of these safeguards will be relatively insignificant. Although it is quite possible that the overall impact of these structural economic changes on the country may be a net welfare gain, particularly when the benefits to future generations are taken into account, there clearly will be major 'losers' from imposing explicit policies based on the safe minimum standards and the precautionary principle. Devising additional mechanisms and policies for ensuring that these 'losers' are adequately compensated would not only be more equitable but also may ensure that appropriate incentives exist for complying with safe minimum standards and the precautionary principle.

Third, as implied by the discussion so far, any policies to safeguard ecological limits will not be sufficient on their own. There will be a need for complementary incentive and management regimes, at the international, national and local level, to begin encouraging all economic activities to become more sustainable and efficient in the use of 'natural' capital and biodiversity. As argued previously, one obvious set of complementary policies would involve compensation to countries and individuals that disproportionately bear the burden of safe minimum standards and precautionary principle strategies. Moreover, as will be seen in the subsequent section, there is also scope for using regulations and market based incentives for reducing the environmental costs of economic activities.

If designed properly, institutional and market mechanisms can minimize the costs of ensuring that economic exploitation of biodiversity becomes more efficient and sustainable. The costs to society are in fact reduced in two ways:

---

2 As we have argued in Chapter 3 and will discuss further in Chapter 10, there are important medium and even short term economic development benefits to be gained by low and lower middle income countries adopting efficient and sustainable management of their natural 'capital'. However, even if these countries adopt such strategies at the national level, the global external benefits associated with biodiversity conservation could mean that the amount of biodiversity each country chooses to conserve may be insufficient to achieve the desired target of global biodiversity conservation. If these countries are not managing their environments efficiently and sustainably, then they will presumably need even greater inducements to adopt conservation strategies to meet global targets.

■ First, the 'optimal' policy will produce the least cost method of 'internalizing' environmental externalities and the most efficient use of natural capital.

■ Second, by encouraging more efficient and sustainable use of natural resources, improved management and incentives will increase the likelihood that economic activities avoid the penalties and restrictions imposed through safe minimum standards and policies enforcing the precautionary principle.

However, as will also be discussed in the next section, the existence of ecological thresholds and uncertainty over the consequences of transgressing them will also mean that conventional market and regulatory instruments alone may not be sufficient to safeguard the welfare of future generations. Hence, there is a rationale for combining these more conventional instruments with innovative policies incorporating safe minimum standards and the precautionary principle, to ensure an 'optimal mix' of policies for efficient and sustainable use of biodiversity.

Finally, as indicated in Box 9.1, there are important risks associated with the implementation of safe minimum standards. Similar, albeit less penurious, risks are also associated with implementing policies based on the precautionary principle. Thus the problem of determining the optimal 'mix' of environmental policies to reduce biodiversity loss is a complicated one. Not only does the traditional problem of deciding whether regulation or market-based instruments will yield the most efficient approach to controlling environmental degradation still remain, but there is the additional factor of determining where and when to apply any 'limits' to overall economic activity and environmental use.

Given all the arguments discussed in this section, it is not surprising that the prevailing opinion is to use safe minimum standards and the precautionary principle as policy guidelines or only in limited circumstances, for example, to protect endangered species from extinction. However, concern over biodiversity loss and increasing ecological scarcity has meant that many ecologists and economists in the Biodiversity Programme suggest that it is time for a rethink of current environmental management strategies. Increasing reliance on safe minimum standards and the precautionary principle for biodiversity conservation is an important policy option worth considering.

In the remaining sections of this chapter, we explore further the contributions of Biodiversity Programme papers to resolving the critical issue of the 'optimal mix' of policies. In the next section, we begin by discussing the merits and limits of regulations and market based incentives, and we return to the problem of designing complementary policies for safeguarding ecological limits based on safe minimum standards and the precautionary principle.

REGULATIONS AND MARKETS: WHEN DO THEY WORK?

Whether safe minimum standards and the precautionary principle will result in specific policies limiting or regulating economic activity, or whether they will serve mainly as guidelines for major policy decisions, is an issue that we cannot hope to resolve in this book. However, as we noted in the previous section, it does raise an important issue of what is the optimal 'mix' of policy instruments to employ in encouraging the appropriate incentives and management regimes to reduce excessive biodiversity loss. Again, our ignorance of ecological thresholds and our uncertainty about transgressing these limits are important factors. Against this background, the traditional debate in economics over the relative merits of regulatory compared to market based instruments needs to be re-examined. In this section we review the debate in the light of the ecological and economic implications of biodiversity loss that have been raised throughout this book.

Traditional discussions of appropriate policy instruments for providing the necessary economic incentives for natural resource management usually focus on the relative merits of regulatory as opposed to economic instruments.

Regulatory, or direct control, instruments involve the direct limitation or reduction of activities that degrade the environment, in accordance with some legislated or agreed standard. Examples include quotas or bans on renewable resource harvesting, restrictions on air pollution emissions, controls on hazardous waste transport and dumping, zoning laws and ambient water quality standards. Such controls are usually mandatory and enforceable through litigation, fines/penalties, revocation of licences, or other judicial or administrative sanctions. Regulatory controls on environmental degradation have an important role to play, but their effectiveness in some countries is limited by poorly functioning judicial, administrative and monitoring/enforcement procedures.

In contrast, economic, or market based, instruments do not directly control or restrict activities that degrade the environment. Rather, they create the economic incentives for individuals to choose freely to modify or reduce their activities, thus indirectly producing an environmental improvement. The aim of market based instruments is to alter private costs and benefits so that any unaccounted social costs (and benefits) of environmental degradation can be 'internalized' to ensure the desired environmental improvement. Box 9.2 provides examples of the main categories of these instruments.

However, the effectiveness of such market based instruments in adjusting private costs to reflect the social costs of environmental degradation may depend on how well market systems reflect private costs in the first instance. As discussed in Chapter 4, the pervasiveness of market and policy failures that are frequently the underlying causes of environmental degradation problems suggest many instances where public policies and incomplete markets reduce the direct costs to individuals of utilizing the environment. Thus many authors stress as a priority the role of policy reforms as an 'economic instrument', that is to say, the removal of subsidies and other public policy interventions that distort the private costs of resource use and pollution discharge (Panayotou 1990 and Pearce 1990). Similarly, institutional reforms such as the improvement or establishment of property and resource right regimes, legal titling, environmental sanctions, contract enforcement and so forth are equally important policy instruments for improved natural resource management in developing countries in that they assist or even establish markets for environmental goods and services. Consequently,

Box 9.2

Market based instruments and incentives

Market based, or economic, instruments do not directly control or restrict activities that degrade the environment. Rather, they create the economic incentives for individuals to choose freely to modify or reduce their activities, thus indirectly producing an environmental improvement. Market based instruments can be narrowly or broadly categorized.

The 'narrowest' classification would include all policy measures that explicitly affect private costs and benefits, so that any unaccounted social costs (and benefits) of environmental degradation can be 'internalized' to ensure the desired environmental improvement. There are five general categories of this type of instrument.

- Charges (taxes), fees or other 'additional' prices to be paid for the social costs arising from environmental damages. Examples would include effluent charges on sulphur dioxide emissions, tax differentiation between leaded and unleaded petrol, user charges for public waste disposal, depletion taxes on mineral exploitation and stumpage fees for timber extraction.
- Subsidies to assist individuals in altering activities or conforming to environmental standards. Examples include subsidies for the development and adoption of 'clean' technologies, tax allowances for energy conservation, soft loans for erosion control investments and price supports for paper recycling industries.
- Deposit/refund or fee/rebate systems, where a surcharge is levied on the price of products leading to resource depletion or pollution which is then refunded if the product (or its residuals) is 'recycled' or if the depleted resource is 'restored'. Examples include deposit/refund schemes for glass bottles, aluminium cans and other containers, and reforestation rebates on timber stumpage fees.
- Tradable or marketable permits, where rights to discharge pollution or exploit resources can be exchanged, either through a free or controlled 'permit' market. Examples include tradable permits for greenhouse gas emissions, marketable quotas for fish harvesting, tradable depletion rights to mineral concessions and marketable discharge permits for water-borne effluents.
- Compensatory incentives, which are similar to subsidies, in that markets or financial inducements are created for certain individuals or groups who either disproportionately bear the risk or costs of environmental improvement, or who possess 'unique' environmental assets. Examples include compensatory financing of 'environmentally friendly' technology transfer to developing countries for compliance with international environmental agreements, debt-for-nature swaps involving biologically diverse tropical forests and increased heating allowances for the poor and aged to compensate for energy or carbon taxes.

Broader definitions of economic instruments would include certain enforcement incentives for compliance with environmental regulations, such as performance bonds that are paid in advance and refunded when compliance is assured, non-compliance fines that are levied when regulations are violated and assigning legal liability for the costs of environmental degradation (Opschoor and Vos 1989).

Other authors extend further the definition of economic instruments to include the removal of subsidies and other public policy interventions that distort the private costs of resource use and pollution discharge (Panayotou 1990 and Pearce 1990). Such distortions are particularly prevalent in developing countries, where public policies frequently reduce the direct costs to individuals of exploiting or converting natural resources and of using the environment as a waste 'sink'. However, such 'policy failures' are also widespread in industrialized countries, particularly with regard to the energy sector.

Finally, institutional reforms such as the improvement or establishment of property right regimes, legal titling, environmental sanctions, contract enforcement and so forth are sometimes categorized as 'economic' instruments, in that they assist or even establish markets for environmental goods and services (Panayotou 1990).

Source: Adapted from Barbier (1993a).

---

as described in Box 9.2, the full range of market incentives for controlling environmental degradation includes additional market based instruments such as taxes and tradable permits, as well as removal of policy distortions that distort private costs and institutional reforms.

As indicated in Box 9.3, there are many important factors that determine whether regulatory instruments are preferred to market instruments and incentives. Cost-effectiveness is an important consideration, but by no means the only criterion. In general, the use of market based instruments for environmental management is on the rise and in the future we can expect a greater policy 'mix' of instruments to improve the efficiency of achieving a desired improvement in environmental quality or resource use. In Chapter 10 we discuss in more detail specific examples from Biodiversity Programme papers of the use of market and regulatory instruments to induce appropriate incentives and management regimes for biodiversity conservation at the international, national and local level.

The cost-effectiveness of economic instruments depends to a large part on their ability to relate incentives to the economic damages of pollution and resource depletion, and, conversely, to the economic benefits of environmental improvements. However, precisely because the effects occur 'externally' to markets, the economic impacts of environmental degradation are difficult to measure and value. For example, the economic damages associated with pollution may vary depending on geographical location, the combined effects of pollution 'mixes', seasonal variations and other factors affecting 'critical loading' of assimilative capacity. To go one step further and measure the various impacts on economic activities and welfare is often difficult. Similarly, to value the full costs of resource degradation and depletion often involves complex and difficult calculations of the 'user' costs of forgone future income from irreversible loss of the resource today, the 'external' impacts on ecosystems and economic activity, and the loss of 'unique' or 'intrinsically' valuable species and environments.

Under conditions of uncertainty, different environmental policy instruments are preferable under different conditions. With economic instruments, the uncertainty usually manifests itself in terms of uncertainty over the reduction in environmental damage, whereas with regulatory controls the uncertainty is over the costs of reduction. Although difficult to generalize, under uncertainty regu-

Box 9.3
Market versus regulatory instruments

An important criterion in the selection of an environmental policy instrument is its cost-effectiveness, or economic efficiency, in achieving the desired improvement in environmental quality or resources. Obviously, an instrument cannot be cost-effective if it is not first appropriate to the environmental improvement at hand. For example, as discovered in Indonesia, the implementation of a reforestation tax/rebate scheme will fail in its objectives if its concession leases are so short that timber companies have no incentive to replant stands (Barbier, Burgess and Markandya 1991). Similarly, tradable permits for extremely toxic discharges may be less appropriate than an outright ban on emissions or user charges to pay for detoxification and disposal. Finally, the success of an instrument in terms of cost-effectiveness is clearly influenced by the overall institutional framework – legal, economic, political and even cultural – in which it is imposed.

If they are appropriate, the potential cost-effectiveness of market instruments and incentives makes them attractive alternatives to regulatory controls. Regulatory instruments require the central authority to determine the best course of action, whereas economic instruments decentralize much of the decision making to the single firm or household, which typically has better information for determining the appropriate individual response to given economic conditions. For example, studies routinely indicate that the costs of direct control of air pollution are 2 to over 20 times more costly than economic instruments (Tietenberg 1990). In addition, market instruments provide cost incentives to adopt 'cleaner' technologies, and 'alternative' resource inputs and processes, or to develop such improvements with time.

However, there are important qualifications to the inherent attractiveness of market instruments and incentives:

- important criteria other than cost-effectiveness may be used to evaluate and select environmental policy instruments (such as the financial objective of raising revenues rather than the incentive objective of reducing pollution or exploitation);
- under certain conditions (such as the presence of uncertainty, threshold effects, pollution 'mixes' and so on) the cost savings from employing market instead of regulatory instruments may be minimal or even negative;
- market instruments are often used in conjunction with regulatory instruments and, in some instances, a 'mix' of instruments may be the most cost-effective approach.

However, in practice, direct controls have been traditionally preferred as the main environmental policy instruments.

Policy makers seem to prefer regulation because:

- a 'regulative' tradition exists such that authorities are more familiar with the direct control approach, whereas switching to economic instruments implies additional information requirements, higher initial administrative costs, bureaucratic opposition and more complex or at least unfamiliar processes;
- the effects of regulation are more certain, whereas the revenue and incentive effects of charges and other economic instruments are seen as too uncertain;
- charges and other economic instruments are perceived as having undesirable impacts on inflation, income distribution and international competitiveness.

Firms and individuals seems to prefer regulation because:

- there is a fear that charges and other economic instruments might be additional to compliance costs or that such instruments might be 'misused' for financial rather than incentive purposes;
- they are also more familiar with the 'regulative' tradition and can influence this process better through negotiation;
- there is a 'risk aversion' to instruments which have variable outcomes that may be difficult to predict or plan for, to the extent that even stricter, but more certain, direct controls are preferred.

Source: Adapted from Barbier (1993a).

latory instruments will tend to produce too little pollution and resource depletion, with a greater share of the economic burden being borne by producers and resource users, whereas economic instruments tend to yield too much pollution and resource depletion, with the burden shifted mainly to consumers and 'victims'. If there are undesirable but unknown 'threshold' effects associated with increased environmental degradation, then regulatory control will be preferred. Similarly, if the damages are uncertain but appear to rise slowly as environmental degradation increases (relative to the decline in benefits), then direct controls will be preferable, as they will minimize expected efficiency losses.

The additional complications of thresholds, uncertainty and multiplier effects surrounding global biodiversity loss make the choice of correct instruments more problematic. As argued in Part I, the value of biodiversity goes beyond the use of biological resources as raw material inputs and amenities, or as living entities worth preserving 'in their own right'. Rather more fundamental is the role of biodiversity in assuring the resilience of ecosystems on which economic activity depends. Assessing the value of this role is extremely difficult, as determining the forgone benefits of irreversible loss of biodiversity today essentially involves determining the value of the 'sustainability' of the economic–environmental system. This in turn means that decisions as to how much society should 'pay' to preserve the benefits associated with biodiversity conservation cannot be made as easily as, say, decisions such as how much of a particular resource to deplete or a specific waste residual to emit. The decision as to how best to 'internalize' the external costs of biodiversity loss in markets and policy actions through the choice of regulatory or economic instruments also takes on fundamentally different characteristics from the more conventional problem of controlling resource extraction or pollution.

For example, most problems of pollution and resource depletion can be distinguished as being either unilateral or reciprocal externalities (Dasgupta 1982). The former are essentially damages uncompensated through markets or through other means that are imposed by one actor on another; for example, pollution by firm X upstream causes damage to be inflicted on fishermen Y downstream. Reciprocal externalities, on the other hand, are also uncompensated damages but they instead result when actors use a common 'pool' resource such that they impose these damages on each other. Examples include open access exploitation of resource stocks (such as fisheries) and pollution of the global atmosphere. As argued by Pearce and Perrings (1994), biodiversity loss is unusual with respect to both the range of people affected (at international, national and local levels), and the degree to which it encompasses both unidirectional and reciprocal externalities. Examples of the complexity of costs arising from biodiversity loss are described more fully in the case studies of forests, wetlands, island, estuarine and marine systems, and rangelands discussed in Part II. In Chapter 10, we focus more closely on the need to develop management and incentive schemes to control biodiversity loss on all three 'levels' where costs are inflicted – international, national and local.

However, the existence of threshold values for the various parameters of the ecological systems on which economic activity depends further complicates the design of appropriate policies. Ecological thresholds suggest that there are limits to the ability of ecosystems to withstand the stress imposed by environmental degradation. If stressed beyond these limits, ecosystems will collapse. By reducing ecological resilience, biodiversity loss increases the likelihood that thresholds will be breached.

Thus policy makers have to address the additional problem that the costs of exceeding thresholds are fundamentally uncertain (Perrings and Pearce 1994). The possibility of a major environmental catastrophe or system collapse cannot be ruled out. As a consequence, any policy which compromises the resilience of ecosystems will have uncontrolled effects and even small policy changes can have dramatic but unforeseen impacts. This would suggest that the protection of ecosystem sustainability, or resilience, should become an explicit and overriding policy objective. To fulfil this objective, limits may have to be imposed on economic activity so as to preclude the possibility of thresholds being crossed, where there is reason to believe that the social costs of system collapse or environmental catastrophe are major.

As indicated in Box 9.4, if the social costs of exceeding ecological thresholds are greater than the private net gains from doing so, then imposing safe minimum standards and penalties for limiting economic activity is the optimal policy. In fact, protection of the thresholds could be met through strict enforcement of the safe minimum standard (such as physical restriction or regulation of economic activity) or, as shown in Box 9.4, through the imposition of 'discontinuous' environmental levies and fines at the level of the threshold. However, what is more significant is not whether a regulatory or market based instrument is used, but that we are once again back to considering non-economic criteria in determining environmental policy. The economic instruments required to protect ecological thresholds are no longer motivated by conventional economic objectives, such as equating marginal net private benefits with marginal external costs. Instead, the motivation is governed by an essentially ethical judgement about the socially acceptable margin of safety in the exploitation of the natural environment and, above all, the acceptable level of biodiversity necessary to maintain ecosystem functioning and resilience (Perrings and Pearce 1994). We are therefore back in the realm of considering safe minimum standards and the precautionary principle – which is where we started this chapter.

Box 9.4

Environmental policies and ecological threshold effects

Policies for controlling environmental damage are usually governed by a standard economic rule for 'internalizing' any environmental externalities. For example, the 'optimal' level of economic activity would be at the point where the marginal net private benefit (namely, private profit) of those who degrade the environment is just equal to the marginal external cost of environmental degradation on the rest of society. Depending on their relative cost-effectiveness and other considerations, either environmental regulations or market based instruments could be used to attain the desired level. However, this environmental policy 'rule' clearly depends on either private costs and revenues or environmental damage functions being well known and clearly defined. In particular, the latter must be 'well behaved' (in other words, continuous and convex or rising 'smoothly' with the level of environmental degradation).

The presence of ecological thresholds would suggest that environmental damage functions are not well behaved but are most likely 'discontinuous', or 'jump', at the point of the threshold. If the threshold costs – the social costs of exceeding the threshold – are greater than the maximum private net benefit of exceeding the threshold, then the standard environmental policy 'rule' described above no longer holds and cannot be used to determine choice of instruments. Instead, the optimal policy would be to devise a penalty function to prevent private actors from degrading the environment beyond the threshold. This is illustrated for the cases where thresholds are known and not known with certainty.

In Figure 9.1, the external costs of biological resource use are discontinuous at some level of economic activity, q^*_s. At that threshold point, the costs 'jump' to some much higher level, and then continue to increase with the level of economic activity. However, the external costs beyond this ecological threshold are uncertain, for example, they consist of adverse but unknown effects on the flow of ecological services to which that resource contributes, including the overall 'resilience' of an ecosystem. The social costs of exceeding the threshold clearly outweigh the net private gains; consequently, it is not optimal to allow economic activity beyond this point, namely, to the maximum level of private profit, Π_p, at point q^*_p. The optimal policy is to combine user charges for the expected social costs of biological resource use below the threshold level of activity, $0a$, and a penalty above the threshold level of activity, bc. If this penalty is enforced, it will be sufficient to protect society against the costs of exceeding the threshold, and the greater the difference between the penalty and private profit, the greater the margin of safety.

However, it is very rare that ecological thresholds are known with certainty. For example, the rationale for safe minimum standards is based on the lack of knowledge of the threshold level for many species and ecosystems (see Box 9.1). Consequently, the standard which triggers the penalty should be set at a level so as to reduce the 'risk' of overshooting the threshold. As shown in Figure 9.2, the standard is imposed at a much lower level of activity than that which actually breaches the ecological threshold – at a level where ecological damages are known but rising. That is, the penalty function $0abc$ lies to the left of the discontinuity at q^*_s. Thus the penalty function is associated with a safe minimum standard policy that ensures the preservation of a minimum stock of the biological resource that is consistent with maintaining ecological services and ecosystem resilience.

Source: Perrings and Pearce (1994).

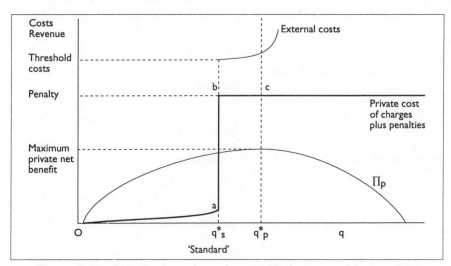

Figure 9.1   *Penalty function: thresholds known with certainty*

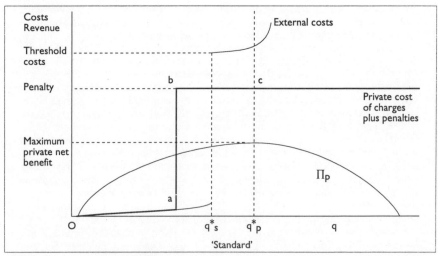

Source: Perrings and Pearce (1994).

Figure 9.2   *Penalty function: thresholds not known with certainty*

CHALLENGES TO BE ADDRESSED

In this chapter we have discussed both the limits to exploitation of ecosystems and the limits to the use of economic policies, particularly traditional regulatory or market based instruments, in controlling environmental degradation and biodiversity loss that threaten ecological sustainability. The conclusion we have reached is that whether one imposes specific limits on economic activity may depend on whether the social costs of crossing ecological thresholds are unknown but believed to be extremely high. This essentially involves an ethical judgement concerning the imposition of a 'margin of safety' on exploitation of the natural environment and, especially, maintaining a minimum level of biodiversity that is necessary to support ecosystem functioning and resilience.

As discussed on pages 171–6, such a judgement is consistent with strong sustainability arguments, particularly concerning the prevention of irreversible loss of essential and non-substitutable biodiversity. Assuming that this perspective is accepted by society, then the optimal 'mix' of policies may be to use safe minimum standards and the precautionary principle to prevent transgression of ecological limits, and traditional instruments to encourage efficiency of economic activities within these limits. Is such an approach feasible or desirable? Deciding on this question requires addressing a number of important issues, which in turn point to the challenges ahead for further research.

First, the evolution of policies based on safe minimum standards and the precautionary principle for safeguarding ecological thresholds is in its infant stage at best. The development of such threshold instruments has largely been restricted to species that are 'endangered' with respect to commercial exploitation (for example, fish stocks, whales and terrestrial mammals). Relatively little attention has been directed to threshold instruments to protect the resilience of ecosystems, particularly where ecological functions and resilience are sensitive to the mix of species, and a change in biodiversity has potentially severe and irreversible consequences (Perrings and Pearce 1994).

Development of instruments to protect ecological thresholds will require greater understanding than at present of the ecological and economic features of 'critical' ecosystems that are the most at risk from economic–environmental interactions. The case studies in Part II provided some examples of the type of information required for management of key natural ecosystems and the economic activity dependent on them. As these examples have revealed, incomplete understanding of ecosystem dynamics may lead to the development of institutions, policies and management strategies that are not adaptive to ecological change. Thus an important challenge for ecological economics is to conduct more research into the inter-relationships between biodiversity, resilience and threshold effects. Without this knowledge, it is difficult to conclude whether there are sufficient benefits to society from employing threshold instruments to restrict the impact of economic activity on biodiversity loss.

Nevertheless, the current 'practical' experience of formulating and developing policies based on safe minimum standards, and the precautionary principle is worth exploring and expanding – even if such policies are limited to protecting 'endangered' species or are used as policy guidelines only. For example, Bishop (1993) notes that safe minimum standards are in effect being employed in the US Endangered Species Act, including the establishment of a high level government committee to grant exemptions to the Act where overriding economic or other concerns are considered to be of greater importance. Other countries are adopting similar legislations, and international treaties, notably the Convention on International Trade in Endangered Species (CITES), operate under the same principle.

However, Bishop (1993) also notes that the real challenge to such policies is implementation, particularly lack of funding. He argues that if safe minimum standards are to be used effectively for overall biodiversity protection, then a guaranteed commitment to funding is required, such as the establishment of a trust fund on a permanent basis. In the US, social security and the highway trust fund are examples of this approach applied to other areas of policy. Such a trust fund could be financed through a 'user' charge or 'tax' on natural resource exploitation. The trust fund could then be allocated to finance safe minimum standards policies and other diversity preservation programmes. Although such a tax could adversely affect economic opportunities of the current generation, such effects would be minimal as the tax would affect only the most marginal uses of natural resources.[3]

Similarly, Costanza and Perrings (1990) suggest that a flexible assurance bonding system based on the precautionary principle has its roots in the user fees and deposit refund schemes currently employed to improving the incentives to recycle materials, such as glass bottles. The important feature of such schemes is that it requires bottle users to pay in advance for the costs they might inflict on the rest of society by throwing bottles away. The bottle deposit is instead refunded if it is presented for recycling.

A flexible environmental assurance bonding system would operate on the same principle. Resource users would have to pay an assurance bond in advance, where the amount paid would cover the projected 'worst case' future marginal costs of resource use. The value of the bond would obviously be higher, the greater the estimate of the worst case costs, and could be sequentially determined to reflect changes in the estimates of environmental damages over time. In the case of biodiversity loss, the amount posted would include estimates of the likely threshold costs of use of particular biological resources.[4] The bond would be refundable in whole or in part if the resource users could demonstrate that their environmental damages are lower than the estimates used in setting the bond and, in particular, are low enough so as not to threaten ecological thresholds. The scheme would provide incentives not only for public and private agents to improve data on the environmental costs of economic activity, but also to reduce these costs through the adoption of more 'environmentally friendly' technology. By incorporating the costs of exceeding thresholds, environmental assurance bonds could also be used to control economic activities that threaten to reduce biodiversity loss below the critical minimum levels necessary to sustain key ecosystems.

These examples suggest that the development of 'threshold instruments' to control biodiversity loss is, in principle, fairly straightforward. Of course, in practice – even if there is sufficient 'political will' for this development (a very

---

3 Bishop (1993) suggests that any additional finances from the trust fund could be used to address other long-run environmental issues, such as global warming, toxic waste clean-up, ozone depletion and so forth. Moreover, the type of revenue raising tax envisioned would not necessarily be so high as to affect resource prices significantly in order to raise substantial funds.

4 For example, in Figure 9.1, worst case estimates of the likely but unknown threshold costs beyond the level of activity q^*s would be included in the value of the bond posted by resource users whose economic activity could exceed that threshold. However, in the case represented by Figure 9.2, where the threshold itself is unknown, the operation of a safe minimum standard and penalty scheme to restrict resource exploitation well within the margin of safety (to the left of q^*s) would be the preferred option to ensure protection of the threshold.

big if!) – the design and implementation of such tools encounters many difficulties. Clearly, more work needs to be done in this area, particularly if, as suggested by this chapter, such schemes ought to receive more consideration in strategies to limit biodiversity loss and ecological disruptions.

However, the problems with safe minimum standards and the precautionary principle discussed on pages 176–8 would suggest caution in the use of threshold instruments. The costs of imposing these tools will multiply where they are badly designed or implemented, or employed indiscriminately and under conditions in which they are not warranted. Although authors of many Biodiversity Programme papers would suggest that some use of threshold instruments may be necessary to control the current problem of biodiversity loss, there remain many unresolved questions concerning the extent to which they should be used and on which resource using activities – as well as the critical issue of the timing or 'phasing in' of their use.

Even if it is agreed that an 'optimal mix' of traditional regulatory and market based instruments, along with threshold instruments, should be employed to combat biodiversity loss, there is still the difficult issue of determining this optimal mix, as well as the sequencing of policy instruments. For example, as discussed in Box 9.1, proponents of safe minimum standards argue that implementation of such policies is a necessary 'first step' in ensuring that our current economy, which is 'unsustainable' in its use of biological resources due to pervasive market and policy failure, is redirected on to a development path that more reasonably safeguards future economic opportunities through conserving biodiversity. Consequently, the use of threshold instruments should come first to preserve threshold limits, and the use of traditional regulatory and market based instruments could follow to control the environmental damage of economic activity that obeys these limits.

However, the counter-argument is that elimination of many market and policy failures concerning resource use and environmental degradation may by itself be sufficient for conserving biodiversity (see Box 9.1). The need for threshold instruments can therefore be overly exaggerated in many cases and thus they may be inappropriately applied. Given that such threshold instruments adversely affect the economic opportunities of the current generation and, if wrongly used, also affect the welfare of future generations, there is a great risk in resorting to such instruments as the 'first step' in policies to control biodiversity loss.

The view taken in this chapter is that there are merits to both arguments. Under ideal conditions, the 'optimal' sequencing of policies would be as follows.

■   To eliminate existing policy distortions that are environmentally damaging, namely, the removal of subsidies and other public policy interventions that distort the private costs of resource use and pollution discharge.
■   To implement regulatory and market based instruments to 'internalize' the environmental costs of economic activities in the most cost-effective manner.

The more punitive threshold instruments should be employed in conditions where policy reform and traditional environmental instruments are not sufficient on their own to control biodiversity loss. However, as argued throughout this chapter, it is precisely the conditions generated by irreversible biodiversity loss with unknown environmental impacts that reduce the likelihood that traditional environmental instruments will be sufficient to deal with the problem. Moreover, there are likely to be critical ecosystems and biological resources that will need urgent protection and safeguards in place sooner rather than later – which may mean that the 'optimal' sequencing of policies is reversed and threshold instruments are implemented as the 'first step'.

In practice, the evolution of actual management and incentive schemes could involve many possible combinations of both traditional and threshold policy instruments for biodiversity conservation. Hopefully, the right combinations will emerge that are appropriate to the particular biodiversity problems being addressed, and that the management and incentive schemes that emerge adequately reflect conditions at the international, national and local level. It is this latter issue that is the topic of the next chapter.

10

Policies and Institutions for Biodiversity Conservation

In the preceding chapter we discussed whether there is a need for innovative policies to limit the risk of ecological 'threshold effects' posed by continued loss of biodiversity, and how such threshold instruments should be combined with traditional regulatory and market based instruments to control environmental degradation. We concluded that progress in formulating the appropriate policy response to the biodiversity problem is dependent upon evolving effective management and incentive schemes at the international, national and local level. Improvements in policies and institutions at, say, the international level will not significantly reduce biodiversity loss if complementary improvements are not forthcoming at the national and local levels.

In the following sections we draw on examples from the Biodiversity Programme papers to illustrate the type of effective management and incentive schemes required to control environmental degradation and maintain biodiversity. We discuss both the challenges to be addressed and possible ways forward at all three levels where progress is needed – international, national and local.

INTERNATIONAL MANAGEMENT AND INCENTIVES

Many aspects of the global biodiversity problem have their roots in a global 'open access' or 'market failure' situation. In addition, as the burden of biodiversity conservation may increasingly fall on the more resource abundant developing countries, issues of international compensation are at stake. In the following section we discuss the views of several Biodiversity Programme papers on these issues and the international policies advocated.

Pearce and Perrings (1994) point out that the need for global management and institutions arises because biodiversity is essentially a 'layered' public good.[1] That is, not only does biodiversity loss generate externalities at the national level – in terms of loss of valuable goods, services and ecological functions – but it also produces externalities at the international level. At the very least, the global community may value the existence of biodiversity. In addition, the many future potential uses that a diverse stock of biological resources may offer also have a global value – in particular, the availability of a diverse 'pool' of genetic material not only to derive new products (such as pharmaceuticals, medicines, crops and chemicals), but also to generate new technologies (such as biotechnologies and

---

1 In economics, the term public good refers to a good or service where consumption is 'non-rival' and 'non-exclusive'. The former implies that consumption of the commodity by one individual does not affect the quantity or the quality of the consumption of others; the latter indicates that it is impossible to exclude others from consuming the commodity.

Box 10.1

The public good aspects of global biodiversity values

Public goods are commodities that can be supplied to additional consumers at no extra cost. 'Pure' public goods are both non-rival and non-exclusive. The former implies that consumption of the commodity by one individual does not affect the quantity or the quality of the consumption of others; the latter indicates that it is impossible to exclude others from consuming the commodity.

There are generally very few pure public goods. However, as indicated in Table 10.1 below, there are many commodities that fall between the extremes of pure public and private goods. For example, Randall (1983) argues that some non-exclusive commodities may be non-rival only up to a certain level of consumption and then potentially rival. These are essentially congestible goods. Consequently, common pool resources are non-exclusive goods that are either rival or congestible. Similarly, Aylward (1992) defines sovereign resources as those commodities which are exclusive but their consumption is either non-rival or congestible.

Table 10.1 *Classifying goods*

	Non-exclusive	Exclusive
Non-rival	'Pure' public goods	Sovereign resources
Congestible	Common pool resources	
Rival		Private goods

This classification is useful for discussing the global public good characteristics of many biodiversity values.

For example, many important commercially exploitable species are common pool resources that cross international boundaries, e.g. fisheries and migratory animals such as elephants, birds and whales. International management of these resources including regulation of exploitation is generally necessary to prevent 'open access' depletion.[2]

Nevertheless, the vast majority of the world's biological diversity appears to be concentrated within national boundaries, and thus individual countries essentially have exclusive rights (i.e. sovereignty) over exploiting the biodiversity contained within their borders. However, this does not mean that all the important values of biological diversity can be easily 'captured' by these countries in the form of private goods tradable on markets. For example, tropical countries are believed to contain most of the world's genetic material, but it may be valued by all countries, particularly industrialized nations, as a source of new crop varieties, pharmaceuticals, chemicals and biotechnologies. However, genetic material is essentially non-rival by nature. The 'extraction' of genetic information by one researcher does not impinge on the ability of others to do the same. Hence the way tropical genetic material is currently being exploited would suggest that it is a sovereign resource. Yet the products that are derived from this information are turned into private, marketable goods through the patent process – which allows companies to exclude others from the new and rival products they create. The failure – and often inability – of developing countries to protect their intellectual property rights, and the lack of global agreements supporting these rights, means that they are unable to appropriate the full contribution of their sovereign genetic material to global values.[3]

In addition, although individual countries have sovereign rights or claims over all or part of the major natural systems of the world, the ecological process and services of these systems may benefit more than one country. Examples include the support of mangroves for marine fisheries, the regional and global climatic influence of forest systems, and the protection and water supply functions of major watershed systems. Ecological functions and services are essentially non-exclusive and congestible, and thus have the characteristics of common pool resources. As ecological processes are degraded, the quantity and quality of ecological services and functions are significantly affected. However, it is unlikely that a country is going to bear the costs of maintaining its biodiversity and ecological processes for the benefit of other countries unless it is adequately compensated. This is particularly the case for developing countries, where the competing demands for exploiting the remaining areas of natural environment and biological diversity, coupled with public and market failures that are biased in favour of increased exploitation and conversion, mean that damage to major ecosystem services is occurring at an alarming rate.

Perhaps the global existence value of biodiversity best approximates the characteristic of a pure public good. This value derives from individuals deriving satisfaction from knowing that a particular species, habitat or natural system exists somewhere on earth. Often, these individuals may reside in a completely different part of the world. However, it is impossible to exclude anyone from holding existence values, and one individual's satisfaction does not prevent satisfaction by others. There are nevertheless problems of free riding. Individuals or groups do not have the incentive to act unilaterally to conserve the species, habitat, or ecosystem if all others who hold existence values obtain the benefits for free. This is particularly the case with regard to global existence values. The disparity between the number of global beneficiaries from existence values and those managing the resource means that the latter cannot easily 'capture' or appropriate these values. Once again, developing countries are especially affected, as they are the custodians for much of the world's remaining biodiversity and natural environments.

Source: Adapted from Aylward (1992).

gene transfers). Finally, as stressed throughout this book, the impacts of biodiversity loss on ecological resilience may also have global impacts, especially if major ecosystems such as forests, marine and coastal environments, rangelands and wetlands are severely affected, and the 'multiplier effects' of ecological interdependencies amplify the scale and magnitude of disturbances across regions and countries.

Box 10.1 illustrates the problem of international management of biodiversity and biological resources that display global public goods characteristics for many important values. Essentially, several international institutional and policy mechanisms are lacking that prevent adequate management of key global biodi-

---

2 Open access exploitation of common pool resources increases the risks of rapid depletion because of the non-exclusivity problem. The absence of common management rules means that access by individuals to the resource is not controlled and each individual has the incentive to exploit the resource as quickly as possible before exploitation becomes 'congested'. Moreover, if it is impossible to exclude others from exploiting the resource, the existence of any access rents (namely, profits) from exploitation will be an incentive for many individuals to undertake this activity or alternatively for the individuals already exploiting the resource to expand their activities.

3 Calculations by Aylward *et al* (1993) suggest that, as the information contained in tropical genetic material is essentially the basic raw material of a highly sophisticated biochemical production process, the 'value added' contribution to products such as pharmaceuticals is much less than previous estimates suggest. Nevertheless, this contribution is still significant enough in value terms for certain tropical countries to improve their ability to 'capture' this value; hence, there is a strong rationale for the development of new institutions for this purpose, such as the Instituto Nacional de Bioversidad (INBio) in Costa Rica.

versity values, including international fisheries and migratory animals, genetic material, ecosystem services and existence values. Countries and individuals managing natural environments that generate these global benefits do not currently capture an adequate share of these values. The result is too little conservation of biodiversity, as countries and individuals do not have the incentive to maintain sufficient biodiversity to continue generating global benefits. Developing countries are especially affected by this incentive problem, as they are the custodians for much of the world's remaining biodiversity and natural environments that are the source of significant global values.

For example, as suggested by Swanson (1992a and 1994), a major constraint on the ability of developing countries to benefit from the potential value of their biodiversity is the lack of an international system of legal rights over the information potential of natural resources. The establishment of intellectual property rights is necessary to protect investments that generate information. More specifically, a monopoly right can be granted for the marketing of a particular range of tangible goods as a basis for compensating both past informational investments, as well as any future ones made on the initial 'idea' or 'piece of information'. Intellectual property rights are currently used to reward informational investments in a wide variety of markets, such as computer software.

However, intellectual property rights do not yet apply to the potential informational value contained in natural resources, such as genetic material. Swanson (1992a and 1994) argues that such an international system of rights should be developed for biological resources in order to compensate countries and individuals for conserving stocks of potentially useful biodiversity. Investments in the retention of natural environments and lands that are rich in biodiversity, and in the research effort necessary to determine the usefulness of genetic material and resources, are essentially information generating investments. The creation and protection of a system of intellectual property rights for these investments would provide incentives to conserve biodiversity in two ways:

■ there would be an exclusive right to market discoveries derived from analysing the useful properties of genetic material from biodiversity; and
■ there would be a subsidiary right to license prospecting for useful biological materials in existing natural habitats.

It is necessary for such rights to be recognized internationally to avoid piracy of identified uses and to ensure their inclusion within existing international patent treaties.

In the absence of an international system of intellectual property rights for the potentially useful genetic information contained in biodiversity, some countries are developing their own 'value added' biological prospecting activities and contractual licensing agreements in order to establish exclusive rights over and returns from genetic information. The most advanced case is the Instituto Nacional de Biodiversidad (INBio) in Costa Rica (Aylward et al 1993). Through collection, curating and prospecting activities, INBio hopes to codify and market genetic information from biotic samples collected from Costa Rica's natural areas as a means of generating financial returns that will flow back into conservation.

Supported by government and government money, INBio also has lucrative commercial licensing contracts with Merck & Co and the British Technology Group (BTG) for the exclusive provision of tested biotic samples. Although these pharmaceutical prospecting contracts cannot sustain biodiversity protection in Costa Rica by themselves, prospecting can provide funds for the development of taxonomic information which may yield many other economic benefits to the country, for example the training of parataxonomists, the development of a national biodiversity inventory, improved biotechnology and scientific capacity in local universities, and educational, ecotourism and research benefits.[4]

A system of intellectual property rights that is internationally recognized would probably support further investments in the information potential of biodiversity like the INBio 'experiment' in developing countries. As more such 'experiments' are established, it may be necessary to evolve such a system to settle disputes over patent rights and exclusive licensing arrangements. Hopefully, increased investments in the information potential of biodiversity will lead to the development of the appropriate international mechanisms and institutions to protect intellectual property rights over biodiversity.

Swanson (1994) suggests that there a variety of other international policies and regulations that could be adopted to improve the incentives for individual countries to manage natural resources that yield important global benefit. The main purpose should be to create and maintain a global premium on investments by individual countries in diverse resources. Such a premium can be created through two mechanisms: international compensation agreements and international market regulation agreements. We will discuss each type of mechanism in turn.

International market regulation

The intellectual property right regime for genetic material discussed above is one example of international market regulation. Another example would be the development of sustainable trade regimes for wildlife and natural resource products to provide sufficient returns to countries to invest in maintaining stocks of these resources. Swanson (1994) cites the example of the trade in elephant ivory. He argues that the ban on the ivory trade by CITES was precisely the wrong incentive for elephant management in Africa. Although the continental populations of elephant have declined by half in recent decades, these populations had fallen precisely in those states that had not been investing their resources and using proceeds from the (legal) trade in ivory to compensate these investments. In other states that had invested in managing their elephants and taken advantage

---

4   There are also important 'spin-off' benefits from particular agreements. For example, the BTG contract is for the development of a demonstrated phloem mobile nematicide (DMDP) which can be derived from a plant grown in Costa Rica. In exchange for INBio's sale of an unspecified amount of pure active ingredient to BTG, the company has granted INBio exclusive production and distribution rights within Costa Rica for the final product, and stipulated that licencees in other countries will seek to source the raw material for this product from Costa Rica. In addition for the spin-off benefits for INBio, there may be additional benefits for Costa Rica in that DMDP may replace the use of chemical nematicides currently used by farmers which can be ecologically damaging.

of the trade to do so, such as Zimbabwe, their elephant populations had vastly increased over the same period (for example, by 100 per cent in Zimbabwe).[5]

A proper sustainable wildlife trade exchange – and ivory exchange in the case of the African elephant – would be one way of ensuring that countries investing their diverse resources would receive a premium and countries that do not would be penalized. For example, only suppliers that show evidence of investing and managing their resources would be allowed in the exchange, and any consumer of products through the exchange would know that the funds would flow to a supplier that invests in the resource. To the extent that consumer countries agree and enforce purchases solely from the exchange, the result would be greatly enhanced prices for the supplier countries allowed to participate in the exchange. The exchange based price differential would therefore constitute the premium for suppliers who invest and maintain their resources, and the penalty for suppliers who do not.

However, international market regulations to improve resource management have to be employed with caution. They appear to be effective mainly when mismanagement of trade incentives appears to be a major factor in resource degradation, and where increased regulation can facilitate increased returns and thus incentives for long-run investment and management in the resource. These conditions require careful analysis of the economic incentives between trade and resource management.

For example, in recent years concerns about tropical deforestation have led to an increased focus on the role of the timber trade in promoting forest depletion and degradation. Despite concern over the state of tropical deforestation and its implications for global welfare, several recent studies have indicated that the tropical timber trade is not the major direct cause of the problem – perhaps less than 10 per cent of total deforestation – whereas conversion of forests for agriculture is much more significant (Amelung and Diehl 1992; Barbier et al 1993b; Binkley and Vincent 1991; Hyde et al 1991). Nevertheless, it is clear that current levels of timber extraction in tropical forests – both open and closed – exceed the rate of reforestation (WRI 1992). Less than 1 million ha, out of an estimated total global area of 828 million ha of productive tropical forest in 1985, was under sustained yield management for timber production (Poore et al 1989). Moreover, timber extraction has a major indirect role in promoting tropical deforestation by opening up previously unexploited forest, which then allows other economic uses of the forests, such as agricultural conversion, to take place (Amelung and Diehl 1992; Barbier et al 1991). For example, in many African producer countries, around half of the area that is initially logged is subsequently deforested, while there is little, if any, deforestation of previously unlogged forested land (Barbier et al 1993b).

Proponents of intervention in the tropical timber trade argue that such a policy is justified in two important respects.

■ Bans, taxes, quantitative restrictions and other interventions could be used to discriminate between the trade in tropical forest products from sustainably

---

5 For further details on the economics of the ivory trade, see Barbier et al (1990).

managed production forests, and products from forests that are poorly managed and harvested. Outright bans are advocated by those who believe that all trade in tropical timber is destructive to the forests.

■ Proponents of intervention also argue that, as virtually all major tropical forest countries are producers and exporters of timber products, intervention in the global timber market – such as a tax on imports – would force these countries to 'internalize' the global values ascribed to their tropical forests that are lost through the depletion arising from timber production.

This is because the major global externalities of tropical forests, such as their role as a 'store' of biodiversity and carbon, and their 'macro' climatic functions, are essentially ignored by domestic policy makers in deciding how much forest land to allocate to timber production and how much timber to produce.

Barbier and Rauscher (1994a and 1994b) use a theoretical model to examine the effect of timber trade interventions on the incentives for tropical timber exporting countries to conserve their forests. Their analysis indicates that if importing nations want the exporting countries to conserve more of their forests, trade interventions appear to be a second-best way of achieving this result. Under certain conditions, they may be counter-productive.[6] These results are consistent with what was said earlier about international market regulation – in order to be effective, such regulation has to provide incentives for improved investment in resources and not penalize resource use indiscriminately.

Recent empirical studies have supported the results of the Barbier–Rauscher model (Barbier et al 1993b; Binkley and Vincent 1991; Hyde et al 1991). For example, an analysis of the implications of trade interventions on controlling timber related deforestation in Indonesia is described in Box 10.2. Generally, these studies have also concluded that trade intervention is a 'second-best' option for controlling tropical deforestation. Rather, as discussed in Chapter 4 of this book, the heart of the problem of biodiversity loss through tropical deforestation arises through market and policy failures in tropical forest countries themselves. The failure to manage production forests sustainably also arises from poor forest sector policies and regulations to ensure that sufficient incentives and invest-ments are available at the forest stand level to maintain the resource over the long run. Rewarding countries that move towards sustainable management of their production forests by opening international markets to their products – and not restricting access to those markets – would be one important incentive for further investments in sustainable management.

International compensation

The model by Barbier and Rauscher (1994a and 1994b) does indicate that, in contrast to trade intervention, international transfers that reduce the dependency

---

6   In their theoretical model, Barbier and Rauscher (1994a and 1994b) demonstrate that trade interventions that decrease the terms of trade of the tropical timber exporting country will lead to reductions in the long run equilibrium of the forest stock, if the country is import dependent. The latter condition is reflected in the elasticity of marginal utility with respect to imported consumption goods; for example, a country is import dependent if the absolute value of this elasticity is greater than one.

Box 10.2

Trade interventions and deforestation in Indonesia

As part of a study of the global tropical timber trade, the effects of a total import ban on a major tropical timber producer, Indonesia, were simulated (Barbier et al 1993a and 1993b). According to the results of the analysis, an import ban would have a devastating impact on Indonesia's forest industry in the short term (see Table 10.2). Although there would be significant diversion of plywood and sawnwood exports to domestic consumption, this would be insufficient to compensate for the loss of exports. Net production in both processing industries would fall. Given its export orientation, the plywood industry would be particularly hurt – reducing its output by over 40 per cent. Net production losses in the sawnwood industry would be closer to 10 per cent. The overall effect is to lower domestic log demand in the short term by around 25-30 per cent.

The policy scenario is, of course, assuming that the import ban is 100 per cent effective. It is unlikely that all importers of Indonesia's tropical timber products – many of which are also newly industrializing or producer countries with processing capacities – would go along with a Western-imposed ban. In any case, one would expect that over the longer term there would be some diversion of Indonesian plywood and sawnwood exports to either new import markets or existing markets that prove to be less stringent in applying the ban (such as other developing or newly industrializing countries).

The long-term implications of an import ban on tropical deforestation are also not encouraging. Even if the ban is 100 per cent effective in the short term, any reduction in tropical deforestation resulting from lower levels of timber harvesting is likely to be short lived. A total import ban would cause a major diversion of Indonesian timber products to meet domestic demand. Although in the short term net production of wood products, and thus log demand, would fall, this situation would not necessarily be sustained over the long run. Even if this is not the case, the ban may be ineffective in permanently reducing tropical deforestation because: (i) timber production is not the main source of deforestation in Indonesia; and, (ii) as the value of holding on to the forest for timber production decreases, the incentives to convert more of the resource to alternative uses such as agriculture will increase.

The timber trade model of Indonesia was also employed to show the effects of import taxes on a major exporter (see Table 10.2). The results suggest that tax rates beyond 1–5 per cent would begin introducing major distortionary effects. However, such low levels of tax would clearly have little impacts on reducing deforestation in Indonesia. Their only purpose would be to raise revenue that could be then transferred to Indonesia and other tropical forest countries for forest conservation and sustainable management initiatives. In addition, it would probably be more effective if Indonesia raised the money itself for 'sustainable management' programmes by imposing revenue raising export surcharges.

Source: Barbier et al (1993a and 1993b)

of the producer country on the exploitation of tropical forests for export earnings are more effective in promoting conservation of the forest stock. Essentially, such transfers would be a form of international compensation to tropical forest countries for holding on to more forests than they would otherwise. The basic

Table 10.2 *Indonesia – timber trade and tropical deforestation simulation model*

Policy senario – import ban and revenue raising taxes (% change over base case)

Key variables	Total import ban [a]	1% revenue raising import tax [b]	5% revenue raising import tax [d]
1. Prices (Rp/m^3)			
Log border equivalent price (unit value)	–	–0.17%	–0.82%
Sawnwood export price (unit value)	–	–0.11%	–0.54%
Plywood export price (unit value)	–	–0.21%	–1.03%
2.Quantities ('000 m^3)			
Log production	–28.33%	–0.04%	–0.19%
Log domestic consumption	–27.37%	–0.04%	–0.18%
Sawnwood production	–10.64%	–0.03%	–0.14%
Sawnwood exports	–100.00%	–0.23%	–1.12%
Sawnwood domestic consumption	30.01%	0.06%	0.30%
Plywood production	–43.84%	–0.04%	–0.22%
Plywood exports	–100.00%	–0.10%	–0.51%
Plywood domestic consumption	214.51%	0.23%	1.12%
3. Deforestation (km^2)			
Total forest area	–	0.00% [c]	0.01%
Annual rate of deforestation	–	–0.41%	–0.72%

Notes: [a] Large price changes were used deliberately to constrain sawnwood and plywood exports to zero in this simulation and therefore are no longer endogenously generated by this model. Also, the functional form of the deforestation equation and its estimation using regional panel data imply that the large changes in log production associated with the import ban scenario cannot be used to predict reliably the effects on forest cover and deforestation. Thus, both price and deforestation effects are eliminated from this policy scenario simulation.
[b] A total of US$23.1 million (1980 prices) in revenue would be raised, with US$5.8 million and US$17.3 million from Indonesian sawnwood and plywood exports respectively.
[c] A negligible increase over the base case forest cover of 53 km^2.
[d] A total of US$113.9 million (1980 prices) in revenue would be raised, with US$28.5 million and US$85.4 million from Indonesian sawnwood and plywood exports respectively.

Source: Barbier et al (1993a).

principle is that, to the extent that all nations benefit from the global external benefits resulting from sustainable management of large tracts of tropical forest lands, the international community should compensate producing nations for the loss of potential income that they would incur by reducing tropical deforestation, timber sales and conversion of forest land to other uses. The revenues for this international compensation should be made available from financial resources in addition to and separate from the trade in tropical timber products.

Empirical studies have confirmed that there is a strong rationale for additional funds to be made available to producer countries for sustainable forest management from sources outside of the tropical timber trade (Barbier et al 1993b). Comprehensive international agreements, targeted financial aid flows and compensation mechanisms to deal with the overall problem of tropical deforestation may ultimately eliminate the need to consider intervention in the timber trade. Given that commercial logging is not the primary cause of tropical deforestation, such approaches would avoid unnecessary, and possibly inappropriate, discrimination against the timber trade. On the other hand, a comprehensive tropical forest agreement seems much more difficult to negotiate and raises its own problems of workability and effectiveness.[7]

More innovative international mechanisms and institutions may be required. For example, Amelung (1993) argues the case for the establishment of an international rainforest fund, as proposed by UNEP, in order to avoid free-riding among non-tropical countries. Similar arguments are put forward by Sedjo, Bowes and Wiseman (1991), although their preference is for the establishment of a global system of marketable forest protection and management obligations (FPMOs).

Similar systems of strategic international payments could be established for a wide variety of biodiversity conservation areas, including tropical forests. Swanson (1994) proposes that such payments could form an international parks agreement or a resource franchise agreement. Under an international parks agreement, the global community would pay the rental price of unconverted land held in national parks and possibly provide a subsidy for management services as well. In complete preservation areas, the rental price of land should approximate the forgone land development opportunities; where some sustainable resource use is allowed, the rental price paid by the international community should equal the difference between the returns on resource use and the returns from conversion or full development.

The latter rental price condition also applies to the resource franchise agreement, which is a three-way agreement between the host country government, the franchisee and the international community. Limited and sustainable resource use of the land would be allowed, but it would be 'franchised' through competitive bidding to a local entity. The franchisee would be responsible for providing management and protection services from the returns it generates from resource use, and the host country government is responsible for monitoring and enforcing the franchise agreement. If it fails to do so, the host country would forfeit the rental payment. Otherwise, the international community would pay a land rent to the host country equal to the difference between the value of the franchisee's bid and the full value of the land if it were developed or converted to other uses.

A different and even more comprehensive system of internationally transferable development rights (TDRs) has been proposed by Panayotou (1994). The basic approach is described in Box 10.3. A market for internationally transferable development rights differs from other international compensation proposals in that TDRs could be issued unilaterally and transferred bilaterally without the need for an international convention on tropical forests or biodiversity. Except for a minimum level of legislation to establish the TDRs, and perhaps the commitment by developed country governments to stimulate demand initially, the system relies on the market to determine the value of TDRs and to achieve

---

7 See Barrett (1990) for a general discussion of the difficulties involved in securing international environmental agreements.

the optimal level of biodiversity conservation for global values. Thus once established, regulation and enforcement of the mechanism is kept to a minimum. Politically, a system of TDRs is likely to be more acceptable to developing countries as it provides a good deal of control over conservation and development decisions, and at the same time ensures that they are paid the full development opportunity costs of biodiversity conservation.

There are nevertheless a number of important obstacles to the implementation of TDRs. In particular, the initial division of land and establishment of the market must be carefully planned and managed, purchasers need to be assured of the level of protection of habitats once TDRs are transferred and a verifiable system of rights attached to TDRs needs to be determined (for example, right of access, dividends from discoveries, division of capital gains from appreciation and so on). There are also long term considerations such as political and economic stability within host countries, and international capital market movements. However, the attraction of the TDR system is that it can be implemented easily on a trial or pilot basis, and gradually extended and replicated once countries have sufficient experience in operating the system.

To some extent, variations of the TDR system already exist in the form of debt-for-nature swaps and the Global Environmental Facility (GEF) (Panayotou 1994).

Debt-for-nature swaps essentially involve the transfer of development rights over conservation land from developing countries to international environmental non-governmental organizations (NGOs) in exchange for payment of part of the national debt. Countries such as Bolivia, Costa Rica, Ecuador, the Philippines and Poland have benefited. However, these deals are very ad hoc, and the values of the development rights determined by these swaps do not necessarily bear any resemblance to the actual costs of forgone development opportunities. To the extent that a market has been created for such swaps, it is a thin one in terms of the amount of land traded and with high transaction costs. Moreover, repayment of debt that is heavily discounted in secondary markets is not generally considered by developing countries as adequate compensation for transference of development rights over large areas of their tropical forests.

Similarly, the GEF is in part a collective arrangement for the transfer of development rights out of environments with global biodiversity values in developing countries, with the compensation for this transfer largely paid by developed countries who are the main donors to the GEF. The facility has funds of about US$1.5 billion to be disbursed over the next few years, and is to be managed by the Programme (UNDP), United Nations Environment Programme (UNEP) and the World Bank. The GEF's mandate is to finance investment, technical assistance and institutional development activities in four areas: global climate change, ozone depletion, protection of biodiversity and water resource degradation. In particular, the GEF would fund activities to protect biodiversity and natural habitats that would provide cost-effective benefits to the global environment, but would not have been undertaken by an individual country because the measurable benefits to a national economy were too low to justify investment by that country on its own (Munasinghe 1992).

Box 10.3

Internationally transferable development rights

A system of internationally transferable development rights (TDRs) could in principle be developed to ensure adequate conservation of global biodiversity values
in tropical countries. TDRs have been used extensively in American and European
cities for the conservation of historic buildings and other sites of cultural heritage,
and are also being used for biodiversity conservation on the Akamas Peninsula of
Cyprus (see Box 10.6).

The first step in establishing TDRs for biodiversity conservation would be to
divide land into conservation and development areas. Individuals owning land in
conservation areas would retain their development rights, but not be allowed to
use them on site. Instead, they would sell or transfer these rights to property in
the development area. Since the development area is likely to be several times
the size of the conservation area, there would be a strong demand for development rights from land owners in the development area (for example, to sidestep
zoning or building regulations). Thus an active market in development rights
would be created through which the land owners in the conservation areas are
fully compensated for their 'frozen' development rights and they will still share in
the financial benefits of economic development.

An international market for TDRs could also be implemented. Tropical countries
could set aside habitats for biodiversity conservation and divide each habitat into
a number of TDRs. Each TDR would indicate the location, condition, diversity and
degree of protection of the habitat, and any special rights that it conveys to the
buyer/holder. TDRs could then be offered for sale both locally and internationally
at an initial offer price that covers fully the opportunity cost of the corresponding
land unit (namely, the net present value of the income forgone from the alternative
development opportunity). If the initial offer price does not clear the market, then
the price could be adjusted. Alternatively, the quantity and/or quality of land under
TDRs could be changed.

The international market for TDRs could be completely wide open. Potential
buyers could include local and international environmental organizations, local
and international foundations and corporations, developed country governments,
chemical pharmaceutical companies, scientific societies, universities and research institutions, and even environmentally minded individuals. The main benefit of the market in TDRs would be that such a diverse group of buyers would be
able to express their preferences for a wide variety of global benefits through an
international market transaction that transfers development values (the supply of
TDRs) into conservation values (the purchase of TDRs to hold land as carbon
offsets, preservation areas, sources of genetic material and so on). Moreover,
such a transfer would require payment of the full opportunity costs of conservation to private and public land owners in tropical countries.

However, the international market in TDRs would not reflect all the environmental benefits of biodiversity conservation, but only the global values. The rights
to other natural land areas that yield other environmental services such as ecotourism, watershed protection and so forth should be retained within the host
country, as the benefits of these services occur locally or nationally, and should
provide motivation for national conservation efforts.

Nevertheless, the global problem of biodiversity loss and increasing ecological
scarcity should lead to a corresponding growth in the value of biodiversity. The
result should be an appreciation in the value of TDRs with time, as scientists,

biotechnologists and pharmaceutical companies seek access to conservation areas for research, and exploration for new substances and products. The owners of TDRs as shareholders in a particular habitat should therefore be entitled to dividends and/or earn capital gains on their TDRs, as the demand for genetic material and information resources increases. The global value associated with the ecological services of biodiversity habitats may also appreciate with time. For example, the carbon sequestration value of tropical forests should be expected to rise with the predicted growth in global greenhouse gas emissions.

Given the public good characteristics and free-riding problems associated with the global values of biodiversity (see Box 10.1), it is possible that there may be insufficient demand for TDRs, at least initially, to conserve enough biodiversity to meet these global values. The governments of developed countries, who appear to be the main beneficiaries of global values, could enhance the demand for TDRs in two ways.

■ These governments could provide credits or offsets against domestic regu- lations in exchange for purchase of TDRs from conservation areas in the tropics.

■ Developed country governments could introduce a conservation tax, and then allow individuals the option of paying this annual tax or purchasing and holding TDRs from tropical countries instead.

Source: Panayotou (1994).

However, the GEF is constrained by its limited funding and its project-by-pro- ject approach which does not represent a TDR-type market mechanism (Panayo- tou 1994). On the other hand, the GEF was never intended to be more than an investment fund and a pilot one at that. It remains an important first step in the mobilization of concessionary funding for protecting natural habitats, as well as encouraging limited and sustainable use of biological resources, and the transfer of technology for this purpose. The next stage would be to develop a better understanding of the functioning of the pilot activities under the GEF, in developing policy measures to control loss of biodiversity, in valuing the costs and benefits of preservation, and in facilitating other complementary interna- tional mechanisms, such as the ones discussed here (Munasinghe 1992).

Perhaps one encouraging sign has been the formulation in recent years of an international Convention on Biological Diversity that, at the very least, endorses the principle of incremental cost financing pioneered by the GEF (Barrett 1994a and 1994b). That is, under the terms of the Convention, developed country signatories have an obligation to provide new and additional financial resources to developing countries to help them meet any portion of the costs that the latter may incur in implementing globally beneficial biodiversity conservation over and above the national benefits of conservation.[8] The important principle is that, unless developed countries offer compensation to developing countries, the latter

---

8   Thus the term incremental costs is somewhat misleading, as it does not relate to the normal usage of the term as the marginal or additional costs of conserving one more unit of biodiversity. Instead, the Convention's interpretation of incremental cost financing is as follows: supposing a developing country conserves an area of forest at a present value cost, C, and receives local or national present value benefits, B (such as watershed protection). However, C > B and so the country will not undertake conservation investments on its own. On the other hand, if the forest also has unknown but positive global biodiversity benefits that make it worth conserving, then developed countries should pay the 'incremental' costs of conservation, which in this case are C–B.

will not undertake additional biodiversity conservation on behalf of the global community.

Barrett (1994a and 1994b) has analysed whether this principle of incremental cost financing for conservation of global biodiversity values can be sustained in a self-enforcing international environmental agreement. His analytical results are not encouraging. Assuming that a system of rewards and penalties can be negotiated to discourage free-riding, when an agreement is signed by many countries, the agreement may not succeed in increasing global net benefits by much. When net benefits could be increased substantially through cooperation, the full cooperative solution may not be sustainable.

What this implies is that the Convention on Biological Diversity, which has been signed by almost all countries, may not increase global well-being substantially. However, this may not be a negative result if developed countries have strong unilateral incentives to conserve global biodiversity in any case, or that global welfare would not really increase substantially if more global biodiversity is conserved. On the other hand, if developed countries have weak incentives to conserve global biodiversity unilaterally and global welfare would increase substantially if more biodiversity is conserved, then the shortcomings of the Convention are all too apparent.

However, Barrett (1994a and 1994b) acknowledges that by focusing on the incremental cost financing aspect alone may be too narrow a criterion for judging the effectiveness of the Biodiversity Convention. Other issues addressed by the Convention that may have significant implications for global biodiversity conservation include the assignment of property rights to biodiversity and the appropriate measure of diversity. In addition, even if its actual implementation as a self-enforcing agreement is unworkable, the importance of the Convention in terms of fostering global commitment to the principles of biodiversity conservation and international compensation, cannot be overlooked. By establishing these principles in the international community, the Convention may facilitate the development of more effective means for conserving globally beneficial biodiversity – such as some of the institutions and mechanisms discussed earlier in this section.

REGIONAL AND NATIONAL MANAGEMENT

Although we have discussed generally the broad issues concerning policy imperatives and instruments in Chapter 9, many of the Biodiversity Programme papers provide specific examples of national and regional management of key ecosystems, notably through the establishment of protected areas. In this section, we discuss these issues in more detail, focusing on the implications for site specific biodiversity conservation.

In addition, in the previous section we raised the issue that international policies and mechanisms should not be concerned with all the environmental benefits of biodiversity conservation but only the global values. The environmental benefits of biodiversity and natural environments that accrue locally or nationally should provide motivation for national conservation efforts. However, as argued in Chapter 4 and illustrated by the case studies of Part II, pervasive market and policy failures often lead to development decisions that are biased against the conservation of biological diversity, even if important benefits to the national economy and human livelihoods are lost. Often, this results from the lack of proper valuation of and accounting for the benefits of biodiversity conservation in national management strategies. We begin this section by briefly examining this issue.

As argued by Wells (1992), one of the critical challenges facing advocates of increased levels of biodiversity protection is to convince policy makers that scarce financial and other resources should be diverted into biodiversity conservation at the expense of other competing programmes. This is particularly the case for developing countries, where the national and local benefits of biodiversity conservation are not often apparent and occur over a long time frame, whereas 'more pressing' development needs such as poverty alleviation are thought to take priority.

In Parts I and II, we provide ample evidence of why much biodiversity conservation through efficient and sustainable management of natural resources is complementary to, rather than at odds with, economic development and poverty alleviation. Improving the incomes and welfare of local communities, especially poor ones, while simultaneously preserving physical and biological systems, offers opportunities for developing countries to pursue the environmental, economic and social goals of sustainable development in a complementary manner (Munasinghe 1993). An important requirement is to develop policy measures that can make market forces work more effectively to improve natural resource use, while also addressing equity concerns, particularly differences between those who bear the costs of environmental improvement and those who benefit. Related to this issue is the appropriate valuation of the contribution of biodiversity, natural habitats and ecological processes in developing countries to human livelihoods and the overall national economy. Failure to take this contribution into account in development implies that economic activities that lead to environmental degradation and biodiversity loss are unnecessarily subsidized.

For example, Munasinghe (1992) argues that, in order to include important environmental values in macro-economic analyses, current methods of accounting for national income – that is, a country's gross national product (GNP) or economic output – need to be modified. He cites three specific shortcomings in the current national accounting frameworks with regards to natural resources.

■ Natural and environmental resources are not included in national accounts, which therefore represent limited indicators of national well-being as they neglect the welfare impacts of changes in environmental assets and conditions.

■ National accounts fail to record the depreciation of natural capital, such as a country's stock of water, soil, air, exhaustible resources and wilderness areas. In developing countries, many resource based goods are unmarketed and those that are marketed are generally underpriced; national accounts are not adjusted for these effects either.

■ Environmental clean-up costs are included as part of national income, whereas the costs of environmental damages, and the benefits of ecological goods and services are not taken into account.

These deficiencies would suggest the need to adjust conventional measures of GNP to integrate better economic and environmental accounting. Already, there have been major initiatives to develop resource accounting methods to ensure that measures of GNP more accurately reflect environmental values and thus better approximate sustainable income.[9]

However, Common and Norton (1994) maintain that currently proposed methods of resource and environmental accounting fall short of being able to account fully for biodiversity values, let alone environmentally 'sustainable' income. Although some theoretical models do indicate the 'optimal' adjustments to national accounts required to reflect sustainability, these models provide very little guidance for actual statistical accounting practices. Much of the environmental information required to compute theoretically 'optimal' values and prices does not yet exist. Moreover, an essential feature of the sustainability problem generally, and the biodiversity conservation problem particularly, is that the reality to be modelled is complex and largely unknown. It is not surprising, therefore, that many empirical attempts to adjust national income for environmental values do not use modelling per se but attempt to account for these values using market and pseudo market prices. Common and Norton (1994) suggest that such adjustments to the national accounts may be neither consistent nor relevant and, as a consequence, will do little by themselves to enhance biodiversity conservation or to promote sustainability.

On the other hand, the authors do believe that better modelling of economic–environmental linkages for environmental and resource accounting purposes does have a positive role in improving our understanding of the welfare implications of these linkages. Such a modelling effort could also assist in identifying management options and informing public debate. Perhaps most importantly, it would generate demand for the physical and biological data necessary to analyse economic–environmental linkages.

Rather than waiting for environmental and resource accounting efforts to provide an indication of the information requirements for biodiversity conservation, Common and Norton (1994) argue that generation of improved environmental data should come first. In particular, the implementation of an integrated, long term ecological monitoring programme at the country, regional and global level will be an essential prerequisite not only for improved environmental and resource accounting but for biodiversity conservation generally. The aim of such a programme would be to increase our knowledge of global biodiversity and to help establish critical thresholds in various ecosystems, so that the ecological significance of the data derived from monitoring and other sources can be properly evaluated and acted upon. In particular our predictive understanding of ecosystem dynamics and the various function roles of biodiversity need improv-

9 For comprehensive reviews and discussions of the various approaches, see Ahmed, El Serafy and Lutz (1989); Common and Norton (1994); Lutz (1993); Pearce, Markandya and Barbier (1989); and UNSO (1990).

ing. The implementation of such a programme would, by itself, not guarantee either biodiversity conservation or sustainability. However, given that ecological monitoring lies at the heart of the analysis of key economic–environmental linkages behind biodiversity loss, it should be given higher priority in the allocation of scarce public funds for sustainability research and policy analysis.

For example, Box 10.4 indicates the role of ecological monitoring as part of Australia's national strategy for biodiversity conservation. Australia is the only 'megadiverse' nation that is not a low or middle income 'developing' economy. Given that it does not have the typical socio-economic conditions of managing biodiversity found in most megadiverse countries, Australia is an interesting case of how a biodiversity conservation strategy could be developed in the absence of major structural economic and ecological constraints. It is clear that such a strategy to prevent future biodiversity loss will require extensions of the reserve system and changes to off-reserve land management practices, as well as in-creased research efforts directed at ecological monitoring as the basis for under-standing economic–environmental linkages. In the case of Australia, sufficient technical and intellectual resources are available to implement a fully operational integrated ecological monitoring programme within ten years, given appropriate institutional and funding commitments.

Australia's affluence relative to other megadiverse countries means that it has the potential to allocate larger absolute amounts of resources, including intellec-tual and technical skills, to addressing biodiversity conservation problems. As discussed on pages 191–204, support for conservation efforts in low and middle income 'developing' countries may come through international mechanisms and agreements, particularly as biodiversity loss is essentially a global problem. However, implementation of any agreed measures will still be through nation states and their governments. Ultimately, this implies that all countries, whether rich or poor, will need to decide how best to protect those natural ecosystems and species under greatest threat. The development of appropriate national and regional policies, and management schemes for protected areas will therefore be an essential component of global biodiversity conservation efforts.

As discussed by Common and Norton (1994), a rationale approach to selection of protected areas for biodiversity conservation would include the following features:

- ecosystems which are subject to intensive human activities and already considered susceptible to threats (such as rare, highly fragmented and modi-fied) due to past human activities or natural processes;
- rare and endangered species, threatened species and vulnerable species, and biologically diverse ecosystems located in areas likely to be most susceptible to climate and other environmental changes.

However, as argued throughout this book, the establishment of any protected areas for biodiversity conservation involves opportunity costs. These typically involve forgoing economic benefits of development activities that would have led to more intensive exploitation or even conversion of resources and land. The case studies in Part II indicated that these forgone development opportunities need

Box 10.4

Biodiversity monitoring and management strategies in Australia

Of the 12 nations classified as 'megadiverse' by the World Bank, Australia is the only high income country. Australia's socio-economic features are more in common with developed economies than with fellow megadiverse nations and, in particular, Australia is distinctive by its very low population density.

Despite its comparatively little resemblance to other megadiverse countries, Australia does share the common feature of continuing biodiversity loss. The country's biodiversity is subject to a high degree of endemism from regional to continental scale, and a significant feature of its biota is the broad geographic distribution of many species and assemblages. For example, the forests of the eastern seaboard occur more or less continuously from temperate to tropical Australia. However, since the arrival of Europeans, significant biodiversity and species loss has occurred through the introduction of exotic plant and animal species and habitat modification in the form of clearing native vegetation for agriculture, timber harvesting, urban development, pollution and similar 'external' impacts of economic development.

The proximate causes of biodiversity loss in Australia are typical of those found in most countries (see Chapter 4). The role of market and policy failures has been especially significant. Government policy has, in particular, determined the management of publicly owned land and influenced the incentives affecting the behaviour of private agents. Some government failures have been addressed, such as the elimination of tax incentives for clearing land, but others remain, such as the underpricing of native timber on public land. Lack of understanding of the role of biodiversity in economic–environmental linkages has been a major factor in policy failure and in more recent years the government of Australia has begun funding efforts to reduce this ignorance.

For example, the Australian Heritage Commission has the primary role of identifying sites for preservation and conservation, including areas of biodiversity importance. The Commission also oversees the preparation of the National Wilderness Inventory, which includes development of a spatial database permitting the identification of areas of high wilderness quality and the analysis of the impact of development proposals on wilderness. In addition, the separate Resource Assessment Commission advises the federal government on options for the use of natural resources, consistent with the requirement of sustainability.

In 1991, the Biological Diversity Advisory Committee was established, with non-governmental membership, to advise the federal minister for the environment on the development of a national strategy for biodiversity conservation. In addition, an Endangered Species Programme has been established with the objectives of protection of endangered species or communities, addressing threatening processes such as the introduction of species, and encouraging community education and involvement. Finally, a special task force, a Working Party to Ecologically Sustainable Development Secretariat, which is expected to make recommendations concerning the extension of ecological databases, assessment and monitoring, off reserve management, reserve extension and research.

Successful implementation of Australia's biodiversity management strategy appears to depend on an institutional and funding commitment to extensions of the reserve system of preservation areas and improved off reserve land management. Without such a commitment, further significant biodiversity losses are likely to occur in Australia. However, successful in situ biodiversity conservation itself will require the development of a reserve system based on sound scientific foundation. Improved research and ecological monitoring is key to this approach.

A pragmatic approach to ecological monitoring is to use ecosystems and species with the latter focused initially on those species and distinct populations under more immediate threat of extinction. Research addressing the taxonomic and functional roles of species, populations and communities which are critical to the maintenance of biodiversity must also be conducted. Monitoring to assess management regimes will require the systematic selection of sites to span protected and non-protected natural areas, as well as measurements of the environmental changes arising from imposed management regimes. Monitoring that addresses the cause of biodiversity loss (for example, endangering processes) is also essential.

Given government funding for such research efforts, Australia appears to be in the forefront of the development of methodologies to assist selection and design of protection areas. These techniques can also be used to develop the required monitoring networks for biodiversity conservation. Two continental scale monitoring networks are proposed for Australia.

- Major continental scale climatic gradients could be identified and monitoring sites selected along these gradients to span protected and non-protected areas. Where ecosystems are the targets for monitoring, the location of sites could be stratified, on meso and micro-scale environmental gradients.
- Alternatively, monitoring sites could be stratified by continental scale environmental domains, as characterized by climate, substrate and catchment parameters. Within these, monitoring sites could be located to span protected and non-protected areas, and selected management regimes for targeted species and ecosystems.

The initial start-up cost is expected to be less than A$40 million, and annual operating and research costs are unlikely to exceed A$20 million. Sufficient intellectual and technical resources are available in Australia to implement a fully operational integrated ecological monitoring programme within ten years, given appropriate institutional and funding commitments.

Source: Common and Norton (1992 and 1994).

to be properly assessed and valued, if correct incentive and management systems for biodiversity conservation are to be put in place. Equally, if not more important, the loss of economic opportunities from the establishment and enforcement of protected areas usually affect local populations disproportionately. In developing countries, these are usually low income rural communities who can ill-afford losses of income, wealth and access to resources. On pages 211–17 we discuss in more detail this key aspect of national biodiversity conservation and protected area strategies: the need to ensure that such conservation measures also provide real and immediate benefits to local people.

Ultimately, the need to assess all the benefits and costs of biodiversity conservation must form the basis of a national or regional strategy. Estimating the economic contribution that biological resources make to the national economy, and establishing new administrative structures for managing biological resources, are important steps in formulating and implementing this strategy. However, as suggested by McNeely (1993), the development of a national or regional conservation strategy should in itself form the basis for reviewing national policies that influence the incentives for conservation of biological resources and diversity. Box 10.5 briefly outlines the basic strategy.

Box 10.5
Establishing national policies for managing biodiversity

The incentives which are needed to conserve biological resources and diversity at the local level usually require commensurate policies at the national level. A national or regional conservation strategy can be an effective means of reviewing such policies and determining what shifts are required to achieve national objectives for biodiversity conservation. The following steps are a necessary component of such a strategy.

- Quantify and bring to the attention of policy makers the many economic and financial benefits of integrating rural development activities with conservation of biological resources and diversity.
- Identify both conflicts and potential for cooperation between the various activities of agriculture, fisheries, forestry, conservation and rehabilitation of degraded lands.
- Formulate legislation consonant with the socio-economic patterns of the target group and the natural resources being utilized, both to institute a system of penalties and rewards, and to ensure that incentives carry the power of law.
- Review policies and legislation in other sectors for possible applications to conservation of biodiversity and community involvement in such work.
- Devise effective incentives to accelerate integrated development to close any gap between what the individual sees as an investment benefit and what the government considers to be in the national interest.
- Establish new administrative structures for managing biological resources. While those resources contained within strictly protected areas are usually government controlled (in theory), biological resources in buffer zones, coastal areas, national forests and communal areas are often 'open access' resources, and need to be brought into some form of management regime.
- Develop the capacity of local communities to participate in conservation efforts so as to ensure that these measures are more likely to yield immediate and real benefits to local people.

Source: McNeely (1993).

For many developing countries – particularly the poorest – a national or regional biodiversity conservation strategy, as described in Box 10.5, would be the most sensible starting point in developing and integrating a protected area system within a complementary national policy framework. The activities and policies of all government sectors that influence biological resources should be reviewed as part of this strategy, with the implications for biodiversity loss and sustainable resource use assessed accordingly. Once established, the next stage in the process would be to move towards the 'Australia-style' biodiversity management strategy, whereby improved ecological monitoring and research into economic–environmental linkages form the basis for selection of protected areas and policy analysis of the causes of biodiversity loss. Clearly, the limited technical, human and financial resources of many developing countries will limit the development of this two-stage strategy – particularly the transition to the more resource intensive second phase. This is one important area where bilateral and multilateral aid could be targeted most effectively to assist the formulation of national strategies and policies for conservation management.

Even with donor assistance, limited financial resources and development priorities will always remain an important constraint. Already, over 130 nations have established almost 7000 legally protected areas covering nearly 5 per cent of the earth's land area (Wells and Brandon 1993). Effective management and enforcement of many of these areas, especially in developing countries, remains a formidable challenge and a burden on national resources. As discussed above, a further disincentive for creating new protective areas is the additional economic cost of forgone development opportunities.

With these real constraints and disincentives in mind, it may be appropriate to begin devising more cost-effective means of establishing protected areas. One possibility is the use of transferable development rights, as described on pages 191–204. TDRs could be employed just as easily, if not more easily, at the national level. Box 10.6 describes one such experiment in the use of TDRs for biodiversity conservation in Cyprus. If properly implemented, a TDR system may be one effective means of ensuring that biodiversity conservation is implemented through full compensation of forgone development opportunities, with limited impact on government resources.

LOCAL MANAGEMENT

Ultimately, policies for improved biodiversity management must be concerned with generating appropriate incentives at the local level. In addition, it may be necessary to undertake specific initiatives at the local level in order to complement international, national or regional policies and management strategies, and to ensure their effective implication. In this final section, we discuss the key lessons for local management described in certain Biodiversity Programme papers. We focus in particular on the need for local participation in conservation measures and the benefits they generate, and the appropriate use of indigenous knowledge about biodiversity.

McNeely (1993) argues that the traditional approach to setting up protection areas and managing biological resources has worked against the interests of local populations. Their traditional rights of access to resources in protected areas are usually abrogated by the state. The responsibility for managing biological resources has often been removed from local people, communities and leaders, and instead transferred to central government agencies in distant capitals. As a result, the mainly poor and rural communities in the vicinity of national parks and protected areas generally bear the brunt of the forgone economic opportunities associated with conservation measures – with little or no compensation in return.

Box 10.6

Transferable development rights and biodiversity conservation in the Akamas Peninsula, Cyprus

The Akamas Peninsula is 250 km^2 and situated in the north-west of Cyprus. It is considered to be the last virgin area in the eastern Mediterranean. The area contains a large concentration of biotopes, making it a unique ecosystem. The flora include at least 20 endemic and rare species.

However, Akamas is threatened with degradation from a number of sources:

- day visitors to the area destroying flowering plants, forests and animal species;
- property owners putting pressure on the government to open the area for tourist development;
- inhabitants in nearby villages demanding increased development.

The government has responded by zoning part of the Akamas area as a non-development area, stopping short of declaring it a national park. This has intensified the conflict between development and conservation interests.

A system of transferable development rights (TDRs), as outlined in Box 10.3, has been proposed to resolve these development versus conservation conflicts, which occur not only in Akamas but all over Cyprus. TDRs have been introduced in Cyprus through recent legislation for the preservation of buildings of unique cultural and historical value. The Akamas Peninsula could be preserved through the same mechanism without depriving those with development claims in the area of their development rights and without the government paying compensation.

The coastal area of Akamas and, in fact, all of Cyprus could be divided into development areas and conservation areas, and a TDRs mechanism established as described in Box 10.3. Land owners in conservation areas would retain their rights but they would not be allowed to exercise them on site. They would instead be allowed to sell or transfer these rights to property in development areas, whereas their own land would remain in a natural state. It is estimated that the net present value (NPV) of preservation benefits in terms of improved quality of tourism in the development areas, combined with ecotourism in the conservation area, would exceed the NPV of forgone earnings from not developing Akamas into a mass tourist area like other parts of Cyprus.

Source: Panayotou (1994).

The consequence is often illegal and/or 'open access' exploitation of resources, and increased conflicts between local people and the state.

In recent years, the traditional 'top-down' approach to conservation management has been revised to encourage more community based conservation. Two general approaches seem to have been advocated (Wells and Brandon 1993).

- Buffer zones have been delineated and established around park boundaries, as sites for both conservation and development related activities.
- New approaches to park and protected area management are being promoted to encourage greater local participation.

The result has been a proliferation of projects in recent years attempting to link biodiversity conservation with community based development.

Wells and Brandon (1992 and 1993) have classified all these initiatives that attempt to enhance biodiversity conservation, while simultaneously attempting to address the needs, constraints and opportunities of local people as integrated conservation development projects (ICDPs). They reviewed 23 of the leading ICDPs in Asia, Latin America and Africa in terms of their effectiveness in terms of achieving their dual objectives of community based development and biodiversity conservation.

On the whole, their conclusions are not encouraging. Despite their rapidly growing popularity, the overall contribution of the ICDP approach to biodiversity conservation has so far been limited. For example, the buffer zone approach has failed in part because most protected area management agencies have no legal authority to establish or manage buffer zones, outside or inside park boundaries. Similarly, attempts to encourage participation have faltered because most ICDPs have treated local people as passive beneficiaries of project activities, and have not involved them in decision making related to the process of change and development.

The relative ineffectiveness of ICDPs can be traced to four important factors.

■   Most ICDPs have been operational for less than five years and are therefore at a relatively early stage of implementation.

■   Many ICDPs are operating on very modest scales and with small budgets (some less than US$50,000 annually), while attempting to implement ambitious and wide-ranging programmes aimed at poverty alleviation, environmental education and conservation in numerous small communities spread over large areas.

■   Many ICDPs should be regarded as demonstration projects and cannot be expected to contribute significantly to biodiversity conservation as standalone initiatives; their value will largely come through showing what is possible and encouraging replication elsewhere.

■   The ICDP approach is innovative and experimental; there are few precedents for linking conservation and development goals within single projects, and a period of learning and making mistakes is inevitable.

However, Wells and Brandon (1993) conclude that, despite these difficulties and shortcomings, the ICDP approach should be reassessed but not abandoned. ICDPs:

> must be reinforced and expanded simply because there seem to be no other choices ... innovative, well-designed projects at carefully selected sites that constructively address local people-park relationships are essential to the conservation of biodiversity and thus to sustainable development. Workable buffer-zone arrangements and more effective local participation will be key elements of such projects.

Southgate and Clark (1993) take a slightly more pessimistic view of ICDPs, particularly with regard to biodiversity conservation in South America. The authors condemn the rather 'naive' view that people who live in tropical forests always have a strong economic interest in keeping habitats intact and note that, for proponents of ICDPs, the idea that local communities are not always willing partners in the campaign to save biological diversity is disheartening. Particularly in Amazonia, conflicts between locals, who resent the loss of access to resources, and park managers and supporters often grow acute, and rarely are these conflicts resolved in favour of conserving flora and fauna.

Where conservation is promoted, it is usually because of the potential for tourism development, for example, the Galapagos National Park of Ecuador and the Mayan ruins at Tikal in the Petén tropical forests of Guatemala. Those officially designated natural reserves in South America that still remain relatively untouched will not do so for long. As local populations multiply and as infrastructure development begins encouraging settlement by outsiders, pressure on natural ecosystems will increase, and the survival of parks and reserves may be threatened.

In Chapter 5, we discussed in detail the 'nutrient mining' thesis as an explanation for increasing tropical deforestation in Latin America and elsewhere. The term describes the process by which a large number of price-taking colonists have unlimited access to large areas of forested land. The frontier is cleared and expanded up to the point where no additional rents are made. As agricultural rents are insignificant on the frontier, there is no investment in wealth or human capital as an alternative to continuing investment in the conversion and exploitation of forest land for the production of crops, livestock and other frontier production. The local population is therefore unable to break its dependence on nutrient mining, and yet once forest lands and soils have been depleted, colonists still remain impoverished. Infrastructure development, particularly road-building, actually accelerates deforestation because colonists respond immediately to any opportunity to deplete forest resources made more accessible from the 'opening up' of the forest through the construction of new roads.

Southgate and Clark (1993) argue that this process is not encouraging for ICDPs. Establishment of these initiatives to encourage participation by local populations must overcome powerful incentives for 'nutrient mining' by the same communities. ICDP activities can themselves encourage environmental degradation, for example, improved roads, trails and infrastructure can make it easier for local people to penetrate previously inaccessible forests and protected areas.

In short, where the incentives for 'nutrient mining' and land conversion are strong among local communities, then successful implementation of ICDPs and park protection initiatives will be extremely difficult. Even attempts to set up extractive reserves, buffer zones or demarcate park boundaries are unlikely to withstand the onslaught of loggers, farmers, ranchers and prospectors.

The authors suggest that natural ecosystems and protected areas can best be saved through promoting environmentally sound intensification of crop and livestock production in areas away from forest and agricultural frontiers.[10] Although field activities such as ICDPs are important for saving threatened habitats

---

10 Southgate (1991) has conducted a statistical analysis that illustrates this point: in Latin American countries where crop and livestock yields have improved, land use conversion has been mitigated, whereas in countries with poor productivity trends land conversion has increased. See also the discussion of statistical analyses of deforestation in Chapter 5.

in developing countries, they are not sufficient and certainly not a substitute for improving sustainable production, income and employment in other areas, including urban zones and rural areas where agriculture is already well established. The authors claim that, unfortunately, most organizations are far more interested in seeing ICDPs and related initiatives funded and implemented, than they are in projects to increase overall agricultural productivity.

This point emphasizes a key issue that has been stressed throughout this book: efforts to conserve biodiversity must not be pursued in isolation but must be complementary to overall economic development, particularly in low income countries. Just as efficient and sustainable use of natural resources is essential to economic development, efforts to improve overall economic performance can provide important incentives for increased conservation. As we argued in the previous section, policies for establishing protected areas and national parks cannot be isolated from an overall national strategy for biodiversity conservation management. Equally, a national strategy for biodiversity conservation cannot be isolated from an overall strategy of sustainable economic development and improved economic performance.

The important focus of integrating economic development with biodiversity conservation is the generation of the correct incentives for biodiversity conservation, while at the same time discouraging perverse incentives that work against conservation. Ultimately, this must translate down to the local level, where the millions of farmers, hunters, herders, ranchers, fishing folk and harvesters interact with the natural environment every day.

As argued by McNeely (1993), overcoming the damage caused by perverse incentives will require new initiatives to promote conservation, applied at a series of levels and in a number of sectors. Changing behaviour at the local level will require reasonably comprehensive packages of direct incentives (tax breaks, subsidies, grants, compensation for animal damage, interest-free loans, differential fees and differential access to resources), indirect incentives (the application of fiscal, service, social and natural resource policies to specific conservation problems) and disincentives (penalties, punishment and other forms of law enforcement accompanied by public information). ICDPs are clearly only part of the solution and should not be seen as the 'panacea' of biodiversity conservation, but they do provide an important lesson: conservation measures are likely to be most successful when they provide real and immediate benefits to local people.

More generally, under the right conditions, efforts to promote community based conservation can be an effective indirect incentive that can form an important part of the overall 'package' comprising a biodiversity conservation strategy. Such efforts are diverse and can include building community level conservation institutions, encouraging community involvement in both management and decision making about resource use, promoting ideas of sustainable agriculture and forestry, conserving and promoting traditional knowledge, providing education to local people and providing special development actions to villages surrounding protected areas. Box 10.7 gives some examples of the type of measures being promoted in and around various protected areas of Africa.

Finally, one important incentive for encouraging biological conservation is to

Box 10.7

Improving local incentives for conservation in Africa

In Kasunga National Park in Malawi, local people have been given the right to harvest tree caterpillars and to establish bee hives in exchange for curbing other uses which are incompatible with the objectives of the park. The gross income of these micro-enterprises is US$198 per hectare (ha) from tree caterpillars and US$230 from bee keeping. These earnings are higher than the income realized from subsistence farming of maize, beans and groundnuts, and could be used to increase agricultural productivity through purchasing scarce inputs.

In the Mount Kulal Biosphere Reserve in Kenya, several incentives have been designed in conjunction with the local people and which take into account their traditional pastoral tribal economy. They include registering tribal rangelands to give them legal status; subsidies for the development of water resources; livestock marketing facilities; banking facilities to store wealth other than 'on the hoof'; providing security against raids from other tribes; conservation education in schools, wildlife extension in adult literacy classes and information for government officials about the value of conservation; employment of local people in the system of protected areas; and income from tourism to the protected areas allocated to local development activities.

In KaNgwane, South Africa, the site of the tourist lodge in the Mthethomusha Game Reserve is leased to the private sector, the lease being paid into a trust fund to be used for community projects selected by the tribal authority. In Richtersveld National Park, South Africa, the land on which the park lies is owned and occupied by the Nama community, which has leased it to the government but has retained rights to graze an agreed number of livestock and to undertake the controlled harvest of natural products. The lease payments are deposited into a trust appointed by the community to manage the lands.

In Zimbabwe, to promote the conservation of the wildlife resources found on communal lands, private game reserves have been established where revenues from hunting are paid to local communities. Through this arrangement, some US$4.5 million has been paid out for development in remote parts of the communal lands over a period of seven years. Recreational hunting is now the most positive and widespread economic incentive for the conservation of large animals in Zimbabwe.

In Namibia, game populations have been conserved by giving ownership rights to ranchers, thereby giving them a financial incentive to protect game. In order to utilize huntable game commercially throughout the year, the property must be game-proof fenced and be larger than 1000 ha. Hunting by people other than the owner is permitted only during the hunting season. The prospective hunter negotiates fees directly with the land owner; typical fees range from US$600 for kudu to US$100 for springbok. As a result, some protected species have now increased in numbers and breeding nuclei are sold to land owners at subsidized prices.

Source: McNeely (1993).

improve the use of local knowledge. As pointed out by Gadgil, Berkes and Folke (1993), indigenous knowledge, or traditional ecological knowledge, is of significance from a conservation perspective and an attribute of societies with continuity in resource use practices. It can be defined as a cumulative body of knowledge and beliefs handed down through generations by cultural transmission about the relationship of living beings, including humans, with one another and with their environment.

For example, it is well known that indigenous knowledge is extremely useful with regard to the medicinal and pharmaceutical value of local biodiversity, as well as habitat preference, natural history and behaviour relevant to efficient foraging for biological resources. Such knowledge is explicit and transferred from individual to individual, and across generations. However, the indigenous knowledge base concerning biodiversity conservation is often less explicit. Conservation usually implies restraint from resource use, and development of local institutions and traditions governing restraint is not a simple matter of information transmission. Rather, implementation of conservation appears to be derived from complex 'rules of thumb' derived from historical experience, with compliance often facilitated through religious belief, ritual and social convention.

Box 10.8 summarizes a number of important features of indigenous knowledge and practices concerning biodiversity conservation that appear relevant today. Understanding these practices may also help to eliminate open access conditions that threaten common pool resources (Gadgil, Berkes and Folke 1993). In areas with traditional peoples, private property is often not feasible as these peoples have social traditions of joint ownership. Instituting resource use rights for the local population or recognizing existing rights is only half of the solution; any well-functioning communal property right regime is the ability of users to limit access to the resource by members of the groups, and to make and enforce rules among themselves. Again, relying on traditional ecological knowledge and institutions for implementing conservation may be essential to this process, and may even contribute to rediscovering new principles for more sustainable uses of the natural environment by communities in the developed world (Berkes, Folke and Gadgil 1994).

CHALLENGES TO BE ADDRESSED

In this chapter we have examined a variety of international, national and local policy issues related to biodiversity conservation and management. The potential range of issues is so broad that it is impossible to be comprehensive. We have instead focused on key perspectives emphasized by Biodiversity Programme papers. Other contributions can be found in Parts I and II.

One important conclusion does emerge, however. For global biodiversity conservation to be effectively implemented, policies and institutions will have to be implemented on all three levels. New international mechanisms and institutions are required to deal with the global public goods characteristic of the biodiversity problem. However, much of the world's biodiversity lies within the sovereign jurisdiction of nation states and any international agreements will ultimately depend on nation states for implementation. In addition, the environ-

---

Box 10.8

Important conservation lessons from indigenous knowledge

Four kinds of indigenous conservation practices are of particular relevance to biodiversity conservation today. They are as follows.

- *Total protection to many individual biological communities including pools along river courses, ponds, meadows and forests.* Sacred groves were once widely protected throughout the old world. For example, in the tribal state of Mizoram in north-eastern India, even after conversion to Christianity the local people continue to protect their sacred groves. They are now called the 'safety forest', while the village woodlot from which regulated harvests are made is called the 'supply forest'. Ecological theory suggests that providing such absolute protection in 'refugia' can be an effective way of ensuring the persistence of biological populations.
- *Total protection to all individuals of certain animal and plant species.* For example, trees of all species of the genus *Ficus* are protected in many parts of the old world. At the same time, *Ficus* is now considered by ecologists as a keystone resource significant to conservation of overall biodiversity. Local people seem to be aware of the importance of Ficus as affording food and shelter for a wide range of birds, bats and primates, and probably this understanding was converted into widespread protection of the *Ficus* tree at some point in the distant past.
- *Special protection of certain particularly vulnerable stages in the life history of a species.* The danger of over-harvest and depletion is clearly greater if these species are hunted during their vulnerable stages, and the protection afforded them is a clear case of ecological prudence. For example, in south India, fruit bats may be hunted when away foraging but not at daytime roosts near villages. Many waders are hunted outside the breeding season but not at heronaries, which again may be on trees lining village streets.
- *Group effort for major events of resource harvest.* Many tribal groups engage once a year in a large scale communal hunt. Such a group event may serve the purpose of group level assessment of the status of prey populations and their habitats. This in turn may help in continually adjusting resource harvest practices so as to sustain yields and conserve diversity.

Source: Gadgil, Berkes and Folke (1993).

---

mental benefits of biodiversity and natural environments that accrue locally or nationally should provide motivation for national conservation efforts. This will require national strategies that will aim to assess the role of biodiversity in economic development, correct pervasive market and policy failures that work against conservation, and develop appropriate investment and institutional frameworks for improved protection and conservation. The eventual aim of such strategies is to influence the incentives of individual actors that use and convert the resource base. Consequently, consideration of what motivates these actors' decisions, as well as encouraging local participation and the use of indigenous knowledge, are important components of any biodiversity conservation and management strategy.

In this chapter we have also pointed to a number of key policy issues for further research at the international, national and local levels.

Although further progress with the GEF, debt-for-nature swaps, CITES and the incremental cost financing principles of the Convention on Biological Diversity is welcomed, these initiatives alone will not conserve sufficient biodiversity to protect global values. Other international market regulation and compensation mechanisms will need to be developed. Some of the proposals suggested in this chapter for developing bilateral and multilateral intellectual property rights, licensing and patent agreements, resource franchise agreements, compensation funds, tradable permits and offsets, and transferable development rights need to be further investigated and promoted. All may have their role to play, particularly in ensuring that countries receive a global premium for investing in biodiversity conservation.

A crucial area for further research is the development of ecological monitoring and analysis capabilities at the global, national and regional levels. Such research will be important both for establishing critical ecological thresholds and the role of biodiversity in ecosystem functioning and resilience, as well as identifying threatened species and ecosystems. On a regional and national level, the resulting biological information will be important for designing national strategies for biodiversity conservation and developing indicators for sustainability such as resource and environmental accounts.

In this chapter, we have not discussed in great detail the necessary steps for correcting market and policy failures underlying biodiversity loss. Chapter 9 and the case studies in Part II provide ample examples of the approach and steps advocated. However, we would like to re-emphasize that a comprehensive national biodiversity conservation strategy must be placed in the context of a thorough review of economic–environmental linkages, economic and social policies, and their implications for the appropriate incentives and institutions for biodiversity conservation and sustainable development. Correction of pervasive market policy, and institutional failures that promote environmental degradation and biodiversity loss will hopefully be one important outcome.

For most developing countries, an important starting point is to initiate the basic strategy steps outlined in Box 10.5. Once established, the next stage in the process would be to move towards the 'Australia-style' biodiversity management strategy, whereby improved ecological monitoring and research into economic–environmental linkages form the basis for selection of protected areas and policy analysis of the causes of biodiversity loss (see Box 10.4). Both increased bilateral and multilateral aid, and improved research, could be of assistance to developing countries in developing this two-stage strategy.

Establishment of new protected areas and national parks, and enforcing protection for existing reserves, will be an important – although limited – feature of biodiversity conservation strategies. The shortcomings to date of many integrated community based development projects (ICDPs) for biodiversity conservation cannot absolve us from the responsibility of analysing carefully the incentives determining local people's decisions to degrade the environment. Perhaps, as in the 'nutrient mining' case of frontier clearing in Amazonia, such analysis will lead us to conclude that investment to improve agricultural productivity elsewhere is the main solution to the problem. In other instances, however, it is possible that encouraging better local participation through community led initiatives, and providing real and immediate benefits to local people from conservation efforts, may be sufficient to ensure success.

Finally, further research into the potential role of indigenous knowledge in biodiversity conservation may also prove beneficial. Not only will such knowledge provide clues to the existing pattern of conservation incentives influencing local people's behaviour, it will also assist in the design of new incentive systems in situations where traditional resource management rules break down or are superseded.

Part IV

CONCLUSIONS

11

Paradise Regained:
The Challenges Ahead

In this final chapter we return to some of the broader issues raised throughout this book and by the Biodiversity Programme papers generally. Our first concern is to revisit the question of whether or not a single disciplinary approach is sufficient for tackling the biodiversity problem. We then explore the potential benefits of forging an ecological–economic analytical 'synthesis'. However, the Biodiversity Programme papers and this book are only the initial steps in an ecological–economic 'learning curve'. We therefore look a little further ahead along this curve and attempt to project where we need to proceed analytically. Finally, as we are ultimately concerned with a 'real world' problem, we conclude by examining the practical challenges that an ecological–economic approach must address in the near future if we are to make progress in controlling and limiting biodiversity loss.

IS A SINGLE-DISCIPLINE APPROACH SUFFICIENT?

If the reader has come this far in the book, it will be obvious that our short answer to this question is 'No'. Perhaps, however, it may be useful to recap the main reasons why we believe this to be the case.

As emphasized from the beginning of this book, we see the process of biodiversity loss to be more fundamental to human welfare than simply the disappearance of increased threat to species. Although species extinction is perhaps the most visible symptom of biodiversity loss, the more profound implication is for ecological functioning and resilience. We believe that biodiversity is essential to ensuring the basic ecological services and resources necessary to maintain human welfare and existence. The fundamental problem is to maintain that level of biodiversity that will guarantee the functioning and resilience of ecosystems on which not only human consumption and production but also existence depends. This does not imply that biodiversity conservation requires complete preservation of all species in the world or an immediate moratorium on all uses of the environment, including habitat conversion. It does suggest that we must ensure that current rates of biodiversity loss do not take humankind beyond the minimum threshold level necessary to sustain human welfare and even existence.

As portrayed in Figures 1.1 and 1.2, and discussed throughout the book, critical to understanding the implications of biodiversity loss and designing appropriate policy responses will be thorough analysis of basic economic–environmental linkages. Both economists and ecologists, as well as scholars from other disciplines, will need to work together on this important endeavour. As explained in Part I, we use the term ecological economics to describe this analytical approach – not because we believe that a new or alternative discipline needs to be forged out of economics and ecology to analyse the biodiversity problem, but because what is required is inter-disciplinary collaboration to extend beyond the current frontiers of economics, ecology and other disciplines to deal with the fundamentally important phenomenon of biodiversity loss. In short, ecological economics is not a new discipline as such, but a new category of analysis or synthesis of approaches, for tackling problems of economic–environmental inter-action where a single discipline approach will not suffice.

TOWARDS AN ECOLOGICAL-ECONOMIC SYNTHESIS

What will this new ecological–economic synthesis look like? We hope that the Biodiversity Programme papers and this book provide some indications of the way ahead. However, clearly they are only the first steps in an ecological–eco-nomic 'learning curve'. We would like to end by providing some indication of what further steps up the curve may entail.

First, and foremost, more independent inter-disciplinary 'think tanks', work-shops and forums like the Biodiversity Programme of the Beijer Institute need to be established and supported with long term research funding. Developing inter-disciplinary academic departments and bodies dedicated to the teaching and research of ecological–economic problems such as biodiversity loss, is important if, first, inter-disciplinary research is to lose its 'stigma' in academic circles, and second, the next generation of scholars are going to become better equipped for working across disciplines, synthesizing analytical methods and dealing effec-tively with economic–environmental problems.

In the mean time governments and inter-governmental organizations could foster and support the creation of policy advisory boards and research committees dedicated to understanding the implications of biodiversity loss for an ecologi-cally sustainable economic development. If economists, ecologists and scholars from other disciplines are encouraged to become involved, then collective ap-proaches to policy issues and options for biodiversity conservation may begin evolving. New ideas for research and data requirements will quickly follow. Non-governmental organizations have also an important role to play in many ways:

- insisting that biodiversity loss stays firmly on the political agenda;
- challenging sympathetic economists and ecologists to cooperate in applying their knowledge on specific environmental and biodiversity problems; and
- ensuring that the outcome of any academic or policy research has practical relevance to 'the man on the street' or 'the woman in the jungle'.

In short, better communication between the disciplines is the first step, and improved research collaboration and inter-disciplinary analysis must follow.

Where the ecological–economic synthesis needs to proceed analytically is more difficult to predict, but a few indications have been provided by this book.

First, our conceptual understanding of economic–environmental linkages must allow for the existence of thresholds and the phenomenon of ecological scarcity acting as potential constraints on human welfare. If we do not accept this possibility, then we should not be fundamentally concerned with the problems posed by biodiversity loss. The latter hypothesis may be perfectly tenable, unless ecologists and economists can demonstrate otherwise. But, as the evidence in this book also makes clear, the alternative hypothesis that biodiversity loss may represent a serious threat to human welfare, particularly the economic opportunities available to future generations, does have a significant body of evidence in support. Or, at the very least, the fact that the consequences of biodiversity loss are unknown, yet the risks to human welfare potentially large, at least challenges us to take seriously the notion that biodiversity conservation may be an important policy issue of our times. It is therefore up to economists and ecologists to continue with this challenge and together investigate more fully the potential welfare implications of biodiversity loss, including the threat of increasing ecological scarcity and threshold effects.

Clearly, it follows that the important starting point is to obtain better understanding of the role of biodiversity in supporting ecological resources and services of various ecosystems, including their resilience. Equally, it is important to investigate further the proximate and underlying causes of biodiversity loss, and how to remedy them, as well as what constitutes the 'value' of biodiversity and natural systems to our economic activity and, ultimately, human welfare.

As indicated in this book, these avenues of ecological–economic investigation can proceed in two ways.

As we saw in the case studies of Part II, we could approach the problem of biodiversity loss by analysing key ecosystems, such as forests, wetlands and rangelands, and island, marine and estuarine systems. This would allow us to identify and analyse key management and policy problems that are common to these major systems, and thus build up our collective knowledge of the role of biodiversity in these economic–environmental systems, and how best to design management and incentive schemes to conserve their biodiversity.

Alternatively, as indicated in Part III, we could examine the various policy instruments, mechanisms and instruments at our disposal, and investigate their relative merits and applications for addressing the global biodiversity problem at the international, national and local level. This investigation has both an economic and an ecological component, for it requires us to think about what instruments are appropriate to deal with fundamental problems of ecological scarcity and threshold effects. Similarly, we need to be clear about the economic and ecological conditions governing the value of biological resources and diversity at the international, national and local level, and the incentives of the various actors at all three levels to conserve biodiversity.

In fact, it is our opinion that both approaches are not only necessary but complementary. That is why we included both in this book. Only through the analysis of key ecosystems and the consideration of the lessons of biodiversity loss for management and policy can we make progress in understanding the full ecological–economic implications of the problem.

THE CHALLENGES AHEAD

Nevertheless, there remain some fundamental challenges ahead if we are going to make significant progress in developing an ecological–economic synthesis in our analysis of the global biodiversity loss.

Perhaps most significant is the problem of 'political will'. Throughout this book we have emphasized that concern for the welfare implications of biodiversity loss requires certain ethical judgements. Doing something today about the global problem of biodiversity loss will only come about if there is sufficient concern about inter-generational equity and intra-generational fairness. Maintaining biodiversity well within the limits necessary to sustain ecological functions and resilience is our guarantee to future generations that we will not be endangering their economic opportunities and welfare. Ensuring that those poorer regions of the world today that contain most of the world's biodiversity will not disproportionately bear the burden of biodiversity conservation not only places a premium on equity considerations but may also be essential to realizing the goal of maintaining biodiversity.

It is not clear that modern society is yet sufficiently motivated by inter-generational and intra-generational considerations to take the necessary steps to conserve biodiversity. A pessimist would argue that the current generation will never accept either of these considerations and that the only true motivation for biodiversity conservation will arise if the threat is an immediate one, and will affect rich and poor alike. An optimist would argue that, although fundamentally self-interested, individuals or at least the societies they comprise care sufficiently about the collective human condition as well as the state of the world that their progeny will inherit. If there is evidence that biodiversity loss today affects the welfare of future generations, and that the costs of conservation fall disproportionately on the poor, then the optimist would hold that society today would be motivated to take appropriate and fair action to conserve biodiversity.

Whatever the outcome of this philosophical debate, it can only be resolved by improvements in our understanding of the basic economic–environmental linkages underlying biodiversity loss, and the implications of this loss for human welfare. This formidable research agenda is precisely why an ecological–economic synthesis must be forged.

More specifically, we have highlighted a number of important areas which such research must explore.

First, ecological and economic monitoring of threatened species and ecosystems must be improved on a global, continental and regional basis – with an emphasis on developing a deeper knowledge of ecosystem dynamics, and the role of biodiversity in ecological functioning and resilience. Such monitoring must inform us of the consequences of biodiversity loss, provide basic information on the proximate and underlying causes of this loss, and provide feedback on the success or failure of various proposed management and incentive schemes. The case studies of Part II give some indication of the type of basic economic and ecological information required to make appropriate conservation and development decisions.

Second, comprehensive reviews of the biodiversity implications of existing economic and social policies and strategies must be undertaken by all countries. The development of national strategies for biodiversity conservation must become a priority and, at the same time, multilateral organizations must take the responsibility of formulating global or regional blueprints or strategies. Of fundamental importance is assessing the contribution of biodiversity to economies and societies, as well as the prospects of improved economic performance in mitigating or exacerbating the problem of biodiversity loss. The key market and policy failures that are contributing to environmental degradation and biodiversity loss must be identified and strategies to ameliorate them formulated and implemented. Above all, these national and international strategies must not be simply public relations exercises, but genuine attempts at policy reform to encourage biodiversity conservation. Clearly, the poorer nations of the world will have to be supported in these efforts through technical and financial assistance, capacity building and institutional development.

Third, it is clear from the discussion in Part III that our 'policy tool kit' needs to be expanded if modern society is to deal effectively with the biodiversity problem. Not only will we need to explore more cost-effective methods of employing traditional market based and regulatory environmental instruments, but we may need to develop new 'threshold' instruments that are better suited to ensuring the ecological and biodiversity limits are not transgressed. Clearly, the conditions under which these threshold instruments are employed need to be investigated carefully, as must be the limits to more traditional policy instruments to control environmental degradation. We have suggested that the optimal approach is to begin by dismantling those market and policy failures that distort the incentives for conservation, then 'internalize' environmental externalities in the most cost-effective manner through application of traditional market based and regulatory instruments, and, lastly, apply threshold instruments when protection of minimum biodiversity levels and ecological limits is still not assured. However, given our lack of understanding of the consequences of biodiversity loss and the potential risks to human welfare, there may be important instances when the application of threshold instruments may become an overriding priority.

Finally, we have suggested that action needs to be taken simultaneously on the international, national and local level. Initiatives on one level alone are not sufficient to address the global biodiversity problem. New and innovative approaches to international market regulation and compensation agreements are necessary because of the global public goods characteristic of biodiversity. Essentially, a global premium must be received by those countries who are willing to invest in and maintain their biological resources and diversity that have value to the international community. Equally, the national biodiversity conservation strategies discussed above must be coordinated with these international efforts and, at the same time, protect sufficient biodiversity that provides essential local and national services and resources. As ultimately all policies must translate into economic incentives for resource users, attention to the motivations of local populations, community based development and indigenous knowledge in biodiversity conservation are also essential.

These issues amount to a formidable list of challenges. However, the potential welfare implications of biodiversity loss may also prove to be the most formidable problem facing us at the turn of this century. Perhaps, if in ten years' time, substantial progress is made in addressing these challenges, books written on the ecological economics of biodiversity will begin with the title 'Paradise Regained'.

Glossary of Selected Ecological and Economic Terms

adaptive management Sustainable management practices for ecosystems and species that are responsive to uncertainties and ecological fluctuations, as well as being reversible and flexible.

biogeochemical cycling The recycling of the chemical elements essential for life between the biotic (living) and abiotic (non-living) components of ecosystems.

biological diversity (biodiversity) The variety of living organisms at all levels, from genes to species, populations and communities, including the variety and hierarchy of habitats and ecosystems which contain different biological communities.

carrying capacity The maximum number of organisms that an area or habitat can support without reducing its ability to support the same number of organisms in the future.

ecological economics The collective application of economics, ecology and other disciplines to develop a new category of analysis for approaching problems of human nature interaction where a single discipline approach will not suffice.

ecological or ecosystem functions Processes among and within the various biological, chemical and physical components of an ecosystem that consist of specific activities or flows, such as nutrient cycling, biological productivity, hydrology and sedimentation; dynamic and sequential interactions that characterize the evolution of the system, such as exploitation, conservation, release and reorganization; and the cumulative effect of these processes and interactions, such as the ability of ecosystems to support life. *See also* ecological services.

ecological or biological resources The biological components, or living organisms, of ecosystems that support human production and consumption activities, or which have some other actual or potential use or value to humanity. Also referred to as ecological 'goods'.

ecological scarcity As natural environments and ecosystems deteriorate the essential ecological resources and services they provide will decline and thus increase in value relative to the human made goods and services produced in economic systems; over the long term, persistent ecological scarcity may result in the loss of essential life support functions and the disruption to the overall resilience of ecosystems, thus leading to ecological collapse or catastrophe.

ecological services Ecological functions that are currently perceived to support and protect the human activities of production and consumption or affect overall well-being in some way, thus impacting on human welfare and even existence.

ecological threshold The point at which further disturbance to or exploitation of an ecosystem or its resources will lead to a sudden increase in adverse but unknown effects on the system's functioning, including its overall resilience.

economic or market based instruments Policy instruments that do not directly control or restrict activities which degrade the environment but rather create the economic incentives for individuals to choose freely to modify or reduce their activities, thus indirectly producing an environmental improvement; common examples include deposit/refund systems for recycling waste, carbon and other emission taxes, tradable permit systems for pollution or harvesting resources, resource access fees or licensing and royalty payments, and licensing agreements for exploiting resources.

ecosystem Biological communities which interact with the physical and chemical environment as a unified system, while simultaneously interacting with adjacent ecosystems and with the atmosphere.

efficiency (economic) An outcome is economically efficient if a change in the allocation of inputs (natural resources, labour and capital) or outputs (intermediate products and final goods and services) can be said to make society better off if it leaves at least one person better off without making someone else worse off; well functioning markets generally promote efficiency by providing opportunities for individuals to achieve mutually agreeable gains from trade.

government or *policy failure* A 'failure' in policy is said to occur when the policy interventions necessary to correct market failures are not taken; it also arises when government decisions or policies are themselves responsible for worsening allocation failures, for example, market failures that lead to excessive biodiversity loss.

institutional failure The extent to which institutions are inadequately designed and are unable to adapt to meet changing conditions and requirements; institutions do not coordinate with other institutions, both within and across levels; or institutions fail to exist.

institutions The rules and conventions of society that facilitate coordination among people regarding their behaviour, and include both formal and informal, governmental and non-governmental rules and conventions

instrumental value The value, or 'worth', of something in terms of an 'instrument' for satisfying individuals' needs and preferences; for example, the instrumental value of biodiversity derives from the role that the mix of micro-organisms, plants and animals plays in providing ecological services and resources vital to human welfare.

inter-generational equity The extent to which the economic opportunities available to the current generation are also available to future generations; for example, whether activities undertaken by the current generation that lead to irreversible loss of biodiversity and increasing ecological scarcity today will affect adversely future generations' welfare, and even threaten their existence.

intra-generational equity The extent to which the economic opportunities available to the current (or a future) generation are equally available to all members of that generation; for example, whether the gains from irreversible loss of biodiversity and increased ecological scarcity are enjoyed disproportionately by some human populations and societies, and the costs borne disproportionately by others.

intrinsic value Having value, or 'worth', in itself, regardless of whether it serves as an 'instrument' for satisfying individuals' needs and preferences; for example, many moral arguments for preserving biodiversity are based on the premise that organisms should be 'saved' from extinction because all living entities have a fundamental intrinsic worth.

keystone process species Species (or groups of species) that, in the short run, appear to drive the critical processes necessary for ecosystem functioning.

life insurance or *passenger species* Species that depend on the niches formed by keystone process species but that are also important for maintaining the resilience of an ecosystem, as they form an 'insurance' against rare or unusually extreme events and, with time, may transform into keystone process species through the internal reorganization of the eco-system.

market failure The failure of market prices to reflect the full value to society of a commodity; for example, because most of the economic values of ecological resources and services are not automatically reflected in markets, their increasing 'relative' scarcity is not readily captured by price signals.

natural capital The characterization of environmental resources as assets in the economy that have the potential to contribute to economic productivity and welfare; for example, the value of a natural resource as an economic asset depends on the present value of its income, or welfare, potential.

open access A property rights regime where access for resource use is effectively unre-stricted; in other words, it is free and open to all.

precautionary principle Caution, 'margins of error' or 'safeguards' should be invoked for those human interventions in the natural environment where (i) our understanding of the likely consequences are limited, and (ii) there are threats of serious or irreversible damage to natural systems and processes.

property rights A bundle of entitlements defining the owner's rights, privileges and limitations to use of a resource; they are usually distinguished in terms of private property, state property, common property and open access.

regulatory or *direct control instruments* Policy instruments that involve the direct limitation or reduction of activities that degrade the environment, in accordance with some legislated or agreed standard; common examples include quotas or bans on renewable resource harvesting, restrictions on air pollution emissions, controls on hazardous waste transport and dumping, zoning laws and ambient water quality standards.

reproducible or *humanmade capital* Economic assets, such as buildings, equipment, plants and machinery, tools, financial assets, skilled labour, that are produced by the economy and capable of contributing to long run economic potential or welfare, usually measured in terms of the present value of the income, or welfare, it generates.

resilience The capacity of an ecosystem to recover from perturbations (disturbances), or shocks and stresses, thus absorbing them.

safe minimum standard The preservation of a sufficient area of habitat or natural environment to ensure the generation of ecological services and the survival of species, sub-species or ecosystems – unless the costs of doing so are intolerably high.

self-organization The capacity of ecosystems to develop and evolve in a dynamic fashion within the constraints set by energy flow and biogeochemical cycling; ecosystems are formed in response to these fluxes, are maintained and developed by them, and will respond continuously to them through numerous feedbacks.

strong sustainability The view that, given the limits to substitution between some natural capital and other economic assets (such as reproducible capital), as well as the problems of irreversibility, uncertainty of threshold effects and the potential scale of social costs associated with loss of certain environmental assets, sustainable development cannot be assured without imposing some conditions on the depletion of natural capital; for example, if some minimum level of biodiversity is essential for ecosystem functioning and resilience, preserving the economic opportunities available to future generations requires the prevention of biodiversity loss that threatens this minimum threshold level.

sustainable development Economic and social development that increases the welfare of current generations without affecting adversely the welfare of future generations; for example future generations have economic opportunities that are at least as large as earlier generations.

threshold instruments Policy instruments designed to restrict exploitation of species that are 'endangered' (such as fish stocks, whales, terrestrial mammals); and, more recently, to protect the resilience of ecosystems, particularly where ecological functions and resilience are sensitive to the mix of species, and a change in biodiversity has potentially severe and irreversible consequences.

weak sustainability The view that sustainable development can be assured through the conservation of aggregate capital alone; that is, although natural capital is being depleted, it is being replaced with even more valuable humanmade capital and thus the value of the aggregate stock – comprising both humanmade and the remaining natural capital – is increasing over time in terms of its ability to maintain or enhance human welfare.

Glossary of Acronyms and Abbreviations

BTG British Technology Group

CITES Convention on International Trade in Endangered Species of Wild Flora and Fauna

CSERGE Centre for Social and Economic Research on the Global Environment

EEEM Environmental Economics and Environmental Management

FPMOs Forest protection and management obligations

GEF Global Environmental Facility

GLASOD Global Assessment of Soil Degradation

ICASALS International Center for Arid and Semi-arid Land Studies

ICDPs Integrated conservation development projects

IIED International Institute for Environment and Development

INBio Instituto Nacional de Bioversidad

ISEE International Society for Ecological Economics

IUCN International Union for the Conservation of Nature and Natural Resources

LEEC London Environmental Economics Centre

NGO Non-governmental organization

ODI Overseas Development Institute

OECD Organization for Economic Cooperation and Development

SBI Sustainable Biosphere Initiative

TDRs Transferable development rights

TFRA Tropical Forest Resources Assessment

UNCED United Nations Conference on Environment and Development

UNDP United Nations Development Programme

UNEP United Nations Environment Programme

UNESCO United Nations Educational, Scientific and Cultural Organization

UNFAO United Nations Food and Agriculture Organization

UNSO United Nations Statistical Office

WCED World Commission on Environment and Development

WCMC Wildlife Conservation Monitoring Centre

WRI World Resources Institute

WWF Worldwide Fund for Nature

References

Adams, W M and Hollis, G E (1989) 'Hydrology and Sustainable Resource Development of a Sahelian Floodplain Wetland'. Report prepared for the Hadejia–Nguru Wetlands Conservation Project, Nguru, Nigeria.

Ahmad, Y, El Serafy, S and Lutz, E (ed) (1989) *Environmental Accounting for Sustainable Development.* The World Bank, Washington, DC.

Allen, T F H and Hoekstra, T W (1992) *Toward a Unified Ecology.* Columbia University Press, New York.

Allen, T F H and Starr, T B (1982) *Hierarchy: Perspectives for Ecological Complexity.* University of Chicago Press, Chicago.

Amelung, T (1993) 'Tropical Deforestation as an International Economic Problem'. In H Giersch (ed) *Economic Progress and Environmental Concerns.* Springer-Verlag, Berlin.

Amelung, T and Diehl, M (1991) *Deforestation of Tropical Rainforests: Economic Causes and Impact on Development.* Kieler Studien 241, Tubingen, Mohr, Germany.

Aylward, B A (1992) 'Appropriating the Value of Wildlife and Wildlands'. In T M Swanson and E B Barbier (eds) *Economics for the Wilds: Wildlife, Wildlands, Diversity and Development.* Earthscan Publications, London.

Aylward, B A and Barbier, E B (1992) 'Valuing Environmental Functions in Developing Countries'. *Biodiversity and Conservation* 1:34–50.

Aylward, B A, Echeverría, J, Fendt, L and Barbier, E B (1993) *The Economic Value of Species Information and its Role in Biodiversity Conservation: Case Studies of Costa Rica's National Biodiversity Institute and Pharmaceutical Prospecting,* A Report to the Swedish International Development Authority. London Environmental Economics Centre, London.

Bailey, C (1988) 'The Social Consequences of Tropical Shrimp Mariculture Development'. *Ocean and Shoreline Management* 11:31–44.

Barbier, E B (1989a) *Economics, Natural Resource Scarcity and Development: Conventional and Alternative Views.* Earthscan Publications, London.

Barbier, E B (1989b) *The Economic Value of Ecosystems: 1 – Tropical Wetlands.* LEEC Gatekeeper 89–02. London Environmental Economics Centre, London.

Barbier, E B (1992a) 'Economic Aspects of Tropical Deforestation in South East Asia'. Paper prepared for the workshop on 'The Political Ecology of South East Asia's Forests', Centre for South East Asian Studies, School of Oriental and African Studies, March. Forthcoming in *Global Ecology and Biogeography Letters* 3, 1993.

Barbier, E B (1992b) 'Economics for the Wilds'. In T S Swanson, and E B Barbier, (eds) *Economics for the Wilds: Wildlife, Wildlands, Diversity and Development.* Earthscan Publications Ltd, London.

Barbier, E B (1993a) *The Nature of Economic Instruments: A Brief Overview* LEEC Gatekeeper GK93–01. London Environmental Economics Centre, London.

Barbier, E B (1993b) 'The Role of Economic Incentives for Natural Resource Management in Developing Countries'. In H Giersch (ed) *Economic Progress and Environmental Concerns.* Springer-Verlag, Berlin.

Barbier E B (1993c) 'Valuing Tropical Wetland Benefits: Economic Methodologies and Applications'. *Geographical Journal*, Part 1, 59 (March):22–32.

Barbier, E B (1994a) 'Natural Capital and the Economics of Environment and Development'. In A M Jansson, M Hammer, C Folke, R A Costanza (eds) *Investing in Natural Capital: The Ecological Economics Approach to Sustainability.* Island Press, New York.

Barbier, E B (1994b) 'Tropical Wetland Values and Environmental Functions'. In C Perrings, K-G Mäler, C Folke, C S Holling and B-O Jansson (ed) *Biodiversity Conservation: Policy Issues and Options.* Kluwer Academic Press, Dordrecht.

Barbier, E B (1994c) 'Valuing Environmental Functions: Tropical Wetlands'. *Land Economics*, 70(2):155–173

Barbier, E B, Adams, W M, and Kimmage, K (1991) *Economic Valuation of Wetland Benefits: The Hadejia-Jama'are Floodplain, Nigeria* LEEC Discussion Paper DP 91–02. London Environmental Economics Centre, London.

Barbier, E B, Bishop, J, Aylward, B and Burgess, J C (1992) 'The Economics of Tropical Forest Land Use Options: Methodology and Valuation Techniques'. Report prepared for the Natural Resources and Environment Department, UK Overseas Development Administration.

Barbier, E B, Bockstael, N, Burgess, J C and Strand, I (1993a) *The Timber Trade and Tropical Deforestation in Indonesia* LEEC Discussion Paper DP 93–01. London Environmental Economics Centre, London.

Barbier, E B, Burgess, J C and Markandya, A (1991) 'The Economics of Tropical Deforestation' *AMBIO* 20(2):55–8.

Barbier, E B, Burgess, J C, Bishop, J, Aylward, B and Bann, C (1993a) *The Economic Linkages between the International Trade in Tropical Timber and the Sustainable Management of Tropical Forests.* Final report to the International Tropical Timber Organization, ITTO Activity PCM(XI)/4). Forthcoming in *The Economics of the Tropical Timber Trade*, Earthscan Publications, London, 1994.

Barbier, E B, Burgess, J C, Swanson, T M and Pearce, D W (1990) *Elephants, Economics and Ivory.* Earthscan Publications, London.

Barbier, E B and Markandya, A (1990) 'The Conditions for Achieving Environmentally Sustainable Development'. *European Economic Review* 34:659–69.

Barbier, E B and Rauscher, M (1994a) 'Policies to Control Tropical Deforestation: Trade Interventions vs Transfers'. In C Perrings, K-G Mäler, C Folke, C S Holling and B-O Jansson (ed) *Biodiversity Loss: Ecological and Economic Issues.* Cambridge University Press, Cambridge.

Barbier, E B and Rauscher, M (1994b) 'Trade, Tropical Deforestation and Policy Interventions'. *Environmental and Resource Economics* 4(1):75–94.

Barrett, S (1990) 'The Problem of Global Environmental Protection'. *Oxford Review of Economic Policy* 6(1):68–79.

Barrett, S (1994) 'Some Economics on the Convention on Biological Diversity'. In C Perrings, K-G Mäler, C Folke, C S Holling, B-O and Jansson, (eds) *Biodiversity Loss: Ecological and Economic Issues.* Cambridge University Press, Cambridge.

Barrett, S (1994) 'The Biodiversity Supergame'. *Environmental and Resource Economics* 4(1):111–122.

Bateman, I J, Willis, K G, Garrod, G D, Doktor, P, Langford, I and Turner, R K (1992) *Recreation and Environmental Preservation Value of the Norfolk Broads: A Contingent Valuation Study.* Unpublished report to the UK National Rivers Authority. Environmental Appraisal Group, University of East Anglia.

Behnke, R H and Scoones, I (1993) 'Rethinking Range Ecology: Implications for Rangeland Management in Africa'. Chapter 1 in R H Behnke, I Scoones, and C Kerven, C (eds) (1993) *Range Ecology at Disequilibrium: New Models of Natural Variability and Pastoral Adaptation in African Savannas* Overseas Development Institute, Regents College, London.

Berkes, F (1985) 'The Common Property Resource Problem and the Creation of Limited Property Rights'. *Human Ecology* 13:187–208.

Berkes, F (ed) (1989) *Common Property Resources: Ecology and Community-based Sustainable Development.* Bellhaven Press, London.

Berkes, F and Folke, C (1992) 'A Systems Perspective on the Interrelations between Natural, Human-made and Cultural Capital'. *Ecological Economics* 5:18.

Berkes, F and Folke, C (1994) 'Investing in Cultural Capital for a Sustainable Use of Natural Capital'. In A M Jansson, M Hammer, C Folke and R Costanza (eds) *Investing in Natural Capital: The Ecological Economics Approach to Sustainability.* Island Press, Washington DC

Berkes, F, Folke, C and Gadgil, M (1994) 'Traditional Ecological Knowledge, Biodiversity, Resilience and Sustainability'. In C Perrings, K-G Mäler, C Folke, B-O Jansson, and C S Holling, (eds) *Biodiversity Conservation: Policy Issues and Options.* Kluwer Academic Publishers, Dordrecht.

Binkley, C S and Vincent, J R (1991) *Forest Based Industrialization: A Dynamic Perspective*, HIID Development Discussion Paper No 389. Harvard University, Cambridge, Massachusetts.

Binswanger, H (1989) *Brazilian Policies that Encourage Deforestation in the Amazon.* World Bank Environment Department Working Paper No 16, Washington, DC

Bishop, J Aylward, B and Barbier, E B (1992) 'Guidelines for Applying Environmental Economics in Developing Countries'. *LEEC Gatekeeper Series* No 91–02. London Environmental Economics Centre, London.

Blamey, R and Common, M (1993) 'Stepping Back from Contingent Valuation'. EEEM Discussion Paper Series, No 9309. Department of Environmental Economics and Environmental Management, University of York, UK.

Bond, W J (1993) 'Keystone Species'. In E-D Schulze, and H A Mooney, (eds) *Biodiversity and Ecosystem Function*, 237–53. Springer-Verlag, Heidelberg.

Bromley, D W (1989) *Economic Interests and Institutions: The Conceptual Foundations of Public Policy.* Basil Blackwell, Oxford.

Bromley, D W (ed) (1992) *Making the Commons Work: Theory, Practice and Policy.* Institute of Contemporary Studies Press, San Francisco.

Brown, G and Roughgarden, J (1994) 'An Ecological Economy: Notes on Harvest and Growth'. In C Perrings, K-G Mäler, C Folke, C S Holling, and B-O Jansson, (eds) *Biodiversity Loss: Ecological and Economic Issues.* Cambridge University Press, Cambridge.

Brown, G M Jr. (1990) 'Valuation of Genetice Resources'. In G H Orians, G M Brown, Jr., W E Kunin, and J E Swierzbinski, (eds) *The Preservation and Valuation of Biological Resources.* University of Washington Press, Seattle.

Burgess, J C (1993) 'Timber Production, Timber Trade and Tropical Deforestation'. *AMBIO.* 22(2–3): 136–43.

Burgess, J C (1994) 'Timber Trade as a Cause of Tropical Deforestation', In C Perrings, K-G Mäler, C Folke, C S Holling and B-O Jansson (eds) *Biodiversity Conservation: Policy Issues and Options.* Kluwer Academic Press, Dordrecht.

Ciriacy-Wantrup, S V (1952) *Resource Conservation: Economics and Policies.* University of California Press, Berkeley.

Clark, C (1976) *Mathematical Bioeconomics: The Optimal Management of Renewable Resources.* John Wiley, New York.

Clements, F E (1916) 'Plant Succession: An Analysis of the Development of Vegetation'. Carnegie Institute, Washington. Pub 242, 1–512.

Cleveland, C J (1991) 'Natural Resource Scarcity and Economic Growth Revisited: Economic and Biophysical Perspectives'. In R Costanza, (ed) *Ecological Economics: The Science and Management of Sustainability,* 289–318. Columbia University Press, New York.

Cole, J, Lovett, G and Findlay, S (eds) (1991) *Comparative Analyses of Ecosystems: Patterns, Mechanisms, and Theories.* Springer-Verlag, Heidelberg.

Common, M S and Norton, T W (1992) 'Biodiversity: Its Conservation in Australia'. *AMBIO.* 21(3):258–65.

Common, M S and Norton, T W (1994) 'Biodiversity, Natural Resource Accounting and Environmental Monitoring'. In C Perrings, K-G Mäler, C Folke, C S Holling and B-O Jansson (eds) *Biodiversity Conservation: Policy Issues and Options.* Kluwer Academic Press, Dordrecht.

Common, M S and Perrings, C (1992) 'Towards an Ecological Economics of Sustainability'. *Ecological Economics* 6:7–34.

Conway, G R and Barbier, E B (1990) *After the Green Revolution: Sustainable Agriculture for Development.* Earthscan Publications Ltd, London.

Cook, L M (1991) *Genetic and Ecological Diversity: The Sport of Nature.* Chapman and Hall, London.

Costa-Pierce, B A (1987) 'Aquaculture in Ancient Hawaii'. *BioScience* 37:320–30

Costanza, R, Kemp, W M and Boynton, W R (1993) 'Predictability, Scale, and Biodiversity in Coastal and Estuarine Ecosystems: Implications for Management'. *AMBIO* 22(2–3):88–96.

Costanza, R, Kemp, W M and Boynton, W R (1994) 'Scale and Biodiversity in Coastal and Estuarine Ecosystems'. In C Perrings, K-G Mäler, C Folke, B-O Jansson, and C S Holling, (eds) *Biodiversity Loss: Ecological and Economic Issues.* Cambridge University Press, Cambridge.

Costanza, R, Norton, B G and Haskell, B D (eds) (1992) *Ecosystem Health.* Island Press, Covelo, CA

Costanza, R and Perrings, C (1990) 'A Flexible Assurance Bonding System for Improved Environmental Management'. *Ecological Economics* 2:57–75.

Costanza, R, Wainger, L, Folke, C and Mäler, K-G (1993) 'Modeling Complex Ecological Economic Systems: Toward an Evolutionary, Dynamic Understanding of People and Nature'. *BioScience* 43:545–55.

CSERGE (1993) 'Saving the World's Biodiversity'. A summary paper from the CSERGE Symposium on the Fundamental Forces Driving the Decline of Biodiversity, Kings College, Cambridge, 19–20 July.

Daily, G C and Ehrlich, P R 'Population, Sustainability, and Earth's Carrying Capacity'. *BioScience* 42:761–71.

Daly, H and Cobb, W (1990) *For the Common Good: Redirecting the Economy Toward Community, the Environment and a Sustainable Future.* Beacon Press, Boston.

Dasgupta, P (1982) *The Control of Resources* .Basil Blackwell, Oxford.

Dasgupta, P (1992) 'Population, Resources, and Poverty'. *AMBIO*, 21(1).

Dixon, J A (1989) 'Valuation of Mangroves'. *Tropical Coastal Area Management* 4:1–6.

Dixon, J A, Carpenter, R A, Fallon, L A, Sherman, P A and Manopimoke S (1988) *Economic Analysis of the Environmental Impacts of Development Projects.* Earthscan Publications in association with the Asian Development Bank, London.

Dixon, J A and Hufschmidt M M (eds) (1986) *Economic Valuation Techniques for the Environment: A Case Study Workbook.* Johns Hopkins University Press, Baltimore.

Dixon, J A, Scura, L F and van't Hof, T (1992) 'Meeting Ecological and Economic Goals: The Case of Marine Parks in the Caribbean'. In C Perrings, K-G Mäler, C Folke, C S Holling and B-O Jansson (eds) *Biodiversity Conservation: Policy Issues and Options.* Kluwer Academic Press, Dordrecht.

Dixon, J A, Scura, L F and van't Hof, T (1993) 'Meeting Ecological and Economic Goals: Marine Parks in the Caribbean'. *AMBIO* 22(2–3):110–16.

Dugan, P J (ed) (1990) *Wetland Conservation: A Review of Current Issues and Required Action.* International Union for the Conservation of Nature and Natural Resources, Gland, Switzerland.

Eggertsson, T (1993) *Economic Perspectives on Property Rights and the Economics of Institutions.* Beijer Discussion Papers No. 40. The Beijer International Institute of Ecological Economics, The Royal Swedish Academy of Sciences, Stockholm.

Ehrlich, P R and Daily, G C (1993) 'Population Extinction and Saving Biodiversity'. *AMBIO* 22(2–3):64–8.

Ehrlich, P R and Ehrlich, A H (1981) *Extinction:The Causes and Consequences of the Disappearance of Species.* Random House, New York.

Ehrlich, P R and Ehrlich, A H (1992) 'The Value of Biodiversity'. *AMBIO* 21(3):219–26.

Ehrlich, P R and Wilson, E O (1991) 'Biodiversity Studies: Science and Policy'. *Science* 253:758–62.

Ellis, G M and Fisher, A C (1987) 'Valuing the Environment as Input'. *Journal of Environmental Management* 25:149–56.

Farber, Stephen J and Costanza R, (1987) 'The Economic Value of Wetland Systems'. *Journal of Environmental Management* 24:41–51.

Faustmann, M 1849. 'Calculation of the Value Which Forest Land and Immature Stands Possess in Forestry'. In W Linnard (trans), 'Martin Faustmann and the Evolution of Discounted Cash Flow'. *Commonwealth Forestry Institute Papers* 42 (1968), Oxford.

Feeny, D, Berkes, F, McCay, B J and Acheson, J M (1990) 'The Tragedy of the Commons: Twenty-Two Years Later'. *Human Ecology* 18:1–19.

Fisher, A C and Hanemann, W M (1987) 'Quasi-option Value: Some Misconceptions Dispelled'. *Journal of Environmental Economics and Management* 14:183–90.

Folke, C (1991) 'Socioeconomic Dependence of the Life-Supporting Environment'. In C Folke and T Kåberger, (eds) *Linking the Natural Environment and the Economy: Essays from the Eco-Eco Group.* Kluwer Academic Press, Dordrecht.

Folke, C (1991) 'The Societal Value of Wetland Life-Support.' In C Folke, and T Kåberger, (eds) *Linking the Natural Environment and the Economy: Essays from the Eco-Eco Group.* Kluwer Academic Publishers, Dordrecht.

Folke, C and Kautsky, N (1989) 'The Role of Ecosystems for a Sustainable Development of Aquaculture.' *AMBIO* 18:234–43.

Folke, C and Kautsky, N (1992) 'Aquaculture with Its Environment: Prospects for Sustainability.' *Ocean and Coastal Management* 17:5–24.

Folke, C, Hammer, M and Jansson, A M (1991) 'Life-support Value of Ecosystems: A Case Study of the Baltic Sea Region.' *Ecological Economics* 3:123–37.

Folke, C, Kautsky, N and Troell, M (1994) 'The Costs of Eutrophication from Salmon Farming: Implications for Management.' *Journal of Environmental Management*, 40:173–182

Folke, C ,Perrings, C, McNeely, J A and Myers, N (1993) 'Biodiversity Conservation with a Human Face: Ecology, Economics and Policy.' *AMBIO* 22(23):62–3.

Food and Agricultural Organization (1993) 'Forest Resources Assessment 1990: Tropical Countries'. Forestry Paper No 112, Food and Agricultural Organization of the United Nations, Rome.

Franklin, J F (1993) 'Preserving Biodiversity: Species, Ecosystems, or Landscapes?' *Ecological Applications* 3:202–05.

Freeman, A M III (1984) 'The Sign and Size of Option Value'. *Land Economics* 60(1):1–13.

Freeman, A M III (1991) 'Valuing Environmental Resources under Alternative Management Regimes.' *Ecological Economics* 3:247–56.

Friend, A M (1993) '200 Years of Natural Capital Erosion: A Case Study of Human Stress on the Great Lakes Ecosystem.' In The Institute for Research on Environment and Economy (ed) Ecological Economics: Emergence of a New Development Paradigm. CIDA and IREE, University of Ottawa.

Gadgil, M (1993) 'Biodiversity and India's Degraded Lands.' *AMBIO* 22(2–3):167–72.

Gadgil, M, Berkes, F and Folke, C (1993) 'Indigenous Knowledge for Biodiversity Conservation.' *AMBIO* 22(2–3):151–6.

Githinji, M and Perrings, C (1993) 'Social and Ecological Sustainability in the Use of Biotic Resources in Sub-Saharan Africa'. *AMBIO* 22(2–3):110–6.

Gren, I-M (1992) *Benefits from Restoring Wetlands for Nitrogen Abatement: A Case Study of Gotland.* Beijer Discussion Paper Series No 14. The Beijer International Institute of Ecological Economics, Stockholm.

Gren, I-M, Folke, C, Turner, R K and Bateman, I J (1992b) 'Wetland Ecosystems:

Primary and Secondary Values of Wetland Ecosystems.' *Environmental and Resource Economics* 4(1):55–74,.

Grima, A P L and Berkes, F (1989) 'Natural Resources: Access, Right-to-use and Management.' In F Berkes, (ed) *Common Property Resources: Ecology and Community-Based Sustainable Development* 33–54. Belhaven Press, London.

de Groot, R S (1992) *Functions of Nature*. Wolters-Noordhoff, Amsterdam.

Grubb, P J and May, R M (1991) 'Comments on the Sustainable Biosphere Initiative.' *Conservation Biology* 5:550–1.

Günther, F and Folke, C (1993) 'Characteristics of Nested System.' *Journal of Biological Systems* 1:257–74.

Hammer, M (1991) 'Marine Ecosystems Support to Fisheries and Fish Trade.' In C Folke and T Kåberger, (eds) *Linking the Natural Environment and the Economy: Essays from the Eco-Eco Group*, Kluwer Academic Press, Dordrecht.

Hammer, M (1994) 'Diversity Conservation in Relation to Fisheries in the Baltic Sea.' In C Perrings, K-G Mäler, C Folke, B-O Jansson and C S Holling, (eds) *Biodiversity Conservation: Policy Issues and Options.* Kluwer Academic Publishers, Dordrecht.

Hammer, M, Jansson, A M and Jansson, B-O (1993) 'Diversity, Change and Sustainability: Implications for Fisheries'. *AMBIO,* 22(2–3)97–105.

Hanemann, W M (1990) 'Commentary on Valuation of Genetic Resources.' In G H Orians, G M Brown, W E Kunin and J E Swierzbinski, (eds) *The Preservation and Valuation of Biological Resources.* University of Washington Press, Seattle.

Hardin, G (1968) 'The Tragedy of the Commons'. *Science,* 162(3859):1243–8.

Hardin, G (1988) 'Commons Failing'. *New Scientist,* 22 October.

Hartwick, J M (1977) 'Intergenerational Equity and the Investing of Rents from Exhaustible Resources.' *American Economic Review* 66:972–4.

Holling, C S (1973) 'Resilience and Stability of Ecological Systems.' *Annual Review of Ecology and Systematics* 4:124.

Holling, C S (1986) 'Resilience of Ecosystem: Local Surprise and Global Change.' In E C Clark and R E Munn, (eds) *Sustainable Development of the Biosphere*, 292317. Cambridge University Press, Cambridge.

Holling, C S (1992) 'Cross-scale Morphology, Geometry and Dynamics of Ecosystems.' *Ecological Monographs* 62: 447–502.

Holling, C S (1992) 'The Role of Forest Insects in Structuring the Boreal Landscape' in H H Shugart, R Leemans, and G B Bonan, (eds). *A Systems Analysis of the Global Boreal Forest* Cambridge University Press, Cambridge. 170–91.

Holling, C S, Schindler, D W, Walker, B W and Roughgarden, J (1994) 'Biodiversity in the Functioning of Ecosystems: An Ecological Primer and Synthesis'. In C Perrings, K-G Mäler, C Folke, C S Holling and B-O Jansson (eds), *Biodiversity Loss: Ecological and Economic Issues*, Cambridge University Press, Cambridge.

Hotelling, H (1931) 'The Economics of Exhaustible Resources.' *Journal of Political Economy* 39:137–75.

Hudson, W E (ed) (1991) *Landscape Linkages and Biodiversity*. Island Press, Washington, DC

Hurlbert, S H (1971) 'The Non-concept of Species Diversity: A Critique and Alternative Parameters.' *Ecology* 52:577–86.

Hyde, W F, Newman, D H and Sedjo, R A (1991) *Forest Economics and Policy Analysis: An Overview*, World Bank Discussion Paper No 134, The World Bank, Washington, DC

IUCN/UNEP/WWF (1980) *World Conservation Strategy: Living Resource Conservation for Sustainable Development*. IUCN, Gland.

IUCN/UNEP/WWF (1991) *Caring for the Earth: A Strategy for Sustainable Living*. IUCN, Gland.

Jackson, J B C (1991) 'Adaptation and Diversity of Reef Corals.' *BioScience* 41:475–82.

Johansson, P-O and Löfgren, K G (1985) *The Economics of Forestry and Natural Resources*. Basil Blackwell, Oxford.

Johnson, H B and Mayeux, H S (1992) 'Viewpoint: a View on Species Additions and Deletions and the Balance of Nature.' *Journal of Range Management* 45: 322–33.

Jones, T and Wibe, S (1992) *Forests: Market and Intervention Failures – Five Case Studies*. Earthscan Publications, London.

Jordan, W R, Gilpin, M E and Aber, J D (eds) (1987) *Restoration Ecology: A Synthetic Approach to Ecological Research*. Cambridge University Press, Cambridge.

Jørgensen, S E (1992) *Integration of Ecosystem Theories: A Pattern*. Kluwer Academic Press, Dordrecht.

Kates, R W (1990) 'Hunger, Poverty and the Environment.' Paper presented at the Distinguished Speaker Series, Center for Advanced Study of International Development, Michigan State University, Lansing, 6 May.

Kay, J J (1991) 'A Nonequilibrium Thermodynamic Framework for Discussing Ecosystem Integrity'. *Environmental Management* 15:483–95.

Kelly, J R and Harwell, M A (1990) 'Indicators of Ecosystem Recovery.' *Environmental Management* 14:527–45.

Kim, O-K and van den Oever, P (1992) 'Demographic Transition and Patterns of Natural Resource Use in the Republic of Korea'. *AMBIO* 21(1):56–62.

Kramer, R A (1993) 'Tropical Forest Protection in Madagascar'. Paper prepared for Northeast Universities Development Consortium, Williams College, 15–16 October.

Kramer, R, Munasinghe, M, Sharma, N, Mercer, E and Shyamsundar, P (1992) 'Valuing a Protected Tropical Forest: A Case Study in Madagascar'. IVth World Congress on National Parks and Protected Areas, Caracas, Venezuela, 14–16 February.

Krebs, C J (1985) *Ecology*. Harper & Row, New York.

Krutilla, J V and Fisher, A C (1985) *The Economics of Natural Environments: Studies in the Valuation of Commodity and Amenity Resources* 2nd edn. Resources for the Future, Washington, DC

Lal, P N and Dixon, J A (1990) 'The Management of Coastal Wetlands: Economic Analysis of Combined Ecologic-Economic Systems.' *Mimeo*. Australian Bureau of Agricultural and Resource Economics, Canberra.

Lane, C R (1991) 'Alienation of Barabaig Pasture Land: Policy Development in Tanzania'. PhD thesis, University of Sussex.

Larsson, J, Folke, C and Kautsky, N (1994) 'Ecological Limitations and Appropriation of Ecosystem Support by Shrimp Farming in Columbia.' *Environmental Management*, forthcoming.

Larsson, U, Elmgren, R and Wulff, F (1985) 'Eutrophication and the Baltic Sea: Causes and Consequences.' *AMBIO* 14:9–14.

Lawton, J H and Brown, V K (1993) 'Redundancy in Ecosystems.' In E-D Schulze,and H A Mooney, (eds) *Biodiversity and Ecosystem Function*, 255–70. Springer-Verlag, Heidelberg.

Leonard, H J (1989) *Environment and the Poor: Development Strategies for a Common Agenda*. New Brunswick: Transaction Books.

Leopold, A (1970) *A Sand Country Almanac*. Ballantine Books, New York.

Likens, G E (1992) *The Ecosystem Approach: Its Use and Abuse. Excellence in Ecology 3*. Ecology Institute, Oldendorf/Luhe, Germany.

Lipsey, R G and Lancaster, K J (1956) 'The General Theory of the Second Best.' *Review of Economic Studies* 24:11–32.

Lipton, M (1968) 'The Theory of the Optimizing Peasant'. *Journal of Development Studies*, 327–51.

London Environmental Economics Centre (1992) 'Economic Analysis of Tropical Forest Land Use Options: A Preliminary Review of the Literature'. Report prepared for the Natural Resource and Environment Department, UK Overseas Development Administration. LEEC, London.

Lovejoy, T E (1980) 'A Projection of Species Extinction.' In G O Barney (ed) *The Global 2000 Report to the President. Entering the Twenty-first Century, Vol 2*. Council on Environmental Quality, US Government Printing Office, Washington, DC

Lubchenco, J, Olson, A M, Brubaker, L B, Carpenter, S R, Holland, M M, Hubbell, S P, Levin, S A, MacMahon, J A, Matson, P A, Melillo, J M, Mooney, H A, Peterson, C H, Pulliam, H R, Real, L A, Regal, P J and Risser, P G (1991) 'The Sustainable Biosphere Initiative: an Ecological Research Agenda.' *Ecology* 72:371–412.

Ludwig, D, Hilborn, R and Walters, C (1993) 'Uncertainty, Resource Exploitation, and Conservation: Lessons from History.' *Science* 260:17, 36.

Lugo, A E, Parrotta, J A and Brown, S (1993) 'Loss of Species Caused by Tropical Deforestation and their Recovery Through Management'. *AMBIO*, 22(2–3):106–9.

Lutz, E (ed) (1993) *Toward Improved Accounting for the Environment*. An UNSTAT–World Bank Symposium. The World Bank, Washington, DC

McArthur, R H and Wilson, E O (1967) *The Theory of Island Biogeography*. Monographs in Population Biology 1. Princeton University Press, Princeton, New Jersey.

McCay, B J (1993) 'Management Regimes.' Beijer Discussion Papers No 38. The Beijer International Institute of Ecological Economics, The Royal Swedish Academy of Sciences, Stockholm.

McCay, B J and Acheson, J M (eds) (1987) *The Question of the Commons: The Culture and Evolution of Communal Resources*. University of Arizona Press, Tucson.

McNeely, J A (1993) 'Economic Incentives for Conserving Biodiversity: Lessons for Africa.' *AMBIO* 22(23):144–50.

McNeely, J A, Miller, K R, Reid, W R, Mittermeier, R A and Werner, T B (1990) *Conserving the World's Biological Diversity*. IUCN, Gland.

Magurran, A E (1988) *Ecological Diversity and its Measurement*. Chapman and Hall, London.

Mahar, D (1989) 'Deforestation in Brazil's Amazon Region: Magnitude, Rate and Causes', in G Schramm and J Warford (eds) *Environmental Management and Economics Development*. Johns Hopkins University Press, Baltimore, USA

Mahatab, F U and Karim, Z (1992) 'Population and Agricultural Land Use: Towards a Sustainable Food Production System in Bangladesh'. *AMBIO*, 21(1):50–5.

Mäler, K-G (1994) 'Sustainable Development.' In C Perrings, K-G Mäler, C Folke, C S Holling and B-O Jansson (eds) *Biodiversity Loss: Ecological and Economic Issues*. Cambridge University Press, Cambridge.

Mäler, K-G, Gren, I-M and Folke, C (1994) 'Multiple Use of Environmental Resources: A Household Production Function Approach to Valuing Natural Capital.' In A M Jansson, M Hammer, C Folke, and R Costanza, (eds) *Investing in Natural Capital: The Ecological Economics Approach to Sustainability*. Island Press, Washington.

Meyer, O (1993) 'Functional Groups of Microorganisms.' In E-D Schulze, and H A Mooney, (eds) *Biodiversity and Ecosystem Function*. Springer-Verlag, Heidelberg.

Miller, J R and Menz, F C (1979) 'Some Economic Considerations for Wildlife Preservation.' *Southern Economic Journal* 45:719–20.

Mills, L S, Soulé, M E and Doak, D F (1993) 'The Keystone-Species Concept in Ecology and Conservation.' *BioScience* 43:219–24.

Mitsch, W J and Jörgensen, S E (eds) (1989) *Ecological Engineering: An Introduction to Ecotechnology*. John Wiley, New York.

Munasinghe, M (1992) 'Biodiversity Protection Policy: Environmental Valuation and Distributional Issues'. *AMBIO*, 21(3):227–36.

Munasinghe, M (1992) 'Environmental Protection Policy: Environmental Valuation and Distribution Issues.' *AMBIO* 21(3):227–36.

Munasinghe, M (1993) 'Environmental Economics and Biodiversity Management in Developing Countries'. *AMBIO*, Vol.22, No.23, pp.126–35.

Munasinghe, M (1994) 'Managing Biological Diversity', In C Perrings, K-G Mäler, C Folke, C S Holling and B-O Jansson (eds) *Biodiversity Conservation: Policy Issues and Options*. Kluwer Academic Press, Amsterdam.

Myers, N (1979) *The Sinking Ark: A New Look at the Problem of Disappearing Species*. Pergamon Press, Oxford.

Myers, N (1993) 'Biodiversity and the Precautionary Principle.' *AMBIO* 22(2–3):74–79.

Narain, U and Fisher, A (1994) 'Modeling the Value of Biodiversity Using a Production Function Approach.' In C Perrings, K-G Mäler, C Folke, B-O Jansson, and C S Holling, (eds) *Biodiversity Conservation: Policy Issues and Options*. Kluwer Academic Publishers, Dordrecht.

Nelson, J G and Serafin, R (1992) 'Assessing Biodiversity: A Human Ecological Approach.' *AMBIO* 23:212–18.

Nihlgård, B and Rundgren, S (1978) *Naturens Dynamik* .Natur och Kultur, Stockholm.

North, D C (1989) *Institutions, Institutional Change and Economic Performance*. Cambridge University Press, Cambridge.

Norton, B G (1992) 'Nature, Culture and Biodiversity Policy'. Paper prepared for the

Second Conference on the Ecology and Economics of Biodiversity Loss held by the Biodiversity Programme of the Beijer Institute for Ecological Economics of the Swedish Royal Academy of Sciences, Stockholm, 29–31 July.

Norton, B G and Ulanowicz, R E (1992) 'Scale and Biodiversity Policy: a Hierarchical Approach'. *AMBIO* 21(3):244–9.

Odum, E P (1975) *Ecology.* Holt-Saunders, New York.

Odum, E P (1983) *Basic Ecology.* Holt-Saunders International Editions, New York.

Odum, E P (1985) 'Trends to be Expected in Stressed Ecosystems.' *BioScience* 35:419–22.

Odum, E P (1989) *Ecology and Our Endangered Life-Support Systems.* Sinauer Associates, Sunderland, Massachusetts.

Odum, H T (1971) *Environment, Power and Society.* John Wiley & Sons, New York.

O'Neill, R V, DeAngelis, D L, Waide, J B and Allen, T F H (1986) *A Hierarchical Concept of Ecosystems.* Princeton University Press, New Jersey.

Opschoor, J B and Vos, H B (1989) *Economic Instruments for Environmental Protection.* OECD, Paris.

Orians, G H and Kunin, W E (1990) 'Ecological Uniqueness and Loss of Species.' In G H Orians, G M Brown, W E Kunin, and J E Swierzbinski, (eds) *The Preservation and Valuation of Biological Resources,* 146–84. University of Washington Press, Seattle.

Ostrom, E (1990) *Governing the Commons: The Evolution of Institutions for Collective Action.* Cambridge University Press, Cambridge.

Paine, R T (1969) 'A Note on Trophic Complexity and Community Stability'. *American Naturalist* 103:91–3.

Panayotou, T 1990, 'Policies, Incentives and Regulations: The Use of Fiscal Incentives', Conference on Environmental Management in Developing Countries, OECD Development Centre, Paris, October 3–5.

Panayotou, T (1994) 'Conservation of Biodiversity and Economic Development: The Concept of Transferable Development Rights'. *Environmental and Resource Economics* 4(1):91–110.

Panayotou, T and Ashton, P (1994) 'Sustainable Use of Tropical Forests in South East Asia'. In C Perrings, K-G Mäler, C Folke, C S Holling and B-O Jansson (eds), *Biodiversity Conservation: Policy Issues and Options.* Kluwer Academic Press, Dordrecht.

Pearce, D W (1990), 'Policies, Incentives and Regulations: Recent Thinking in OECD Countries', Conference on Environmental Management in Developing Countries, OECD Development Centre, Paris, October 3–5.

Pearce, D W (1994) 'Biodiversity Conservation and Economic Development: Local and Global Dimensions'. In C Perrings, K-G Mäler, C Folke, C S Holling and B-O Jansson (ed)s *Biodiversity Conservation: Policy Issues and Options.* Kluwer Academic Press, Dordrecht.

Pearce, D W and Markandya, A (1989) *Measuring Environmental Benefits.* Organization for Economic Cooperation and Development, Paris.

Pearce, D W, Markandya, A and Barbier, E B (1989) *Blueprint for a Green Economy.* Earthscan Publications, London.

Pearce, D W and Perrings, C (1994) 'Biodiversity Conservation and Economic Development: Local and Global Dimensions'. In C Perrings, K-G Mäler, C Folke, C S Holling and B-O Jansson (eds) *Biodiversity Conservation: Policy Issues and Options*. Kluwer Academic Press, Dordrecht.

Pearce, D W and Warford, J J (1992) *World Without End: Economics, Environment and Sustainable Development*. Oxford University Press, Oxford.

Perrings, C (1991) 'Reserved Rationality and the Precautionary Principle: Technological Change, Time and Uncertainty in Environmental Decision Making'. In R Costanza (ed) *Ecological Economics: The Science and Management of Sustainability*. Columbia University Press, New York.

Perrings, C (1993) 'Stress, Shock and Sustainability of Optimal Resource Utilization in a Stochastic Environment'. In E B Barbier, (ed) *Economics and Ecology: New Frontiers and Sustainable Development*. Chapman and Hall, London.

Perrings, C, Folke, C and Mäler, K-G (1992) 'The Ecology and Economics of Biodiversity Loss: The Research Agenda'. *AMBIO* 21(3):201–11.

Perrings, C, Folke, C, Mäler, K-G, Holling, C S and Jansson, B-O (1994) 'Framing the Problem of Biodiversity Loss'. In C Perrings, C Folke, K- G Mäler, C S Holling and B-O Jansson (ed) *Biodiversity Loss: Ecological and Economic Issues*. Cambridge University Press, Cambridge.

Perrings, C and Pearce, D W (1994) 'Threshold Effects and Incentives for the Conservation of Biodiversity'. *Environmental and Resource Economics* 4(1):13–28.

Perrings, C and Walker, B (1994) 'Biodiversity Loss and the Economics of Discontinuous Change in Semi-Arid Rangelands'. In C Perrings, K-G Mäler, C Folke, C S Holling, and B-O Jansson, (eds) *Biodiversity Loss: Ecological and Economic Issues*. Cambridge University Press, Cambridge.

Persson, A (1994) 'Macroeconomic Policies behind Deforestation in Costa Rica'. In C Perrings, K-G Mäler, C Folke, C S Holling and B-O Jansson (eds), *Biodiversity Conservation: Policy Issues and Options*. Kluwer Academic Press, Dordrecht.

Pezzey, J (1989) *Economic Analysis of Sustainable Growth and Sustainable Development*. Environment Department Working Paper No 15. The World Bank, Washington, DC

Pianka, E R (1986) 'Ecological Phenomena in Evolutionary Perspective'. In N Polunin, (ed) *Ecosystem Theory and Application*, 325–36. John Wiley & Sons, New York.

Pigou, A C (1920) *The Economics of Welfare*, 1st edn. Macmillan, London.

Pimm, S L (1991) *The Balance of Nature?* University of Chicago Press, Chicago.

Pomeroy, L R and Alberts, J J (eds) (1988) *Concepts of Ecosystem Ecology*. Springer-Verlag, Heidelberg.

Pomeroy, L R, Hargrove, E C and Alberts, J J (1988) 'The Ecosystem Perspective.' In L R Pomeroy, and J J Alberts, (eds) *Concepts of Ecosystem Ecology* 117. Springer-Verlag, Heidelberg.

Poore, D, Burgess, P, Palmer, J, Rietbergen, S and Synnott, T (1989) *No Timber Without Trees: Sustainability in the Tropical Forest*. Earthscan Publications, London.

Primavera, J H (1993) 'A Critical Review of Shrimp Pond Culture in the Philippines.' *Reviews in Fisheries Science* 1:151–201.

Randall, A (1991) 'The Value of Biodiversity.' *AMBIO* 20(2):64–8.

Raven, P H (1988) 'On Diminishing Tropical Forests.' In E O Wilson (ed) *Biodiversity*. National Academy Press, Washington, DC

Regier, H A and Baskerville, G L (1986) 'Sustainable Redevelopment of Regional Ecosystems Degraded by Exploitive Development.' In E C Clark and R E Munn, (eds) *Sustainable Development of the Biosphere*. 75–101. Cambridge University Press, Cambridge.

Reid, W V (1992) 'How Many Species Will There Be?' In T C Whitmore and J A Sayer (eds) *Tropical Deforestation and Species Extinction*. Chapman and Hall, London.

Reid, W V, McNeely, J A, Tunstall, D B, Bryant, D A and Winograd, M (1993) *Biodiversity Indicators for Policy-Makers*. World Resources Institute, Washington, DC

Reid, W V and Miller, K R (1989) *Keeping Options Alive: The Scientific Basis for Conserving Biodiversity*. World Resources Institute, Washington, DC

Reis, E J and Marguilis, S (1991) 'Options for Slowing Amazon Jungle Clearing'. Paper prepared for conference on Economic Policy Responses to Global Warming, Rome.

Repetto, R and Gillis, M (1988) *Public Policies and the Misuse of Forest Resources*. Cambridge University Press, Cambridge.

Resource Assessment Commission. (1991) *Forest and Timber Enquiry*. Draft Report, Vols 1 and 2. Australian Government Publishing Service, Canberra.

Richards, J F (1990) 'Land Transformation.' In B L Turner, W C Clark and W C Kates (ed) *The Earth as Transformed by Human Action: Global and Regional Changes in the Biosphere over the Past 300 Years*. Cambridge University Press, Cambridge.

Roughgarden, J, May, R M and Levin, S A (ed) (1989) *Perspectives in Ecological Theory*. Princeton University Press, Princeton, New Jersey.

Ruddle, K, Hviding, E and Johannes, R E (1992) 'Marine Resources Management in the Context of Customary Tenure.' *Marine Resource Economics* 7:249–73.

Ruitenbeek, H J (1992) *Mangrove Management: An Economic Analysis of Management Options with a Focus on Bintuni Bay, Irian Jaya*. Environmental Management Development in Indonesia Project, Jakarta and Halifax.

Schindler, D W (1990) 'Experimental Perturbations of Whole Lakes as Tests of Hypotheses Concerning Ecosystem Structure and Function.' *Oikos* 57:25–41.

Schneider, R, McKenna, J, Dejou, C, Butler, J and Barrows, J (1990) 'Brazil: An Economic Analysis of Environmental Problems in the Amazon'. World Bank, Washington, DC

Schulze, E-D and Mooney, H A (eds) (1993a) *Biodiversity and Ecosystem Function*. Springer-Verlag, Heidelberg.

Schulze, E-D and Mooney, H A (1993b) 'Ecosystem Function of Biodiversity: a Summary'. In E-D Schulze, and H A Mooney, (eds) *Biodiversity and Ecosystem Function* 497–510. Springer-Verlag, Heidelberg.

Scoones, I (1993) 'Economic and Ecological Carrying Capacity: Applications to Pastoral Systems in Zimbabwe'. In Barbier, E B (ed) (1993) *Economics and Ecology: New Frontiers and Sustainable Development*. Chapman and Hall, London.

Sedjo, R A Bowes, M and Wiseman, C (1991) *Toward a Worldwide System of Tradeable Forest Protection and Management Obligations* ENR 9116, Energy and Natural Resources Division, Resources for the Future, Washington, DC

Sedjo, R A, and Lyon, K S (1990) *The Long Term Adequacy of World Timber Supply*. Resources for the Future, Washington, DC

Serafin, R and Nelson, J G (1992) Biodiversity in Decision-making for the Coast. Paper prepared for the Second Conference on the Ecology and Economics of Biodiversity Loss held by the Biodiversity Programme of the Beijer International Institute of Ecological Economics of the Royal Swedish Academy of Sciences, Stockholm, 29–31 July.

Simberloff, D (1986) 'Are We on the Verge of A Mass Extinction in Tropical Rain Forests?' In D K Elliott (ed.) *Dynamics of Extinction*. John Wiley, New York.

Simberloff, D (1988) 'The Contribution of Population and Community Biology to Conservation Science.' *Annual Review of Ecology and Systematics* 19:473–511.

Smith, V K (1983) 'Option Value: A Conceptual Overview.' *Southern Economic Journal* 50:654–68.

Smith, V K (1991) 'Household Production Functions and Environmental Benefit Estimation.' In J B Braden, and C D Kolstad, (eds) *Measuring the Demand for Environmental Quality*. North-Holland, Amsterdam.

Smith, V L (1977) 'Control Theory Applied to Natural and Environmental Resources: An Exposition.' *Journal of Environmental Economics and Management* 4:1–24.

Solbrig, O T (1991) 'The Origin and Function of Biodiversity'. *Environment* 33:16–38.

Solbrig, O T (1993) 'Ecological Constraints to Savanna Land Use'. In M D Young and O T Solbrig (eds) *The World's Savannas: Economic Driving Forces, Ecological Constraints and Policy Options for Sustainable Land Use*. Man and the Biosphere Programme/UNESCO Vol 12. Parthenon Publishing Group, Paris.

Solbrig, O T (1993) 'Plant Traits and Adaptive Strategies: Their Role in Ecosystem Function'. In E-D Schulze, and H A Mooney, (eds) *Biodiversity and Ecosystem Function* 97–116. Springer-Verlag, Heidelberg.

Solow, R M (1974) 'Intergenerational Equity and Exhaustible Resources.' *Review of Economic Studies,* Symposium on the Economics of Exhaustible Resources 29–46.

Solow, R M (1986) 'On the Intertemporal Allocation of Natural Resources.' *Scandinavian Journal of Economics* 88(1):141–9.

Soulé, J D and Piper, J K (1992) *Farming in Nature's Image: An Ecological Approach to Agriculture*. Island Press, Washington, DC.

Southgate, D (1991) *Tropical Deforestation and Agricultural Development in Latin America* LEEC DP 91–01. London Environmental Economics Centre, London.

Southgate, D and Clark, H L (1993) 'Can Conservation Projects Save Biodiversity in South America?' *AMBIO* 22(2–3):163–6.

Steele, J H (1991) 'Marine Ecosystem Dynamics: Comparison of Scales.' *Ecological Research* 6:175–83.

Swanson, T M (1992a) 'Economics of a Biodiversity Convention.' *AMBIO* 21(3):250–7.

Swanson, T M (1992b) 'The Global Conversion Process: The Fundamental Forces Underlying Losses of Biological Diversity'. *CSERGE Working Paper*, GEC 9241, Centre for Social and Economic Research on the Global Environment, London.

Swanson, T M (1994) 'Biodiversity and Intellectual Property Rights.' In C Perrings, K-G Mäler, C Folke, C S Holling, and B-O Jansson, (eds) *Biodiversity Loss: Ecological and Economic Issues*. Cambridge University Press, Cambridge.

Swanson, T M (1994) 'The International Regulation of Biodiversity Decline: Optimal Policy and Evolutionary Product.' In C Perrings, K-G Mäler, C Folke, C S Holling and

B-O Jansson (eds) *Biodiversity Loss: Ecological and Economic Issues*. Cambridge University Press, Cambridge.

Swanson, T M and Barbier, E B (1992) *Economics for the Wilds: Wildlife, Wildlands, Diversity and Development*. Earthscan Publications, London.

Tietenberg, T (1990) 'Economic Instruments for Environmental Regulation', *Oxford Review of Economic Policy* 6(1):17–33.

Toulmin, C (1993) 'Combatting Desertification: Setting the Agenda for a Global Convention'. *Dryland Networks Programme Issues Paper* No 42. Drylands Programme, International Institute for Environment and Development, London.

Trenbath, B R, Conway, G R and Craig, I A (1990) 'Threats to Sustainability in Intensified Agricultural Systems: Analysis and Implications for Management.' In S R Gliessman, (ed) *Agroecology*. Springer-Verlag, New York.

Turner, M G and Gradner, R H (eds) (1990) *Quantitative Methods in Landscape Ecology*. Springer-Verlag, New York.

Turner, R K (1991) 'Economics and Wetland Management.' *AMBIO* 20(2):59–63.

Turner, R K (1993) 'Sustainability: Principles and Practice.' In R K Turner (ed) *Sustainable Environmental Economics and Management: Principles and Practice*. Belhaven Press, London.

Turner, R K, Folke, C, Gren, I-M and Bateman, I (1994) 'Wetland Valuation: Three Case Studies.' In C Perrings, K-G Mäler, C Folke, C S Holling and B-O Jansson (eds), *Biodiversity Loss: Ecological and Economic Issues*. Cambridge University Press, Cambridge.

Turner, R K and Jones, T (ed) (1991) *Wetlands: Market and Intervention Failures*. Earthscan Publications, London.

Twilley, R R (1991) 'Properties of Mangrove Ecosystems Related to the Energy Signature of Coastal Environments.' *Mimeo*. Department of Biology, University of Southwestern Louisiana, Lafayette.

Unemo, L (1994) 'Environmental Impact of Government Policies and External Shocks in Botswana – A CGE Model Approach'. In C Perrings, K-G Mäler, C Folke, C S Holling, and B-O Jansson, (eds) *Biodiversity Conservation: Policy Issues and Options*. Kluwer Academic Press, Dordrecht.

United Nations Environment Programme (1991) 'Status of Desertification and Implementation of the United Nations Plan of Action to Combat Desertification'. UNEP, Nairobi.

United Nations Environment Programme (1992) *Biodiversity Country Studies: Synthesis Report*. UNEP, Nairobi.

United Nations Environment Programme (1993) *Guidelines for Country Studies on Biological Diversity*. UNEP, Nairobi.

United Nations Food and Agricultural Organization (1991) *Second Interim Report on the State of Tropical Forests by Forest Resources Assessment 1990 Project*. Presented at the Tenth World Forestry Congress, September, Paris.

United Nations Statistical Office (1990) *SNA Handbook on Integrated Environmental and Economic Accounting* Preliminary draft. UNSO, New York.

Vincent, J R and Binkley, C S (1991) *Forest Based Industrialization: A Dynamic Perspective*, Development Discussion Paper No 389, Harvard Institute for International Development (HIID), Cambridge, Massachusetts.

Vitousek, P, Ehrlich, P R, Ehrlich, A H and Matson, P A (1986) 'Human Appropriation of the Products of Photosynthesis.' *BioScience* 36:368–73.

Walker, B H (1992) 'Biodiversity and Ecological Redundancy'. *Conservation Biology* 6:18–23.

Walker, B H (1993) 'Rangeland Ecology: Understanding and Managing Change'. *AMBIO*, 22(2–3):80–87.

Walters, C J (1986) *Adaptive Management of Renewable Resources*. McGraw-Hill, New York.

Weissinger, A K (1990) 'Technologies for Germ Plasm Preservation *Ex Situ*'. In G H Orians, G M Brown Jr., W E Kunin and J E Swierzbinski (eds) *The Preservation and Valuation of Biological Resources*. University of Washington Press, Seattle.

Weitzman, M L (1994) 'Diversity Functions.' In C Perrings, C Folke, K–G Mäler, C S Holling and B–O Jansson (eds) *Biodiversity Loss: Ecological and Economic Issues*. Cambridge University Press, Cambridge.

Wells, M P (1992) 'Biodiversity and Conservation, Affluence and Poverty: Mismatched Costs and Benefits and Efforts to Remedy Them.' *AMBIO* 21(3):237–43.

Wells, M P and Brandon, K E (1992) *People and Parks: Linking Protected Area Management with Local Communities*. The World Bank, Washington, DC

Wells, M P and Brandon, K E (1993) 'The Principles and Practices of Buffer Zones and Local Participation in Biodiversity Conservation'. *AMBIO* 22(2–3):157–62.

Westoby, M, Walker, B H and Noy-Meir, I (1989) 'Opportunistic Management for Rangelands not at Equilibrium'. *Journal of Rangeland Management*, (44):427–433.

Wibe, S (1991) *Market and Intervention Failures in the Management of Forests*. Report to the Environment Committee, Organisation for Economic Cooperation and Development, Paris.

Wildlife Conservation Monitoring Centre (WCMC). (1992) *Global Biodiversity: Status of the Earth's Living Resources*. Chapman and Hall, London.

Williams, M (1990) 'Forests.' In B L Turner, W C Clark and W C Kates (eds) *The Earth as Transformed by Human Action: Global and Regional Changes in the Biosphere over the Past 300 Years*. Cambridge University Press, Cambridge.

Wilson, E O (1992) *The Diversity of Life*. The Penguin Press, London.

Wisniewski, J and Lugo, A E (eds) (1992) *Natural Sinks of CO2*. Kluwer Academic Publishers, Dordrecht.

Woodward, F I (1993) 'How Many Species are Required for a Functional Ecosystem?' In E–D Schulze, and H A Mooney, (eds) *Biodiversity and Ecosystem Function* 271–291. Springer-Verlag, Heidelberg.

World Commission on Environment and Development. (1987) *Our Common Future*. Oxford University Press, Oxford.

World Resources Institute (1990) *World Resources 1990–91*, Oxford University Press, New York.

World Resources Institute (WRI). (1992) *World Resources 1992–93*, Oxford University Press, London.

Worldwide Fund for Nature (1989) *The Importance of Biological Diversity*. WWF, Gland, Switzerland.

Wright, D (1990) 'Human Impacts on Energy Flow through Natural Ecosystems, and Implications for Species Endangerment'. *AMBIO*, 19:189–94.

Yañez-Arancibia, A and Day, J W (eds) (1988) *Ecology of Coastal Ecosystems in the Southern Gulf of Mexico: the Terminos Lagoon Region*. UNAM Press, Mexico.

Young, M D and Solbrig, O T (eds) (1993) *The World's Savannas: Economic Driving Forces, Ecological Constraints and Policy Options for Sustainable Land Use*. MAB/UNESCO Vol 12. Parthenon Publishing Group, Paris.

Zucchetto, J and Jansson, A M (1985) *Resources and Society: A Systems Ecology Study of the Island of Gotland, Sweden*. Springer Verlag, Heidelberg.

Index

Aber, J D 49
abiotic environment 156; disturbances 97, 98; matter 120
Aborigines 63
Acheson, J M 164n
accounting frameworks 205–6, 219
Adams, W M 123n, 127, 128
adult literacy classes 216
affluence 207
afforestation 112
Africa 213, 215; decline in food production 64; east and southern 156; elephant management 195; green revolution technologies 65; improving local incentives for conservation 216; sub-Saharan 79, 80, 81, 165; tropical forest area 92; wetland areas under threat 117; *see also* Botswana; Ghana; Kenya; Madagascar: Namibia; Nigeria; South Africa; Tanzania; Zaire; Zimbabwe
agriculture: activity no longer possible 95; already well established 215; arable farming 165; clearing native vegetation for 208; conversion 36, 107; expansion 62; floodplain, losses to 127; freshwater and seawater fish pond integrated with 142; inappropriate farming practices 67; increased taxes on output 109; 'marginal' areas 37; mixed subsistence farming 150, 163; over-use and mis-use of resources 67; poor farming practices 37; population pressure affecting the sustainability of development 67; productivity 107, 138, 215, 220; rapid development 51; released resources from the sector 110; rents 106; shifting, fertile land for 103; soil 26; sustainable 215; yield 107; *see also* crops; livestock
Ahmed, Y 206
Alberts, J J 42, 43
algae 27, 33, 133; plankton 136
Allen, T F H 47

Amazonia 99, 106, 214, 219
Amelung, T 196, 200
animals 61, 63, 103, 208, 218; compensation for damage by 215; husbandry 36; large, conservation of 216
anthropocentric perspectives 24, 49, 50, 83
Antilles 32n, 147
aquaculture 141; combined, in coastal waters 144; intensive 142; sustainable use of biodiversity 139
aquifer systems 123
arable farming 165
ash 106
Ashton, P 104, 107, 108
Asia 119, 213; East 142; perverse incentives for deforestation 104; South-east 107, 141; tropical forest area 92; wetland areas under threat 117
assets: alternative income-yielding 53; distribution of 72; economic 54, 55; environmental 56, 205; humanmade 173; productive 68
assimilative capacity 66; 'critical loading' 181
assurance bonding system 188
Australasia 117
Australia 63, 207, 208–9
Aylward, B A 32, 74, 120, 123, 125n, 192, 193, 194

bacteria 26
Bailey, C 141
balsam fir 96, 97, 98
Baltic Sea 125, 132, 135, 147; annual input of nitrogen 138; changes in composition of nearshore fisheries 32; cod fisheries 137; depletion of fish stocks 61; loss of ecological functions and services 33
Bangladesh 64, 66, 67
banking facilities 216
bans 179

competition for 96; reducing outlets of 143; removal of 67; runoff 138

Oceania 117, 142
Odum, E P 24, 27, 30, 43, 44, 45
OECD countries 111
Ontario 98
open access 158, 163, 192, 210; exploitation 75, 78, 107, 212; global 191
Opschoor, J B 180
organisms 24; micro- 26, 27, 30, 43, 50; natural interactions among 42; pelagic 133, 135; resident, easy mobility for 134; soil 96; 'visible' 30; *see also* living organisms
Orians, G H 43
outcomes 39; catastrophic 172; 'second best' 75; variable 183
overcropping 37
ownership 162–6, 216; joint 217
oxygen 33, 134, 141
oysters 134
ozone depletion 62, 201

Pacific 92, 142
Paine, R T 28
Panayotou, T 82n, 104, 107, 108, 179, 180, 181, 200, 201, 203, 212
Paraguay 92
parasites 65, 142
parataxonomists 195
Parrotta, J A 11–12, 49, 62n, 93, 95
pastoralism 80, 154, 164, 216; nomadic 150, 162, 165
pastures 106
patents 192, 219; international treaties 194
PCBs (polychlorinated biphenyls) 138
Pearce, D W 34, 50, 51, 53n, 55, 56, 84n, 179, 180, 183, 184, 185, 187, 191, 206
penalties 177, 179, 204, 210, 215
Perrings, C 16, 18, 26, 28, 32, 34, 37, 38n, 43, 44, 46n, 47, 49, 50, 51, 55n, 56, 60n, 66, 79, 80, 82, 84, 157, 158, 160, 161, 162, 164, 165,# 172, 175, 176, 183, 184, 185, 187, 188, 191
Persson, A 107, 108
perturbations 25, 26, 27; ability to survive 46; resilient to 41

pesticides 65; demand for 147; problems sometimes aggravated by use 65
pests 65, 106, 147
Pezzey, J 38
pharmaceuticals 195, 202–3
Philippines 64, 92, 108, 201; island of Leyte, Bao and Mahiao rivers 125
photosynthesis 24, 96; energy captured in 66
phytoplankton 33, 133
Pianka, E R 42
Pigou, A C 51n
Pimm, S L 25n, 42
Pinus radiata 110
Piper, J K 49
plankton 133, 136
plantations 92–3, 95, 110; coniferous 112; establishment of 12, 96, 111; forest conversion to 106; subsidizing 112; tropical monoculture 49
plywood 86, 198, 199
Poland 145, 201
policies 20–1, 191–220, 225, 227; advisory boards 224; conservation, appropriate 42; economic 74, 105, 106; environmental 185; government 57, 78, 158, 162–6; interventions 72; macro–economic 73, 107, 166; monetary 75; national, for managing biodiversity 210; threshold 190; *see also* policy failures
policy failures 71–5, 78, 82, 205, 219; affecting forests 104–12, 114; assessing 130; key 227; major factor in 208
political and ideological factors 81
'political will' 226
pollution 18, 51, 117, 179, 181, 208; air 33, 70, 182; controlling 183; costs 52, 182; stresses imposed by 27, 47; surcharge on products leading to 180; tradable permits for 175; water 138
Pomeroy, L R 42, 43
Poore, D 196
poplar 96
population: density 107, 208; growth 64, 68–9, 70; Malthusian constraints 5; pressure 65–9, 106; scale 66–8
poverty 80, 107; alleviating 69, 205; countries/ nations 102, 227; extreme 68; rural households/communities 71, 211

Solow, R M 54
Soul, J D 49
Soul, M E 26, 28
South Africa: KaNgwane,
  Mthethomusha Game Reserve 216;
  Richtersveld National Park 216
South America *see* Latin America
Southgate, D 76, 99, 107, 113, 213, 214
Spain 112
spatial diversity 29
specialization and scientific disciplines
  56–7
species 26, 35, 85; algal 133; animal 61,
  63, 208, 218; area relationship 93–4;
  beyond hope 9; biological 49; broad
  geographic distribution 208; collection
  and classification 6; composition of 96,
  159; crop 61; domesticated 14, 16, 61;
  dominant, rapid turnover of 61;
  'driver' 99; endangered 28, 62, 178,
  207; endemic 134, 212; estuarine 134;
  ex situ conservation of maintaining,
  away from natural habitats 8–9; exotic
  63, 208; fish 133, 138; flora and fauna
  120; freshwater and oceanic 133;
  genetic difference among 16;
  homogenization, for production of
  economic goods and services 61;
  important commercially exploitable
  192; individual conservation 62;
  introduction of new 160; island 63;
  key 114; keystone process 41;
  legislation ensuring preservation of
  175; life history of 218; life insurance
  28–9, 41, 99; loss of 11–12, 27, 41, 96;
  major group wiped out 134;
  non-human 68; origin of 6;
  over-exploitat- ion of 8, 137;
  'passenger' 28, 99; plant 36, 63, 153,
  208, 218; preservation of 175, 223;
  rapid resource degradation of 78; rare
  207, 212; refuges for 95; resilience of
  48; role of 27; survival of 50;
  sustainable utilization 9; targeted 209;
  taxonomic and functional roles 209;
  temperate zone 27; threatened 95, 207,
  219, 223, 226; tree 95, 98, 95, 104,
  218; 'unique' or 'intrinsically' valuable
  181; variation in genetic make-up 7;
  vulnerable 207; widespread destruction
  of 63; wild 13, 14, 16, 62; *see also*

species diversity; species extinction;
  'species richness'
species diversity 12, 14, 16, 28, 30, 50;
  changes in 123; determined 98;
  domesticated 14; highest 44; lower 33;
  management actions for 95;
  unparalleled 134
species extinction 3, 17, 37, 40, 68, 79,
  95; based on tropical deforestation 13;
  extremely vulnerable to 62; factors
  affecting 95; future damages associated
  with 173; increased 10–11;
  irreversibility of 173, 175; loss and
  fragmentation of habitats leads to 65;
  mainly confined to medium-sized
  mammals 63; objective to minimize
  12; probability of 15; protecting 178;
  threats 8, 33, 60, 61, 209, 223
'species richness' 3, 8, 11, 49, 99
spruce 96, 97, 98
squatters 109, 110
Sri Lanka 64
stability 64, 162
state and transition decision tree 161
Steele, J H 135
stewardship responsibility 48
Stockholm 9
storm prevention functions 32, 123
strategic international payments 200
strategies: international 227; national 218,
  227; risk minimizing 81
stresses 27, 29, 47, 62, 79, 184; external
  164, 167; important source 66;
  prolonged 55; threshold 146
stumpage: fees 106, 180; prices 110
subsidies 73, 164, 180, 200, 215;
  development of water resources 216;
  export, in the meat processing sector
  166, 167; forest plantations 111, 112;
  livestock production 166; logging 106;
  price 216
subsistence 36, 80
substitution 55, 56, 173
sulphur 67
supply: demand and 81, 110; monetary 75
'supply forest' 218
'survival algorithms' 81
sustainability 9, 98, 183, 206; agricultural
  development, population pressure
  affecting 67; ecological 186; ecosystem
  24–30, 66, 184; green revolution and

Index compiled by Frank pert